The Nature of Cont Organization Devel...

The nature of contemporary Organization Development (OD) is often written about by both scholars and practitioners, yet there is little evidence of these descriptions (or debates on key issues) having been based on reliably collected data. This book compares academic and practitioner perspectives on the profession of OD in the UK and how it has evolved over four decades. The research which informs this book was designed to investigate similarities and differences in the perspectives between these two communities. Where practitioners and academics views varied in the data, reasons for this are explored in this book, through the theory lens of Institutionalism, Fashions, Fads and the Dissemination of Management Ideas.

The empirical data on how OD has evolved in the UK in the underpinning research to this text was gathered through content analysis of job advertisements from over a four-decade period. This provided information on changes in the magnitude in the take-up of the profession in the UK as well as significant developments in the content of the job roles over the period.

It will not come as a surprise to find that American thinking dominates in OD as it does in many other domains of management. What is a surprise is the extent to which OD practice in the UK is so very different from what the academics tell us it is.

This book also identifies the extent to which institutional theory is at play in the development of professions; with agency as a driver in shaping professions. This manifests itself in terms of the perceived interests of what will give leverage for success in practitioner and academic careers.

The Nature of Contemporary Organization Development is key reading for researchers, scholars and practitioners of organizational change and development, organizational studies, management philosophy and related disciplines

For the detailed methodology underpinning the empirical evidence please see: https://research-portal.uws.ac.uk/en/persons/anne-clare-gillon/publications/

Anne Clare Gillon is Senior Lecturer in Management at the University of the West of Scotland, a Chartered Fellow of the CIPD and a Senior Fellow of the HEA. Prior to her academic career, she worked at a senior level in HR roles in the private and public sectors. Anne Clare has held several active roles in the British Academy of Management (BAM), including as a member of the BAM Council and as a Vice-Chair of The Academy.

Routledge Studies in Organizational Change and Development

Series editor:
Dr. Bernard Burnes

The management of change is now acknowledged as being one of the most important issues facing management today. By focusing on particular perspectives and approaches to change, particular change situations, and particular types of organization, this series provides a comprehensive overview and an in-depth understanding of the field of organizational change.

Titles in this series include:

Agency and Change
Rethinking Change Agency in Organizations
Raymond Caldwell

The Sustainability and Spread of Organizational Change
Modernizing healthcare
*Edited by David A. Buchanan, Louise Fitzgerald
and Diane Ketley*

Managing Organizational Change in Public Services
International Issues, Challenges and Cases
Edited by Rune Todnem By and Calum Macleod

Organizational Change, Leadership and Ethics
Leading Organizations toward Sustainability
Edited by Rune Todnem By and Bernard Burnes

Organizational Change for Corporate Sustainability 3rd edition
Suzanne Benn, Dexter Dunphy and Andrew Griffiths

Managing Change in Extreme Contexts
Edited by David Denyer and Colin Pilbeam

The Nature of Contemporary Organization Development
Anne Clare Gillon

For a full list of titles in this series, please visit www.routledge.com

The Nature of Contemporary Organization Development

Anne Clare Gillon

Routledge
Taylor & Francis Group

NEW YORK AND LONDON

First published 2018
by Routledge
605 Third Avenue, New York, NY 10017

and by Routledge
2 Park Square, Milton Park, Abingdon, Oxon, OX14 4RN

First issued in paperback 2020

Routledge is an imprint of the Taylor & Francis Group, an informa business

© 2018 Taylor & Francis

The right of Anne Clare Gillon to be identified as author of this work
has been asserted by her in accordance with sections 77 and 78 of the
Copyright, Designs and Patents Act 1988.

Library of Congress Cataloging-in-Publication Data
Names: Gillon, Anne Clare, author.
Title: The nature of contemporary organization development /
    Anne Clare Gillon.
Description: New York : Routledge, 2018. | Series: Understanding
    organizational change | Includes index.
Identifiers: LCCN 2017058284 | ISBN 9780815371298 (hardback) |
    ISBN 9781351106801 (wed pdf) | ISBN 9781351106795 (epub) |
    ISBN 9781351106788 (mobipocket)
Subjects: LCSH: Organizational change.
Classification: LCC HD58.8 .G545 2018 | DDC 302.3/5—dc23
LC record available at https://lccn.loc.gov/2017058284

ISBN 13: 978-0-367-73448-0 (pbk)
ISBN 13: 978-0-8153-7129-8 (hbk)

Typeset in Sabon
by Apex CoVantage, LLC

Contents

Tables

Preface

In his study of the professions, Abbot (1988) alludes to the trust we place in, and the reverence we pay to professionals. In particular, he cites these sentiments with regards to long established professions, such as the medical, legal and clerical professions.

Those in the professions of medicine, the law and the clergy might have an extremely significant impact at critical moments in our lives. That cannot be said for those who consider themselves to be Organization (or Organizational) Development (OD) professionals. However, throughout our adult years, most of our waking hours are spent in work mode. The efforts of OD practitioners might not be present in acute life situations, but any profession which could contribute to our existence as human beings at work must surely be of importance.

Reference

Abbot, A. (1988) *The System of Professions: An Essay on the Division of Expert Labour*. The University of Chicago Press: Chicago.

What Exactly Is Organization Development?

The nature of contemporary Organization Development (OD) is often written about by both scholars and practitioners, yet there is little evidence of these descriptions (or debates on key issues) having been based on reliably collected data. This book compares academic and practitioner perspectives on the profession of OD in the UK and how it has evolved over four decades. The research which informs this book was designed to investigate similarities and differences in the perspectives between these two communities. Where practitioners and academics views varied in the data, reasons for this are explored in this book, through the theory lens of Institutionalism, Fashions, Fads and the Dissemination of Management Ideas.

The empirical data in how OD has evolved in the UK in the underpinning research to this text was gathered through content analysis of job advertisements from over a four-decade period. This provided information on changes in the magnitude in the take-up of the profession in the UK as well as significant developments in the content of the job roles over the period. Semi-structured interviews were also carried out with subject experts and a third set of data came from a bibliometric search. This was carried out in order to understand who dominates and influences thought on what constitutes OD. It will not come as a surprise to find that American thinking dominates in OD as it does in many other domains of management. What is a surprise is the extent to which OD practice in the UK is so very different from what the academics tell us it is.

This book also identifies the extent to which institutional theory is at play in the development of professions; with agency as a driver in shaping professions. This manifests itself in terms of the perceived interests of what will give leverage for success in practitioner and academic careers.

For the detailed methodology underpinning the empirical evidence please see https://research-portal.uws.ac.uk/en/persons/anne-clare-gillon.

1 The Beginnings of a Puzzle

The Beginnings of a Puzzle

As with all research, the investigations which led to this book were iterative in nature. I first became motivated to study the difference between academic and practitioner perspectives on the development of the OD profession in the United Kingdom (UK) in 2008. This resulted from my experience of a move from a practitioner to academic career in 2007, and I was keen to identify a subject of personal interest and relevance for research.

I had previously held a senior practitioner job role which had both Human Resource (HR) and OD in the title. Whilst I had had formal post graduate education and professional development in HR and Human Resources Development (HRD), I was less confident on having had such a firm and comprehensive education in and foundation on theory from the field of OD. I often thought:

> I do hope nobody asks me what OD actually is, because I am not sure that I can give a correct answer. I am very confident in my skills in leading on Change Management projects, but if anyone tests the theory on which I am basing my work, then my professional credibility could be questioned.

No one ever did question me, so in that regard I was *safe* but for my own satisfaction, I wanted to make sure I would close this gap in my knowledge. Therefore, OD seemed to be an ideal topic for research.

My first impression had been OD was deemed by practitioners to be a particularly important and influential specialist area within HR. I was therefore keen to understand the academic perspective on OD and as a first step took a random sample of HR texts from library bookshelves. I examined book indexes for reference to OD, and was surprised and perplexed to find no references to OD. This did not correspond with my perception of the importance of OD in the HR practice world, and aroused my curiosity. I carried out a small-scale exploratory study to confirm my perceptions of the importance of OD amongst practitioners using content analysis data from 2008, and subsequently published in 2011 (Gillon, 2011).

After commencing the research contained within this text, in late 2009 I again examined the prevalence and importance of OD roles in HR practice, by initially examining a small sample of job advertisements through the online job search facility on the Chartered Institute of Personnel Development (CIPD) website. In this search, six relevant advertisements were identified that had OD in the job title. Two of the job roles were for *Head* of function roles, one of which was for a *Director of Organizational Development* with a *Salary: £105000—£110000 per annum + excellent package*. In 2009, this was arguably a very high salary for a professional role, indicating that irrespective of the status of OD amongst HR scholars, some organizations did consider it to be valuable and important.

I subsequently repeated the survey of library literature in preparation for a presentation to practitioners, by searching a selection of HR core textbooks. On this occasion, the search was less random and titles were specifically chosen as being expected to include reference to OD, such as *Human Resource Management Theory and Practice* (Bratton and Gold, 2012), *The Strategic Managing of Human Resources* (Leopold and Harris, 2009) and *Contemporary Human Resource Management Text and Cases* (Redman and Wilkinson, 2009). However, again no index listings for OD were found in any of these textbooks. In *The Strategic Managing of Human Resources*, the *Quakers* made the reference list. So it appeared to have been judged that the *Quaker Movement* was deemed of relevance to *Strategic HR*, but OD was not! How puzzling was that?

Research Aims and Research Questions for the Study

Research Aims

In the early stages of the research the broad aim was to investigate the nature of the profession of OD in the UK, and whether this had changed over the period of forty years between 1970 and 2010. As part of the work for this research, the content analysis data from the first tranche of the main study was written up and published (Gillon et al., 2014). This tranche of research focused on a comparison between the evolution of the OD profession in the UK and the United States of America (US). The data on the magnitude (i.e. extent) of the presence of job roles with OD in the title, between 1970 and 2010, fed directly into the findings of the research study contained within this book. Following the publication of that research, the focus reverted to the exploration of the evidence of variance in the academic and practitioner perspectives on the UK form of the OD profession.

Having found indication of a difference between academic perspectives on, and practice of, OD the initial broad aim was developed to include an investigation of how the profession had developed in UK; why it had developed in that way; and what and who had influenced change(s). The two communities whose perspective on these issues was of interest were OD professionals and OD academics. Additionally, the study aimed to apply theoretical perspectives to identify the forces of influence in operation in the development of the profession in the UK.

Research Questions for the Study

From this research aim, the following research questions were developed:

1 To what extent is there a difference between the academic literature and practitioners' perspective of the development of the OD profession in the UK?
2 What does the empirical data of this study evidence on the development of the OD profession in the UK in respect of its form, magnitude and perceived importance?
3 What are the forces at work which influence the development of the OD profession in the UK?

These questions will be revisited in the Chapter 7 (The Puzzle Solved but not Resolved).

The Research Methods Adopted and the Theoretical Proposition

Three methods were adopted to address the research questions. The first comprised content analysis of job advertisements with OD in the title over a period between 1970 and 2010, in order to assess representation of changes in the magnitude and form of the OD profession in the UK. This data was collected with the purpose of providing a comparator with the depiction of OD in the academic literature.

The second method was a bibliometric search, which aimed to provide a quantitative measure of who had publishing journal articles, reports and books with OD in the title, when they were published, and as far as possible to clarify the national context of the work. It was intended that this data would identify sources of authority in the development of OD and any changes in trend on that influence.

The third method utilized semi-structured interviews with OD, HR and Human Resource Development (HRD) subject experts. A range of academics, senior practitioners, business leaders and leading influencers were interviewed to gain an understanding of variance in perspectives from these different communities, and the data compared with scholarly work on OD.

Institutional theory and the diffusion of ideas, fashions and fads in management were selected through which to analyze the data and understand the forces at work in the development of OD. In terms of my objective to achieve the aims of the study, the context of Whittington and Mayer's

(2000: 4) proposition was applied: 'Between the extremes of universalism and contextualism, we conclude for the value of a modestly generalizing social science of management'.

It is not contended that this research will result in an *objective and generalizable truth* on the development and form of OD in the UK. Nevertheless, it is intended is that through the adoption of these methods the study will produce a *modestly generalizable* understanding of the development of the OD profession in the UK.

Evidence on the Nature of Practitioner OD—Content Analysis

In order to carry out the analysis of job advertisements (to determine the nature of how OD practice developed in the UK), various forms of media were scoped and investigated. In terms of the viability of media sources, the CIPD trade press publication People Management, and its predecessors, were selected as the most suitable source. As a trade publication, it is automatically sent to all CIPD members; has good geographical coverage across the UK profession; and has carried job advertisements since 1967.

All issues of the publication between 1967 and 2010 were searched with the first advertisement with OD in the job title being found in 1972. The search terms for the job roles which would be included in the study were defined as all job advertisements which had OD, Organization Development or Organizational Development (and the same terms with UK spelling). The count was logged for each month of publication and this data is presented in Chapter 3 to show the growth in OD job roles.

A sampling mechanism was applied to select job advertisements for content analysis, with a resulting 220 job advertisements subject to analysis of their content. A coding dictionary had been developed in an exploratory phase of this research (Gillon, 2011), and this was further developed and applied in this latter phase of the research study. Through the application of content analysis, the form of OD as it developed through each decade between 1970 and 2010 is presented in Chapter 3.

Bibliometric Searches: Understanding the Academic Perspective of OD

To establish the field of writing on OD, with a view to then understanding the influence and impact of that work on developments within the profession, a bibliometric search was conducted.

The bibliometric search first identified the databases to search, and three of these were selected for search for academic and practitioner sources. The databases and libraries selected for search were the Web of Science, Copac and the CIPD library. The Web of Science was used to identify relevant academic journal articles and Copac was used to identify relevant academic texts. The CIPD library holds an extensive collection of books, academic and practitioner journals, and materials of interest to the practitioner community. The CIPD practitioner library catalogue was searched using the same search terms used for the job advertisement and academic publication searches, which were: Organization Development, Organizational Development, Organization Development, Organizational Development and OD. The findings from the bibliometric search are presented in Chapter 4.

Subject Expert Views

The method adopted for garnering subject expert views was semi structured interviews. A primary purpose of the interviews conducted with these experts was to compare academic and practitioner perspectives on the nature and development of UK OD between 1970 and 2010, and to explore the sources of influence in the dissemination of changes in practice. Exploring the views of the professional association (in this case the CIPD) and identifying leading thinkers was also important.

To achieve a degree of comparison of perspectives, a broadly similar number of academic (n=8) and practice/business leader interview subjects (n=10) were selected and a smaller number (n=3) of leading influencers. More interviewees were selected in the practice than academic group, as the practitioner group included two types of interviewee; subject practitioners and business leaders.

Initially, a broad target of twenty-five interviews was set. However, saturation (Bryman, 2012) was reached after twenty-one interviews, with no new themes arising from interviews. The number of interviews was deemed sufficient (Mason, 2012). As reported above, the final number of subject expert Interviews, by type of subject expert is shown in the Table 1.1 below.

In selecting experts for interview, an attempt was made to gain access to interviewees from a variety of sectors and experience bases, ensuring an element of stratification (Saunders et al., 2012).

Significant consideration was given to whether interviewees should be given prior information on OD to prompt their responses (Cassell, 2009). However, it was decided that to avoid leading or influencing interviewees, no information would be provided on the findings from the content analysis prior to interview. The order of questions in the interview was arranged to build rapport, with time for critical incident, probing and follow up questions fitting with the aims of the project (Silverman, 2011). The interview was designed to ensure the inclusion of introductory questions and questions

Table 1.1 Categories of Subject Experts

Academics	Senior Practitioners & Business Leaders	Leading Thinkers/ Influencers
8	10	3

to interpret and clarify meaning (Bryman and Bell, 2011), with pauses and silences included to allow the interviewee time to reflect, consider and add further comment.

The Plan of the Book

Chapter 1. The Beginnings of a Puzzle

This chapter has introduced the puzzle that led to the desire to investigate the nature of OD, the background and context of the work, and summarized the research aims and research questions. The methods adopted in gathering data were described.

Chapter 2. Academic Perspectives of OD

This chapter will provide a comprehensive review of literature on OD. It details the origins of the term Organization Development, and outlines its definition, boundaries and history. The chapter also provides a description of traditional OD and the context and challenges around core OD in the UK, with reference critiques of OD, debates on its value and the prognosis for its future.

Chapter 3. Evidence on the Nature of Practitioner OD, Chapter 4 The Evolution of Published Work on OD and Chapter 5. Subject Expert Views

Chapters 3, 4 and 5 comprise the presentation of empirical evidence on the nature of OD.

Evidence on the form and nature of OD (as found in the analysis of job advertisements over a forty-year period) will be presented in Chapter 3. This provides evidence on the magnitude and form of OD in the UK and on how it has evolved over forty years.

The bibliometric data presented in Chapter 4 will inform the reader on the findings from a variety of bibliometric searches. Since much of the writing on OD influences what academics and scholars think OD is, not only is the content of literature examined in the previous chapter, but it is also important to examine who is writing the accounts of OD of influence and when and where they are writing.

In Chapter 5 the findings from subject expert interviews are documented.

Chapter 6. Comparing the Literature on OD with the Evidence

This chapter will be comprised of three parts. Part 1 discusses discrepancies between the OD literature and data collected in this study. Part 2 will compare insights from the theoretical positions with the data collected for this study. Part 3 will examine debates on the value of OD, contemporary OD and the prognosis for its future.

Chapter 7. The Puzzle Solved but not Resolved

The concluding chapter will deliver a summary of the key findings of the study, will consider how it has added to knowledge on the nature of contemporary OD, and will provide a review of the way in which the research questions have been answered. It will discuss the implications of the findings for OD practice, professional associations and academics. Areas of future potential for research will be identified.

My view of what OD is has changed significantly since I first started to research into OD. It has been an illuminating journey and it has been interesting to find out that some of what I thought at the outset was indeed correct, some of it was incorrect, but most of all there was a lot I didn't know! *The Nature of Contemporary Organization Development* is the recount of the years of research into OD.

References

Bratton, J., and Gold, J. (2012) *Human Resource Management Theory and Practice* (5th edn.). Palgrave MacMillan: Basingstoke.

Bryman, A. (2012) in Baker, S., Edwards, R. (eds.) 'How many qualitative interviews is enough'. Discussion Paper. NCRM accessed online at: http://eprints.ncrm. ac.uk/2273/ (24th March, 2015)

Bryman, A., and Bell, E. (2011) *Business Research Methods* (3rd edn.). Oxford University Press: Oxford.

Cassell, C. (2009) 'Interviews in Organizational Research' in Buchanan, D., and Bryman, A. (eds.) *The Sage Handbook of Organizational Research Methods*. Sage: London. Pp. 500–515.

Gillon, A. C. (2011) 'Does OD Practice Within the HR Profession in the UK Reflect the Academic Rhetoric?' *Leadership and Organization Development Journal* 32 (2) 150–169.

Gillon, A. C., Braganza, A., Williams, S., and McCauley-Smith, C. (2014) 'Organisation Development in HRM: A Longitudinal Study Contrasting Evolutionary Trends Between the UK and USA' *International Journal of Human Resource Management* 25 (7) 1002–1023.

Leopold, J., and Harris, L. (2009) *The Strategic Managing of Human Resources* (2nd edn.). Pearson Education: Harlow.

Mason, J. (2012) in Baker, S., and Edwards, R. (eds.) 'How Many Qualitative Interviews Is Enough' *Discussion Paper. NCRM* accessed online at: http://eprints. ncrm.ac.uk/2273/ (24th March 2015)

Redman, T., and Wilkinson, A. (2009) *Contemporary Human Resource Management Text and Cases*. Pearson Education: Harlow.

Saunders, M., Lewis, P., Thornhill, A. (2012). Research Methods for Business Studies 6th edn. FT Prentice Hall, Harlow.

Silverman, D. (2011) *Interpreting Qualitative Data* (4th edn.). Sage: London.

Whittington, R., and Mayer, M. (2000) *The European Corporation: Strategy, Structure and Social Science*. Oxford University Press: Oxford.

2 Academic Perspectives of OD

Having set out the background, this chapter provides an overview of academic perspectives through a thorough review of the literature on OD. It details the origins of the term 'Organization Development'. Difficulties in defining OD and its broad nature are considered. Blurred boundaries and confusion with close subject areas are examined with a view to identifying 'what is not OD' as well as what is (or at least might be). Scholars' accounts of the origins of OD, those named as important contributors, its development as a profession since its founding are all set out.

An outline of what might be considered to be core, traditional, US-developed OD: open systems, process and more recent evolutions of core OD is set out. Following this, other aspects of OD are investigated. The practice of OD, competencies and skills required to be an OD practitioner are reviewed, as are opinions on what makes an effective practitioner; amongst these is the need to challenge organizational orthodoxy. Since Change Management and OD are often thought to be linked, as a boundary area to OD, the nature of scholars' accounts of Change Management and the application of OD practice in Change Management is looked at in more detail. Other subjects found in the literature are identified: its assumed consultancy orientation, the underpinning conceptual foundation in behavioral science, with the move of emphasis to being strategic in approach, including organizational culture within its remit and with a focus on organizational effectiveness.

Various contextual issues impacting on the nature of OD are considered: social change, national and organizational differences and the influence of professional associations (including their impact on legitimacy and status). In the UK in particular, the CIPDs role in embedding OD within its professional map and ODs relationship to HR and Human Resource Development (HRD) are scrutinized. The seemingly taken for granted link between values and ethics embedded in OD are also probed.

Towards the end of Chapter 2, critiques of OD and debates on its value are reviewed as is the prognosis for its future. Having examined the nature of contemporary OD from the academics' perspective, a working definition of OD is presented. The chapter ends with a summary of the key themes from the literature.

The bibliometric search findings in Chapter 4 will demonstrate that writing on OD was dominated by work from the US, followed by the UK. A special issue of the *Journal of Applied Behavioural Science* specifically invited articles to review the state of practice in international OD, with the conclusion being that the international deployment of OD practice was still 'very much at the beginning of these phenomena' (Neumann et al., 2009: 184). As such, the United States (US)/Anglo-centric accounts provided in this review are a reflection of the geographical spread of publication, rather than of author bias in literature searching.

Also noteworthy was that, in comparison to other academic subject areas in business and management, the number of OD scholars was found to be comparatively small. For example, a 2014 journal article by Cummings and Cummings dedicated to the divergent perspectives on OD contained only twenty-eight lead author sources, the work of many of whom were also referred to in this chapter. It was not intentional to draw continuously from the same authors, or from somewhat dated sources, but this serves as a reflection of OD as an area of research with neither a large number, nor a diverse range, of published scholars. In terms of the nature of what was published, some OD topics had more coverage and few reports on empirical research data had been gathered and analyzed. Not all, but much of, the writing was descriptive and prescriptive rather than critical in nature. In summary: reviews of OD 'are now out of date, the textbooks tend to be sketchy, and the OD readers, by their nature, do not present a coherent picture' (Burnes and Cooke, 2012: 1396). All of the factors noted above have influenced the literature reviewed in this chapter.

The Origins of the Term and Definitions of OD

In considering the history and trajectory of OD, it is first useful to understand the origins of the term itself. The term OD was coined simultaneously in two or three places, 'through the works of Robert Blake, Herbert Shepard, Jane Mouton, Douglas McGregor, and Richard Beckhard' (French and Bell, 1999: 41). The name itself came from the T-group movement, run by two groups of National Training Laboratory (NTL) consultants: Richard Beckhard and Douglas McGregor working on a project at General Mills, and Robert Blake and Herbert Shepard working at Esso (Burnes and Cooke, 2012).

In 1959 Douglas McGregor and Richard Beckhard carried out a company-wide culture change project at General Mills in Dewey Balch using a 'bottom up' approach. Thinking that the term 'bottom up management' would not be accepted in academic circles, they decided to use the term 'Organization Development' (Cheung-Judge and Holbeche, 2011: 16). In the same year Herbert Shepard and Robert Blake were carrying out a culture change program at the Esso Refinery in Bayway, New Jersey, entitled the *Managerial Grid* educational program. The objective of the program was to improve organizational health through culture change throughout the total system, and they decided to use the term 'Organizational Development' for their work (Cheung-Judge and Holbeche, 2011: 17). Both of these program shared characteristics which have continued to be the five core characteristics of OD: (1) 'system-wide'; (2) 'planned change efforts'; (3) 'focused on the total system and not just one aspect of it'; (4) 'targeted at the human side of the enterprise'; and (5) 'aimed at improving organisation effectiveness' (Cheung-Judge and Holbeche, 2011: 17).

Definition and the Broad Range of OD

In order to understand OD, it is important to first understand its founding essence. OD 'is an approach to change developed in the US. It is based on the work of Kurt Lewin and, originally at least, was concerned with improving the effectiveness of the human side of the organisation through participative change programmes' (Burnes, 2004a: 601).

The CIPD (2014a: n/p) notes that OD is concerned with ensuring an organization has a committed:

> fit for the future workforce needed to deliver its strategic ambition. It plays a vital part in ensuring that the organisation culture, values and environment support and enhance organisation performance and adaptability. Provides insight and leadership on development and execution of any capability, cultural and change activities.
>
> (CIPD, 2014a: n/p)

However, there are multiple definitions of OD. In the words of Pettigrew (1985: 3): '(OD) has almost as many definitions as it has practitioners', and the copious number of definitions of OD tells a story in itself. However, despite their number, these definitions do little to clarify the understanding of OD and if anything, add to the confusion and difficulties of providing a clear definition. A recurring theme amongst scholars is the lack of consensus on the basic goals of OD (Schein, 2006). There is little agreement about what OD is or what it does (Bradford and Burke, 2004), and several authors provide multiple definitions and characteristics (e.g. Cheung-Judge and Holbeche, 2011; Cummings and Worley, 2015; French and Bell, 1999; Senior and Swailes, 2010). Though OD has 'maintained a conceptual core'—a focus on change and processes with an explicit and implicit goal to improve organization effectiveness—there is less agreement in the literature on 'which values should inform the concept of "organizational health"' (Schein, 2006: xvii).

Over the four-decade period between 1970 and 2010 applied to the data collection for the content analysis, the nature of the field of OD has changed. As would therefore be expected, the characteristics of definitions have also changed. Nevertheless, to give some context to the field an early definition which is still quoted (see Cummings and Worley, 2015) is that: 'Organization development is an effort (1) planned, (2) organization-wide, and (3) managed from the top, to (4) increase organization effectiveness and health through (5) planned interventions in the organization's "processes" using behavioral-science knowledge' (Beckhard, 1969: 9). This definition includes many of the features covered by Cheung-Judge and Holbeche (2011) in the five core characteristics noted above with planned, organization /system-wide approach and a focus on effectiveness included in both. Whilst Beckhard (1969) refers to the application of behavioral science, Cheung-Judge and Holbeche (2011: 17) use a broader rhetoric of 'the human side of the enterprise'. Beckhard's (1969) inclusion of top down management and the use of a process approach are both absent from Cheung-Judge and Holbeche's (2011) characteristics. However, given the time gap between the definitions, they are broadly similar.

A categorization of the main themes of OD definitions are outlined by Stanford (2012: 47:

- Mention of 'change'
- Includes reference to improving 'organizational effectiveness' or other organizational aspect
- Suggests a consciously planned approach to change or improvement
- Indicates that OD is applied to an organization's 'processes'
- Focus on the 'human side' of the enterprise and/or mentions of behavioral science
- Views the organization as a system

However, many of the definitions from which the above themes are drawn from are dated. With the 'Element inherent in definitions', we have moved from:

- *relatively stable contexts* to instability and continuous change;
- *improving effectiveness* to measured and evaluated effectiveness emanating from the creation of *continuous adaptability effectiveness* label is beginning to be replaced by *health*;
- *new state* arrived at through planned change to *flexible approach to various types of change* (planned and/or unplanned radical change, planned and/or unplanned incremental change);
- *human process* to *human and business process, structures, technologies*;

- *behavioral social/science* to ethnography, anthropology, neuro-economics, positive psychology; and
- *systems theory* to complexity theory, chaos theory, quantum theory.

(Stanford, 2012: 50)

Whilst providing a useful typology of themes within OD, the variation between definitions is noteworthy. The boundaries of early definitions of OD were much clearer and the world was more predictable, so defining OD was a simpler task (Garrow, 2009). However, in a world that has become increasingly unpredictable and uncertain, having a standardized OD definition is more difficult (Garrow, 2009). There is increased blurring of the boundaries of the field of OD, alongside significant development in new techniques and approaches. As a result, it has become more difficult to define and describe the concept (Greiner and Cummings, 2004).

OD was not well understood by those from outside the field, for a number of reasons. It was perceived as being eclectic, had a number of conflicting definitions, and did not have a place either in the academic or the corporate world (Marshak, 2006). The diverse nature of OD may be a weakness and a strength 'but leaves many thoroughly bemused' (Marshak, 2006: 835). Stanford (2012: 50) questions if it was a problem that OD had 'no standard definition'? Where the lack of standard definition was a problem was in the assessment of OD's contribution. Evaluation was difficult as the field of OD had blurred boundaries and consequently, this led to difficulty in the maintenance of credibility and reputation (Marshak, 2006).

As organizations changed and the challenges they faced changed, then so should have OD. As an action science, it therefore moved with the times and new applications and methods were developed (Stanford, 2012). The lack of a coherent definition was not necessarily negative, as it reflected that OD utilized knowledge from a range of subject areas. However, a consequence of this was that it reduced the possibility for the development of 'a unifying theory' (Stanford, 2012: 50). This suggests the need for a multi-attribute definition and, in turn, the need to consider the boundaries between OD and other areas.

Blurred Boundaries and Confusion with other Particularly Close Subject Areas

Although the blurred boundaries of the field of OD in both literature and practice have been acknowledged, fuzziness endures even in areas where there is potential for more clarity. The terms of organization and organizational development have often been used as though they were the same (see Francis, 2012). Rothwell et al. (1995: 12) are amongst the few who have differentiated, noting that 'organizational development refers to any effort to improve an organization. Unlike' OD, 'it does not imply assumptions about people, organizations, or the change process'.

Crossover exists between OD and other fields such as Quality of Working Life, Human Resource Management, Human Resource Development, Total Quality Management, Organization Transformation, Organizational Effectiveness and Management Development (Church and Burke, 1995). There is a little more clarity on the difference between Organization Design and OD (for these purposes referred to as Organization Development, in order to differentiate it from Organization Design), and the CIPD professional map differentiates between these (CIPD, 2014a). Though separate fields, Organization Development and Organization Design complement each other as core capabilities required in the design and delivery of strategic change (Cheung-Judge and Holbeche, 2011: 214).

Organization alignment is the goal of Organization Design (Cheung-Judge and Holbeche, 2011), and includes explicit and visible 'focussing on aligning the non-people (hard) parts of the organisation' (Stanford, 2012: 55). Organization Design differs from Organization Development on the issues of people, process, technology and physical infrastructure (Stanford, 2012). However, although Organization Design is the driver for structural change, this in turn impacts on the need to address cultural change (Cheung-Judge and Holbeche, 2011). In contrast to Organization Design, the objective of Organization Development is sustained organizational effectiveness (Cheung-Judge and Holbeche, 2011) and relates 'to elements of the organisation that are implicit and cannot be so easily codified or explained: culture, behaviours, relationships, interactions, the way a written process operates in practice' Stanford (2012: 55). Organization Development and Organization Design are required to work together integrally as it is essential that changes in structure and interpersonal systems legitimize and reinforce each other (Beer and Huse, 1972).

Further clarification of the boundaries of OD is provided by Burke (1971). In reflecting on the work of Warren Bennis, he describes the similarities and differences between OD and Operational Science. He explains that they have much in common, as both started about the same time: both are postwar phenomena; both rely on the application of empirical science; both emphasize improvement and optimization; and both are applied, problem centered and normative in approach. They also; use a systems approach; take interdependencies in the internal system into account; are best applied in a fast-changing complex and sciences-based system; and are dependent on relationships with clients underpinned by communication and trust. For all their similarities the most crucial difference identified is in the identification of strategic variables for intervention (Burke, 1971). Where Operations Science concentrates on routing, inventory and allocation, OD concentrates on mission and values, conflict, human relationships, leadership, resistance of change, human resource usage, communications staff and Management Development (Burke, 1971).

An area where there is also confusion is in the relationship of OD to HRD. Organization-wide training programs, including large-scale programs of managers attending human relations training laboratories, have often been referred to as OD efforts (Burke, 1971). However, the difference

> between these and a genuine OD effort . . . is that they are not specifically related to the organization's mission; they are not action-oriented in the sense of providing a connecting link between the training activity and the action planning which follows it.
>
> (Burke, 1971: 21)

OD is more often confused with Management Development than with other practices or concepts (Burke, 1971). OD and Management Development are often treated as though they are a single entity (e.g. Patching, 1999). However, a primary differentiating character is the customer. In Management Development, the client stakeholders are the managers and the interventions are restricted to their development rather than focusing on the development of the wider organization (Beckhard, 1969). However, OD and Management Development can be compared on a variety of other categories: 'Reasons for Use . . . Typical Goals . . . Interventions for Producing Change . . . Time frame . . . Staff Requirements . . . Values' all of which had different features (Burke, 1971: 572–573). Nevertheless, although the strategies are different, they can be compatible and Management Development is identified as one of the techniques which can be used as an intervention in an OD process (Burke, 1976).

History

Having reviewed the issues around defining OD, its history must be examined in order to consider how it has developed. Since the content analysis data on the development of the profession of OD in the UK covered a forty-year period between 1970 and 2010, it is vital to understand what has been written about the roots of the profession and how it has changed over time. There remains confusion in terms of the timing of the origin of OD (Burnes and Cooke, 2013) and 'the cohering and naming of somewhat disparate social-psychological . . . concepts and practices as the managerial field of . . . (OD)' is normally acknowledged as emanating from the US in the 1950s (Burnes and Cooke, 2013: 768). The origins of OD have been linked to the post World War II era, as part of the ethos of the need to rebuild, reorganize and manage in a new world (Stanford, 2012). It was considered as being a postwar answer, acting as a countervailing influence to the dehumanizing practices of scientific management (Garrow, 2009).

Academics Identified as Important Contributors in the Founding Field of OD

Given that an objective of this research is to understand the dissemination of management ideas, it is important to know who was identified as having had an influence on the development of others understanding of OD. Many scholars writing on OD acknowledged key figures in the early development of OD, especially those who influenced its early development. The key figures acknowledged by three authors of being of importance to OD are detailed in Table 3.3.

Many of the key individuals listed in Table 3.3 are featured in at least two of the lists, with Lewin, Lippitt, McGregor, Argyris, Beckhard, Shepard and Blake having appeared in all three. Lewin died on the 11 February 1947 (Burnes, 2004b) and as such, his direct work ended early in the history of OD. By that time he had founded *Field Theory*, developed thinking on *Group Dynamics*, coined the phrase *Action Research* and developed a *3-Step Model* for change (Burnes, 2004b).

Although Stanford (2012: 43) describes Kurt Lewin as a 'significant other', this is in marked contrast to the primary founder position normally attributed to him: such as being the first name listed by French and Bell (1999). He is considered to be the 'critical founder of OD . . . Schein commented that there is little question that Lewin is the intellectual father of contemporary theories of applied behavioural science, action research and planned changed' (Cheung-Judge and Holbeche, 2011: 14).

Lippitt was also influential at the outset of OD and was in the first group to train in T-group methodology in 1946 (Cheung-Judge and Holbeche,

Table 2.1 Important Contributors in the Founding Field of OD

Cheung-Judge and Holbeche (2011)	Stanford (2012)	French and Bell (1999)
Lewin	Beckhard	Lewin
Lippitt	Bennis	Radke
Schein	Blake	Festinger
McGregor	Mouton	Lippitt
Likert	Lawrence	Cartwright
Argyris	Lorsch	Benne
Tannenbaum and Shedline	McGregor	Bradford
Beckhard	Schein	Tannenbaum
Shepard	Argyris	Argyris
Blake	Shepard	McGregor
	Burke	Shepard
	Greiner	Mouton
	Kolb	Beckhard
	Lewin	Bennis
	Lippitt	Schindler-Rainman
	White	Likert
	Emery	Mann
	Revans	Bion
	Trist	Rickman
	Jaques	Trist
		Emery
		Blake

2011), and along with Benne, he is attributed as the inventor of the T-group (French and Bell, 1999). The association of early OD with T-groups is significant as there was a distinct link between those involved in the NTL and those who became leading names in the OD movement (Burnes and Cooke, 2012). Those involved in early T-groups and the NTL also 'shared its zealot-like commitment to the promotion of T-Groups' which in turn produced an environment suitable for a 'rapid expansion of OD in the 1960s' (Burnes and Cooke, 2012: 1399). Lippitt was also a member of the original staff at MIT's *Research Center for Group Dynamics at MIT*, as well as being one of the founders of NTL (Cheung-Judge and Holbeche, 2011: 14).

Likert is known for the founding of organization survey methodology (Cheung-Judge and Holbeche, 2011). Along with Mann, he developed the survey research and feedback stem, which linked with the Lab and Survey Feedback stems (French and Bell, 1999). Other contributors to developments in the laboratory stem were Tannenbaum, Argyris, McGregor, Shepard, Blake, Mouton, Beckhard, Bennis and Schindler-Rainman (French and Bell, 1999). Argyris authored several books on OD, some of which are considered as classics in the field (Cheung-Judge and Holbeche, 2011). Tannenbaum worked with Shedline to launch the first non-degree training program on OD, with Beckhard creating an early 'non-degree training' OD program at the NTL (Cheung-Judge and Holbeche, 2011: 16). Shepard is credited with establishing the 'the first doctoral programme' in OD 'at the Case Institute of Technology' in 1960 (Cheung-Judge and Holbeche, 2011: 16). He was influenced by work at the Tavistock Institute, particularly in their approach to family group therapy, where he spent sixteen months (Cheung-Judge and Holbeche, 2011). At a later stage he was 'significant in shaping the changes in T-group', spending six years on the NTL staff at Bethel (Cheung-Judge and Holbeche, 2011: 16).

By far, the majority of those identified above are US-based scholars, and the field of OD has been dominated by US-based academics. With respect to the UK influence in early OD, key contributors to developments in the *Sociotechnical/Socioclinical* stem and to *Visioning* and *Future Search*, were Bion, Rickman, Trist and Emery (French and Bell, 1999). Other UK-based contributors include Revans and Jaques (Stanford, 2012). In the founding era of OD, there were links between US- and UK-centered scholars such as Trist, Bion, Lewin, Likert and Argyris, characterized by the joint launch of the *Human Relations Journal* by Tavistock and MIT Research Centre for Group Dynamics (French and Bell, 1999). Bennis and Blake also crossed the US/ UK divide by studying at The Tavistock Institute as did Argyris, who 'held several seminars with Tavistock leaders in 1954' (French and Bell, 1999: 45).

Not all US-based scholars acknowledge the UK-based contribution to the development of early OD. In their 10th edition, Cummings and Worley make no reference to *Sociotechnical Systems*, The Tavistock Institute, or to the work of Trist or Emery (Cummings and Worley, 2015). However, in reviewing the UK contribution to OD, Burnes and Cooke (2013) examine the formal establishment of The Tavistock Institute. In a 1945 document which constituted an application for a funding application to The Rockefeller Foundation to found the Institute, mention was included of 'OD's specific cluster of social-psychological ideas to business and management' (Burnes and Cooke, 2013: 769).

Lewin met Trist, a founder of The Tavistock Institute, in London in 1933 and they met again in 1936 in the US when Trist visited Yale (Burnes and Cooke, 2013). Scholarly accounts of these meetings were that Lewin impressed and influenced Trist, implying a one-sided relationship (Burnes and Cooke, 2013). However, in Trist and Murray's history of The Tavistock, Lewin is only mentioned with respect to his field theory and his visit to Yale, and it is a 'Professor Sapir at Yale whom Trist names as having had a significant impact on him' (Burnes and Cooke, 2013: 775). Trist and Emery were also pioneers in their own right in the founding of the *search conference* real time participative approach to planning in rapidly changing environments (Anderson, 2000). Their approach has been identified as the founding of dialogic OD (Bartunek and Woodman, 2015). However, in more recent accounts, Lewin and his 'immediate US followers' are still situated 'at the centre of OD history' (Burnes and Cooke, 2013: 775). Ultimately, The Tavistock Institute's role in founding the field of OD had not been recognized or sufficiently acknowledged (Burnes and Cooke, 2013). The account of the founding of OD as having been entirely US- and Lewin-centric should be challenged (Burnes and Cooke, 2013).

Another UK-based academic who was influential in the development of OD was Pettigrew, with a 1985 text reporting on an in-depth eight-year study of ICI. With such a groundbreaking study it would be reasonable to expect Pettigrew (1985) to have appeared in the lists of influential scholars in OD. However, here again is a UK-based scholar who had shaped understanding of OD, but has not been fully recognized by academics reporting on the development of OD. Pettigrew's seminal study on ICI was referenced widely (see Beer and Walton, 1987; Burnes, 2004b; Burnes and Cooke, 2012 and Grieves, 2000), and French and Bell cite other work by Pettigrew (1979) as being amongst the 'Important contributions to OD literature' (French and Bell, 1999: 300).

Although judged as an important work by some, Pettigrew (1985) does not feature in other works where it might be expected to appear. So, for example when making reference to OD's history and development (see Bazigos and Burke, 1997; Cheung-Judge and Holbeche, 2015; Church et al., 1992; Cummings and Worley, 2015; Garrow, 2009; Shull et al., 2013; Stanford, 2012), authors have referred to US-based scholars, but missed reference to this formative UK study.

The majority of the names in Table 3.3 above are of those who were influential in the early development of OD. Since the field of OD was not clearly defined up to the 1960s, Schein and Beckhard (1998: v) commissioned an Addison-Wesley series and invited a number of scholars in the field to contribute. The six books were authored by 'Beckhard, Bennis, Blake and Mouton, Lawrence and Lorsch, Schein and Walton' (Schein and Beckhard, 1998: v), suggesting that they were considered to be eminent in the field of OD at that time. Also influential in the development of the field of OD were Schein, who promoted that process consultation was not just a tool but a key philosophy which underpinned OD (Cheung-Judge and Holbeche, 2011: 15); and Burke, for establishing the US-based OD Network (Stanford, 2012).

Although the founding of OD included the underlying intention to improve the working life of the many, it also had an elitist tendency (Golembiewski, 1989). This came from an 'intellectual elitism' derived from its research orientation (Golembiewski, 1989: 43). It could be argued that this intellectual elitism is still a feature of contemporary OD.

The Development of OD as a Profession since its Founding

Having examined the leading names in the founding field of OD, this section will examine its development as a profession. The date of origin of the field of OD is contested, but 1947 is a year commonly given for its foundation (e.g. Cheung-Judge and Holbeche, 2011). Stanford (2012) dates its inception a year earlier, in 1946, claiming that OD has a shorter history than HR with its roots in 'behavioural science . . . psychological concepts' and 'social and humanist values relates to openness, trust and harmony' (Stanford, 2012: 43). However, a case was made for OD originating in 1939, with both the publication of Lewin's autocracy-democracy studies and his participative/action research studies with the Harwood Manufacturing Company (Burnes and Cooke, 2012). In terms of development, the rapid growth in OD was as a result of the 'promotion of T-Groups', but by the end of the 1960s it was under attack (Burnes and Cooke, 2012: 1399).

Scholars have often described the development of the profession as being chronological and an order of succeeding forms. Four accounts of this chronological development are presented in Table 3.4.

Table 3.4 outlines the perspectives of Burke (2004), Cheung-Judge and Holbeche (2011) and Garrow (2009) in relation to the earlier origins of OD, whereas Palmer (2006) and French and Bell (1999) extend their descriptions into later decades. Burke (2004) mentions earlier influences prior to OD, and describes sensitivity training and socio-technical systems as setting the stage for the inception of OD. Broadly speaking, Burke (2006), Cheung-Judge and Holbeche (2011) Palmer et al. (2009) and French and Bell (1999) all describe similar origins and developments, whilst Garrow's (2009) description corresponds less well as a comparison: using the categorization of *roots* she does not follow a chronological order.

Table 2.2 The Development of the OD Profession as an Order of Succeeding Forms

Burke (2004)	Cheung-Judge and Holbeche (2011: 13)	Garrow (2009: 3–4)	Palmer et al. (2009)	French and Bell (1999)
Scientific management The Hawthorne studies Industrial psychology Survey Feedback Sensitivity Training Socio-technical systems Organization development (OD) The managerial grid and OD Coercion and confrontation Management Consulting	NTL 'on group dynamics and leadership' ... 'founded in 1947' 'The birth of the T-group and other forms of laboratory education' ... 'Pioneered in the US by Lewin ... and in the UK by the Tavistock Group' ... 'Carl Rogers labelled the T-group the most significant social invention of the century (1968)' 'The larger human relations movement in the 1950s' 'The socio-technical system (STS) thinking from the British Tavistock Institute' commencing with studies conducted in British coal mining in 1947 'The development of survey research methods' e.g. survey of the Detroit Edison Company	Root 1: The Human Relations Movement Root 2: Training and development Root 3: Employee feedback Root 4: Action research and change Root 5: Systems thinking	40s 50s NTL and T-groups, Action Research and Survey Feedback 50s 60s Participative Management, Productivity and Quality of Working Life (QWL) 70s, 80s Strategic Change	Laboratory Training Stem Survey Research and Feedback Stem Action Research Stem Socio-Technical and Socio-Clinical Stem Second generation (1999) Organizational Transformation Organizational Culture Learning Organization Intensified interest in teams Total Quality Management (TQM) Visioning and Future Search Large meetings and getting whole system participants in the room

The Development of OD as Portrayed in the Academic Literature

Having explored its founding and broad development, this section will examine how the literature on OD unfolds. The earliest book/journal that included the label 'organisation development' was Richard Beckhard, 1969 text (Stanford, 2012). Also in 1969, Schein et al. (1969: iii) introduced a series of six books as 'we felt there was a growing theory and practice of something called "organisation development," but most students, colleagues, and managers knew relatively little about it'.

In the 1970s, OD was still in the process of 'growing up' (Burke, 1976: 23). At this point it had moved from being involved only in industrial applications to having a wider scope of organizational applicability, and had also adopted more of a contingency approach (Burke, 1976). Democracy was no longer the primary value, but authenticity was. The focus had changed from the OD consultant being the change agent, to line managers taking that role. At this point, Burke (1976) was calling for a more unifying theory and research base.

The emphasis in the 1970s, and into the 1980s, was on profit rather than on people (Burnes and Cooke, 2012). There was a move from a behavioral and small group orientation to whole system approaches in which strategy, structure and organizational effectiveness became more important, and the perspectives of a range of organizational stakeholders were considered (Burnes and Cooke, 2012).

Characteristics of this change were:

- practitioners viewing organizations as whole systems and contextually 'building on socio-technical and contingency theories';
- emphasis on organizational culture over group values and norms; and
- a similar shift in the focus on learning from group to organizational learning and organizational transformation prevailing over group change.

(Burnes and Cooke, 2012: 1405)

In the 1980s, techniques such as Business Process Engineering (BPR), Six Sigma and Total Quality Management (TQM) came to the fore (Burnes and Cooke, 2012). Whilst OD specialists had been successful in having their group-level work accepted, their whole systems transformation approaches were less clear. A quandary for OD practitioners was that whilst organizations sought interventions which contributed to organizational economic performance, they were less collaborative or group-based (Burnes and Cooke, 2012). Not all stakeholders had equality of voice, which was against OD's central tenet of democratic and humanist values (Burnes and Cooke, 2012).

An era of rapid top down approaches to change became more common and often the methods involved unpleasant consequences for people, such as business closures and redundancies. The spirit of participation in change for positive impact for all seemed out-of-date (Burnes and Cooke, 2012). This resulted in OD's failure to address power relationships, and this became a focus of academic critique (Burnes and Cooke, 2012).

The range of views on OD from the 'early 1980s and 1990s' varies: from being considered as critical to business success, through to being 'a flash in the pan' (Sharkey, 2009: 12). However, in this climate, OD became practitioner driven, although its academic wing still continued to contribute new ideas and models, especially in terms of large-scale transformational change (Burnes and Cooke, 2012). Once the field became dominated by practice, OD's credibility, effectiveness and rigor was on less stable footing. Nevertheless it expanded into Japan, Latin America and Europe from its origins in the US and UK(Burnes and Cooke, 2012). The notion of strategic OD also developed in the 1980s (Anderson, 2009).

The 1990s and 2000s saw 'the renaissance' of OD (Burnes and Cooke, 2012: 1409). This was as a result of three separate developments: 1) the OD community engaged in soul searching; 2) a new generation of scholars began to give critical yet supportive attention to Kurt Lewin's work; and 3) there was increasing use of OD practice in HR and HRD (Burnes and Cooke, 2012). Additionally, OD and its membership bodies became more internationally dispersed (Burnes and Cooke, 2012).

More recently, there has been a shift in emphasis with OD paying more attention to the external environment in which it operates, with a focus on achievement of alignment and strategic organizational objectives (Austin and Bartunek, 2006). Areas of interest for development have included diversity awareness, socio-technical systems design, self-managed teams, congruent reward systems (e.g. gain-sharing), community, and spirituality (French and Bell, 1999). There has also been a widespread interest in BPR. However, the extent to which BPR is congruent with OD values has been questioned (French and Bell, 1999).

A key question is how the development of OD compares with the development of HR and HRD, particularly in the US? The histories of OD, Human Resource Management (HRM) and HRD in the US came from distinctly separate professional roots, and each has evolved in different timeframes (Ruona and Gibson, 2004). According to Ruona and Gibson (2004), HRM originated in the mid-1980s, HRD originated in the late 1970s, and OD was considered as the oldest of the disciplines with its inception in the mid- to late 1970s. However, this date is much later than most other scholars determine, and may be based on the founding of the OD Network in the early 1970s. In giving the date as mid- to late 1970s Ruona and Gibson (2004) have failed to acknowledge many fellow scholars who place OD's origins from the late 1940s. The development of the profession in the UK did not follow either the same chronological or developmental path, as will be demonstrated in the findings of this study.

There is also a view of OD as having a short history, which started in the 1950s and moved forward into the 60s with the 'hippy counter culture, after which it lost its relevance and coherence and fizzled out in the 1980s' (Burnes and Cooke, 2012: 1396). Aligned to this short historical perspective was a labelling of *classical OD* and *new OD* (Marshak and Grant, 2009): a classification readily adopted by others such as Bartunek and Woodman (2015), Bryant and Cox (2014), Francis et al. (2012). However, arguably, OD has had a longer presence, with its origins in 1939 and remains the leading and most applicable approach to achieving organizational change (Burnes and Cooke, 2012).

OD has moved considerably from its roots in planned and group-based change, and much of early and later OD practice has become mainstream, such as action research and T-groups, self-managed teams and job design change (Burnes, 2004a). Although crucial to its relevance, the organization-wide transformational approaches of OD have not been as well refined, focused and established as its expertise in group/team-level work. Ironically, the more OD has focused on organization-wide issues, the more loosely connected it has become to what is happening with teams and individuals (Burnes, 2004a).

In reporting on documented history and historical developments, as has been done in this section with regards to the development of OD, it is important to always retain a caveat. That is that the documentation is of itself reflective of two eras, the era that is being written about and the era and context in which it was written. For example, norms of the social era at the time of writing could also lead to assumptions pervading the reporting of historical facts. In reviewing two different editions of a French and Bell text, Cooke (1999) demonstrated that in listing key scholars of influence in the development of OD, in the 1984 text no females were mentioned, yet in the 1996 edition, female scholars' names were included!

Core Attributes of OD

Traditional OD: Open Systems, Process and More Recent Additions

During the founding period of OD, Lewin wrote about field theory, group dynamics, action research and the 3-step model of planned change (Burnes, 2004b). All of these elements were integrated into the field of OD practice.

The core of traditional OD was often associated with open systems and process approaches, and the application of tools. There are four broad OD approaches: process consulting; application of systems models; Appreciative Inquiry (AI) and a CIPD toolkit based on a 'seven—step change management approach' Stanford (2012: 54). Schein developed the OD focus on process (Schein, 1969 followed by Schein, 1987; Schein, 1988; Schein, 1999) and continued to emphasize process over content (2006: xix), noting that 'Process at the individual, group, or intergroup levels is what OD practitioners understand and can improve' (2006: xix). Continuing to improve human processes within organizations legitimized OD as being essential to the general field of people in organizations (Beckhard, 1969).

There are several similar descriptions of the OD process. For example, stages in the process model have been defined as being 'diagnosis, strategy planning, education, consulting and training, evaluation' (Beckhard, 1969: 105). Cheung-Judge and Holbeche. (2015) outline processes as consisting of: the overview, entering and contracting phase; followed by diagnosis, intervention and evaluation. Models in Rothwell et al. (1995) also follow related process stages: entry, start up, assessment and feedback, action planning, interventions in large systems, interventions in small groups, person focused interventions, evaluation, adoption and separation.

As a general model of planned change Cummings and Worley (2015: 28) outline parallel steps, with feedback loops for all steps. The four steps in the model are:

- *Entering and Contracting*
- *Diagnosing*
- *Planning and Implementing Change*
- *Evaluating and Institutionalizing Change*

(Cummings and Worley, 2015: 28)

Senior and Swailes (2010) propose a refined process model for a change program. Step 1a consists of diagnosing the current situation, with the data collection methods being the social science type methods also recommended by Cummings and Worley (2015). Step 1b involves developing a vision for change. Step 2 focuses on gaining commitment to the vision and need for change. Step 3 involves developing an action plan, in which the role of the change agent is clearly outlined and responsibilities identified, allocated and charted. Step 4 consists of implementing change, using survey feedback to evaluate, and Step 5 involves assessing and reinforcing the change. Whilst the chronological process models outlined above have been part of OD for decades, in a rapidly changing external world there has been increasing need to fast cycle through the process (Anderson, 2000).

Conceptualizing OD as having a systems orientation, Cheung-Judge and Holbeche (2011: 10) cited Schein (1988) in explaining that 'OD is about building and maintaining the health of the organization as a total system'. In a similar vein Cheung-Judge and Holbeche's (2011: 11) own definition emphasizes a 'focus on the "total system" even if we are asked to look at a specific organization issue'. Cummings and Worley (2015) use open systems thinking for their primary diagnostic model, delineating diagnosis and interventions at organization, group and individual level, as do Senior and Swailes (2010). In the diagnosis stage Cummings and Worley (2015) apply an open systems model. Their comprehensive model contains more detailed information than the overarching open systems model, with organization, group and individual levels all set out in full. The Cummings and Worley (2015) diagnostic model is based on the overarching open systems model which consists of 'Inputs . . . Transformation and Outputs' (Cummings and Worley, (2015: 92).

At the intervention stage, Cummings and Worley (2015) categorize four types of intervention; human process, techno-structural, human resource and strategic change. They also provide a matrix map of which form of intervention is suitable for the particular level the intervention is aimed at, such as individual, group or organizational level (Cummings and Worley, 2005).

Senior and Swailes (2010) devoted a chapter to soft systems models for change and described OD as being an acknowledged example of this approach. They also outlined process oriented change and challenged the notion of rationality underpinning change. An OD approach tackles change by viewing the organization as a whole system, in addition to being made up of interconnected parts. As such, evaluation of OD interventions is difficult, as there was no way to identify single causes of change and the clear effects of these causes (Senior and Swailes, 2010).

Using an OD approach on the whole organization system is time consuming and is not a quick fix. Essentially, it involves a process of facilitating planned change which involves anticipation, diagnosis and evaluation of the alternatives, and the management of change (Senior and Swailes, 2010). This is due, in part, to behavior from senior management determining the culture used to achieve change. However, organizations tend to be made up of a balance of forces that have developed over time and changing this balance automatically generates resistance as various parties adjust (Senior and Swailes, 2010).

Traditional OD, as described above, has continued to develop in form. More recent approaches to traditional OD have divergent perspectives, with four identified stances: development versus change, episodic versus continuous change, planned versus emergent change and diagnostic versus dialogical OD (Cummings and Cummings, 2014). In particular, the relationship between diagnostic and dialogical OD has been extensively explored (Bushe and Marshak, 2009; Oswick, 2009; Wolfram Cox, 2009; Marshak and Bushe, 2009). A dialogic approach to OD has also been introduced. Although pitched as a new form of OD, and for example, appearing in the second edition text of Cheung-Judge and Holbeche (2015) but not in the first (2011) the dialogic approach has been in place since the 1980s. The dialogical approach is coherently pulled together by Marshak and Grant (2008) and Bushe and Marshak (2009) (Bartunek and Woodman, 2015).

Changes in traditional OD over time led to two different eras termed 'Classical OD' and 'New OD (1980 onwards)'. New OD includes practices such as 'appreciative inquiry, large group interventions, changing mindsets and consciousness, addressing diversity, and multicultural realities, and advancing new and different models of change' and the 'emerging field of organizational discourse offers sympathetic concepts' (Marshak and Grant, 2008: S7). This approach utilizes the construction of metaphors in OD practice (Jacobs and Heracleous, 2006) and applying discourse approaches to change (Grant and Marshak, 2011; Oswick et al., 2010). Action research was reframed to include dialogical, critical and conventional forms of the process (Maurer and Githens, 2009). Additional forms of intervention which had not traditionally been under the label of OD began to be included in the field, such as Kaizen (Anderson, 2000) and leadership coaching, which had the power to make sustainable change to behavior (Smith et al., 2009). The recommendation to include a sense making perspective to OD interventions was made (Werkman, 2010).

In terms of the move to using large group organizational change interventions were the following methods:

- Future Search Conference
- Large-Scale Interactive Process Methodology Real-Time Strategic Change)
- Managing Organizational Change (MOC)
- Open Space Technology (OST)
- Search Conferences/Participative Design
- Self-Design for High Involvement
- Simu-Real
- Technology of Participation (ToP)
- Total Transformation Management Process (TTPM).

Schmidt Weber and Manning (1998: 236)

However, these larger group interventions were not as popular with OD practitioners as was expected, as they preferred to work at group level (Burnes and Cooke, 2012). In addition, these approaches were not as well received as earlier OD interventions due to being supported by little in the way of theory development or research (Burnes and Cooke, 2012).

This section has explored the nature of the characteristics of traditional OD with a focus on open systems, process and more recent variation. However, there is a need to explore whether traditional OD, and in its more recent forms, are reflected in contemporary UK practice. Therefore, writing on practitioner issues in OD will now be considered.

OD Practice, Competences and Skills

Given the changing nature of academic understanding of OD, it is important to explore the development of OD practice, competence and skills in the US and UK. There is debate about the US and UK tradition in the scholarly foundation of OD (Burnes and Cooke, 2013) and as part of that, the extent of divergence in professional practice traditions should also be explored. Some have argued that there is a need for OD practice to be codified, with the fields and definitional boundaries clarified (Cummings and Feyerherm, 2003), and published information on practice, competence and skills has been examined by professional organizations such as the CIPD in the UK, and the Strategic Human Resource Management (SHRM) and the OD Network in the US.

In the UK, the CIPD (2014b) developed a professional map which (from its inception in 2007) includes OD as one of the eight core specialist areas. The CIPD (2014a) details the following topics as falling within the scope of the OD specialism: OD strategy, planning and business case development; organization capability assessment; culture assessment and development; organization development intervention and development; change management and communications; OD methodology; and project and program management.

Further detail lists descriptors for four levels at which these areas might be performed. However, it is important to note that the professional map was only developed in 2007 (Gillon, 2011), and prior to this OD was not included in the benchmark standards published by the CIPD. In contrast, the US-based OD Network has focused entirely on OD from the outset. It provides more detail on the nature of OD, with 141 points under seventeen main competence headings:

> Marketing, Enrolling, Contracting, Mini-Assessment, Data Gathering, Diagnosis, Feedback, Planning, Participation, Intervention, Evaluation, Follow-Up, Adoption, Separation, Self-Awareness, Interpersonal, Other
> (Sullivan et al. (2001, n/p)

The OD Network (2014, n/p) describes OD as evolving. In providing detail on the competences required, they state their intent to provide 'principles of practice' to serve as a compass for future training and development of OD practitioners, and as a ruler for current practitioners to assess their practice. In addition, the detail is intended to provide a base for researchers to add new or changed principles, and one of the criteria was developed for clients to evaluate internal and external OD consultants. The Principles of Practice are outlined as being: values-based; supported by theory; systems focused; the application of action research; process focused; informed by data; client centered and focused on effectiveness and health (OD Network, 2014).

What is Required to be an Effective OD Practitioner?

A 1988 SHRM survey concluded that OD practitioners require more general knowledge than those working in other areas of HR specialism (Rothwell et al., 1995: 35). The survey found that it is important for OD practitioners to possess linking skills and 'the requisite background, knowledge, theory base and proficiency of skills' including: self-awareness, understanding of others, interaction skills, toleration of ambiguity and persistence (Wigglesworth, 1995: 424). It was also found to be essential that OD practitioners develop a clear professional identity, and that OD education programs emphasize OD's core ideologies, role concept and key characteristics, and an understanding of the vision of the founders of OD (Gottlieb, 1998).

An additional view is that to be effective an OD practitioner must have conceptual, technical, interpersonal and integrative skills (Neilson, 1984). Integrative skills are viewed as the binding for a practitioner to be able to integrate and synthesize conceptual, interpersonal and technical skills (Neilson, 1984). In addition, capability and competence in understanding financial aspects of organizations had become increasingly sought after, although rarely found in the skill-set of OD practitioners (Dunn, 2009).

Conceptual competence for the OD practitioner is not simply concerned with possessing knowledge of behavioral sciences, but also having a voracious appetite for learning about people and organizations (Neilson, 1984). OD practitioners must be capable of conceiving and applying their knowledge in a full and cohesive scheme of approach (Neilson, 1984). OD technical skills should include the ability to accurately diagnose and apply interventions at each level, and practitioners should also have design skills in terms of putting component technical skills together, in addition to applying this appropriately to a given situational context (Neilson, 1984). In developing interpersonal skills, practitioners should develop a *mastery of self* (Neilson, 1984). The concept of the self as instrument should be practiced through the development of life-long learning habits, working through issues of power, building emotional and intuitive self-awareness, and committing to self-care (Cheung-Judge (2001). In terms of understanding oneself, the practitioner should know how he or she is affected by others, and how he or she affects others (Burke, 1976).

The OD specialist must understand their own biases, be actively conscious of their own values and aware of how these have changed over time (Burke, 1976). Awareness of self is critical to understanding the effect of formative influences on identity, motives, prejudices, self-image and assessment of personal capability (Cummings and Feyerherm, 2003). Developing knowledge of self should be combined with a commitment to continuously learn theory and research in the subject area of behavioral sciences (Burke, 1976). However, mastery of self for an OD practitioner does not mean seeking to meet personal needs, which would lead them to become detached and objective in action (Cummings and Feyerherm, 2003). Practitioners must also have the personal conviction to challenge for truth when faced with power (Cummings and Feyerherm, 2003).

Experience of combining knowledge and skill (Grieves, 2000) is important for the OD practitioner and, like a journeyman, a process of learning is essential before they can consider themselves to be competent. Familiarity with different Change Management processes is also essential for professional development (Schein, 2006). Having a fluent knowledge of business, including an understanding of finance and financial decision making, is essential as is having a knowledge of 'strategic formulation tools and conceptual models' (Anderson, 2000: 7). However, not only process skills are important: having an in-depth knowledge of the industry and organization context in which they work is key to the success of the OD professional (Anderson, 2000).

Eisen, et al. (1995: 493) completed a four-year study that explored the 'competencies OD would need in the future', through their activity in the Fulcrum Network at an Organization Development Network (OD Network) conference. The Fulcrum Network was an online service for OD consultants who were keen to contribute experiences and discuss ideas (Eisen, et al., 1995). Trends and competencies were considered for each of the themes of Fulcrum which included: broadened frameworks in a global environment; clients and client systems; cultural and demographic diversity and change; values and ethics; and trends within OD such TQM, emotional intelligence and quality of working life (Eisen, et al., 1995).

In the series on contemporary trends in OD, Colwill (2012) noted that OD competencies and skills requirements had typically been developed by those who had been in the field for decades and were looking back in terms of what made them successful, rather than looking forward. The tradition of inherent intellectual elitism in OD (Golembiewski, 1989) appeared to remain. For example, The (American) Academy of Management had a Division of *Organization Development and Change* for some time (Academy of Management, 2015). The primary focus of the Colwill (2012) scholar practitioner text was on doctoral education for OD practitioners, and although not suggesting that doctoral-level education was necessary for OD professionals, with seven pages of fifteen dedicated to applying what practitioners could learn from OD doctoral students (Colwill, 2012), the emphasis was clear.

The Requirement to Challenge Organizational Orthodoxy

Challenge is a theme which recurs in the literature on OD. Whether working as an internal practitioner or as an external consultant, to be successful an OD practitioner must be able to contest assumptions made at all levels within the organisation. The key for OD practitioners to be effective in challenge is that they 'need to be confident, highly influential and credible to those they are helping, even if their own presence is low key' (Cheung-Judge and Holbeche, 2011: 209). In the past, OD has been viewed as failing to achieve a position of power and influence (Beer, 1976: 47). The advice of Kotter on how people can build effective relationships with their bosses might enlighten OD specialists in how they might best become influential and credible experts (Cheung-Judge and Holbeche, 2011). Kotter recommends that executives:

1   make themselves aware of their boss's working style, pressures and strengths and weaknesses;
2   are self-aware—they understand their own goals, needs, personal style and weaknesses;
3   set clear mutual expectations—through applying 1 and 2; and
4   are reliable and honest with their boss, they are respectful in their use of their boss's time and resources—and build a good relationship through these actions.

(Cheung-Judge and Holbeche, 2011)

OD and the Field of Change Management

The relationship between OD and Change Management is complex. Sometimes they are distinct and separate, but they are often intertwined. In the foundation of OD, Change Management was part of OD. As the decades passed, Change Management became a significant subject field in its own right and would often subsume OD within its field. With Lewin's approach to planned change, Change Management was a feature of OD from the outset (Burnes, 2004c). Whilst it is not the purpose of this study to provide a comprehensive and systematic review of Change Management literature, the two fields are inexorably linked with OD tools and techniques suitable for use in the management of change programs (Burnes, 2004a).

There are differences in the traditional approach to change and the OD approach to change, with traditional Change Management focusing on 'outcomes' which are 'elite processes—expert led', whereas OD focuses on process as well as outcomes and is participative in nature, as it is 'people-led with clear parameters set by senior leaders' (Cheung-Judge and Holbeche, 2015: 155). The focus in Change Management is economic, whereas OD takes a humanistic approach, considering people to be the key to 'economic gain'. Traditional Change Management is directed and top down, whereas OD is facilitative in nature, seeking to engage and 'give people a voice' (Cheung-Judge and Holbeche, 2015: 155).

Traditional OD was originally associated with planned change, but other forms of change discussed in Change Management theory from the 1980s were processual and emergent perspectives of change (Livne-Tarandache and Bartonek, 2009) with processual analysis (Pettigrew, 1997) developed as a tool to research the impact of the change process on the organization. Lewin's work on change had been criticized as being no longer relevant and there was a broad range of perceptions of change, such as emergent, punctuated, continuous or incremental (Burnes, 2004c). Of these, emergent change replaced planned change as it 'was consistent with the free-market, winner-takes-all spirit of the last 25 years' (Burnes, 2009). Nevertheless, there were similarities between Lewin's approach to change and the influential ideas of complexity theory (Burnes, 2004c). In any case, it was not helpful to treat planned and emergent change as being in conflict. Indeed, an inclusive view of these two types of change may provide new possibilities for OD research (Livne-Tarandache and Bartonek, 2009).

It is notable that many Change Management scholars rely on mainstream OD scholar sources. Burnes is a primary source for many of the UK-based authors, such as Hughes (2006), who are influenced by Burnes' view that the most recent fore-runner to organizational change tools comes from the domain of OD. However there is also a view that Change Management is new and does not come out of OD (Hughes, 2006). In addition there is a perspective that Change Management is informed by management consultancy (Worren et al., (1999).

In 1969 Beckhard described Change Management as being a new approach which was, at that time, a decade old (therefore Change Management emerged c 1959). In that era, Change Management was about aligning the structures of 'organizations so that they can better adapt to new technologies, markets and challenges, and the dizzying rate of change itself' (Beckhard, 1969: 9). The timeline for the beginning of Change Management identified as a new approach ten years earlier by Beckhard in 1969, is approximately ten years out from the founding of OD. The timeline for the origins of Change Management (c1959) given by Beckhard (1969) does not tally with the view that planned change had been a feature of OD from the outset (which is generally placed as being c1947), and the concept of change agent originating with the founding father of OD Kurt Lewin (Burnes, 2004a).

The global context of change was significant to the way that both the OD and Change Management terrain developed. Since the postwar third quarter of the 1900s was relatively stable, change could be participative, incremental and slow (Hayes, 2014). However, external economic conditions began to change rapidly from the 1970s, meaning that organizational changes were far larger scale and much more rapid in response to that, resulting in the OD participative approach to change being no longer viable (Hayes, 2014).

How OD features in the Change Management literature

OD received relatively little attention in the Change Management literature. Mabey and Mayon-White's (1993) edited text on Change Management includes twenty-two papers from a range of esteemed scholars. Amongst the articles, one presents OD process, one uses a team member as agent of change focus, another refers to team building, and the conclusion of a chapter recommends using OD processes. So, of the twenty-two chapters, only four reflect any sort of OD orientation. However, Palmer et al. (2009: 192) portrays OD as now taking a coaching approach to change as well as professing that OD has dominated Change Management for over fifty years. One chapter entitled *Implementing Change*, appears to be heavily influenced by conventional OD, and Chapter 8 on the subject of OD, contains debates on Change Management.

Palmer et al. (2009) suggests that those in the OD camp consider those aligned with Change Management as having the pushy approach of the global consultancy firms: focusing on the needs of senior managers to improve financial performance. Palmer's (2009) view is that those under the Change Management banner necessarily lack the humanistic value system of OD, although some OD practitioners were influenced by Change Management. For example, Palmer proposes that some OD practitioners have a more vendor oriented approach in terms of selling their services to senior management as the client/customer (Palmer et al., 2009). In this view, the shift from humanistic democratic values to bottom line concerns and the ambiguity of what OD consisted of, acted as terminal threat to OD (Palmer et al., 2009).

Hayes (2014) includes reference to OD roots when discussing the change process by including reference to Lewin's model and force field analysis, and outlines more contemporary approaches including action research and AI. Hayes' (2014) description of the change process is similar to that of the traditional OD process: with both recognizing the need for change, diagnosis, vision of future desired state, planning, implementing and sustaining change. Hayes depicts three strategies for change: economic, OD and the '*third way: a combined economic/OD strategy*' which could be implemented either simultaneously or sequentially (Hayes, 2014: 286). Using these approaches sequentially, John Birt focused on implementing change at the BBC by first concentrating using an economic strategy to make the organization more efficient, whereas Greg Dyke later adopted a more OD influenced approach to change which engaged employees and was managed in-house. He was seeking ownership and 'buy in' and brought in the concept of the 'big conversation' to seek the views of employees (Hayes, 2014: 285).

Whilst Change Management approaches are driven by strategy and focus on several organizational components simultaneously, OD is criticized for not being directly linked to strategy and focusing on only one component at a time (Worren et al., 1999). In addition, whilst Change Management draws on OD techniques it arguably replaces, rather than develops from, the field of OD in three ways (Palmer et al., 2009). First, Change Management has a broader scope: it includes strategy, operations and technology as well as human performance. Secondly, classic OD acts as a third party in a coach or facilitator role whereas, change managers are directly involved, have technical skills and are members of a team of others with a range of skill-sets, including organizational areas and strategy: meaning that change managers are more involved and accountable. Thirdly, OD presumes that change in behavior and attitude results in other changes such as structural change, whilst the Change Management perspective is that changes in structure would drive change in attitude and new behavior (Palmer et al., 2009).

The role of the change agent in OD is that of a process consultant or a facilitator, whereas in Change Management the role is more likely to be in a cross functional team, a content expert or in a project team (Worren et al., 1999). The purpose of OD is to change values in order to change behaviors, whereas in a Change Management approach, the behavior is changed first with the modification in values following on later (Worren et al., 1999). Change Management is promoted as being a field which could integrate theories from OD, strategy and technology and using a coordinated approach could deliver on a strategic change agenda (Worren et al., 1999).

However, Farias and Johnson (2000) strongly disagreed with the Worren et al. (1999) perspective, defending the OD perspective and challenging the validity of Worren et al.'s argument. Hornstein (2001) also defended OD, noting that its failure to find favor with global business stakeholders who focus on short-term business goals and financial reward should not lead to it being considered as being defunct.

In terms of which of the fields holds more influence, Palmer et al. (2009) compared the prominence of OD with that of Change Management over the period between 1980 and 2006 through presenting an ABInform graph of journal article titles. In the 1980s, OD articles outnumbered those with Change Management in the title. However, over the period of study, there was a decrease in the number of articles focused on OD and an increase in Change Management focused articles. The study found that trend reversed in 2006 with a dramatic increase in OD articles, and a decrease in Change Management articles (Palmer et al., 2009). In terms of the literature, OD had been prominent, became overshadowed by Change Management, but by 2006 was returning to a position of influence.

One view of OD and Change Management was that OD, HR and leaders had to work together to achieve successful change. In organizations that managed change well there was effective partnership between leaders '(the real OD practitioners), OD and HR experts working together to achieve both the short-term requirements for aligning people and resources with business goals while also working towards the longer term of building future organizational capability' (Cheung-Judge and Holbeche, 2011: 201).

Although the concept of a learning organization approach to Change Management might have been considered to be inherent to an OD approach, surprisingly little was written on it within the OD literature. One Change Management text (Senior and Swailes, 2010) included a section on the importance of organizations being learning organizations. In creating a learning organization, OD aims to put systems in place to enable the organization to cope with future challenges (Watkins and Golembiewski, 1995). Technical, structural and psychosocial subsystems must all be addressed, and formal and informal systems taken into account (Smither et al., 1996). As well as having a future capability orientation, effort have to be made to include others beyond just working with the top level (Watkins and Golembiewski, 1995).

The spirit of learning organizations is indirectly embraced in the literature on OD, with Garrow (2009: 6) noting that 'The concept of flexible, agile and adaptable organisation remains central to OD . . . one of the distinguishing factors of OD as being reflexive and self-examining to facilitate constant organisational renewal'. Cheung-Judge and Holbeche (2011: 11) also imply an organizational learning imperative as being central as 'We aim to improve an organization's problem solving and renewal processes'. Organizational learning is not often referred to explicitly by OD scholars, possibly because it is assumed to be a fundamental part of OD.

A Consultancy Approach to OD

Threaded throughout the OD literature is the view that internal or external specialists hold consultancy oriented roles, and that 'External consultants have played a central role in' OD 'from its inception' (Gallos, 2006: 363). The role of OD practitioners as consultants was assumed by Rothwell et al. (1995), who noted that OD consultants already carried out the role of change agent, but that there was a requirement for them to acquire more formal knowledge of organizational practice and theory (Rothwell et al., 1995).

In order to be successful, an internal consultant must understand the business issues, provide bespoke solutions, and communicate effectively, efficiently and proactively (Weiss, 2006: 471). Internal consultants should also do the foundation work by learning the business through working in other roles and seeking interaction, and regular feeding back, on the process(es), avoiding the use of jargon and applying only validated tools (Weiss, 2006). Additionally, it is important that consultants set and evaluate progress against metrics, take and share credit, use supporter testimonials and document success. One significant part of the consultancy role is to disagree and be able to challenge any 'the emperor's new clothes' rhetoric (Weiss, 2006: 471). Furthermore, as long-term participants in an organization, internal consultants are also accountable for producing sustainable outcomes aligned with organization strategy.

However, Beer and Walton (1987) advocate moving away from a consultant centered approach to OD where its functions are within the remit of the general manager. OD should also lead organizational leaders in placing an increased focus on the selection and development of leaders (Beer and Walton 1987). Getting the selection and development of organizational leaders right, has long been an issue (Burke, 2011).

A Behavioral Science/Organizational Culture Focus in OD Practice

The term *behavioral science* was coined in the US, to cover a broad spectrum of social-psychological practices and concepts (Burnes and Cooke, 2013). One interesting perspective on the context in which this term was chosen was that in the era of McCarthyism, *social science* was considered as sounding too much like socialism, and therefore a term that was best avoided (Burnes and Cooke, 2013)!

French and Bell (1999: 25) noted that 'All authors agree that OD applies behavioral science to achieve planed change'. Cheung-Judge and Holbeche's view of the importance of knowledge of human behavior to the OD, HR and HRD professions was confirmed by the addition of a chapter on behavioral change in the second edition of *Organization Development—A practitioner's guide for OD and HR* (Cheung-Judge and Holbeche, 2015). Historically, a behavioral science approach, principally in the guise of sensitivity and laboratory training, dominated much of the early development of OD. As such, it was important to provide more detail as to what this entailed.

Reflecting its importance, Bennis had, in 1969, devoted a chapter to sensitivity training, which was developed alongside T-group training, describing it as:

> laboratory training is a small group effort designed to make its participants more of aware of themselves and of the group process. The group works under the guidance of a professionally competent behavioural scientist and explores group processes and development through focussing attention on the experienced behaviour of its members.
>
> Bennis (1969: 61)

The use of these groups aroused curiosity, they also caused anxiety, and although their use was considered controversial they were popular (Bennis, 1969). Some expressed strong support for the use of laboratory training and were labelled as 'cultists' by those who were against it (Bennis 1969). Laboratory training was not designed to tackle emotional difficulties but to enhance working life; presupposing that participants already had a 'higher degree of emotional health' (Bennis, 1969: 62). Participants with less open personality types and those who were more structured in their approach may have found sensitivity training more difficult to cope with (Bennis, 1969). A manifestation of the potential problems associated with this approach included, at its most extreme, 'an attempted suicide by one of the participants in the training shortly after his return from the week' Bennis (1969: 62). However, there were situations in which the training worked and proved to be helpful (Bennis, 1969).

In contemporary OD, the importance placed on behavioral science is linked to the extent that organizations believe change is essentially a social process that comes primarily from modification of human behavior (Stanford, 2012 citing Cummings, 2004). Attention to the roots of the psychological foundations of OD supports the acceptance of its relevance (Stanford, 2012, citing Cummings, 2004). Drawing on this field of knowledge remains of relevance to OD, and it is argued that 'We use the technology of applied behavioural science to support the organization towards healthy development' (Cheung-Judge and Holbeche, 2011: 11). In the US, the NTL still run 'Human Interaction Laboratories' (NTL, 2014: n/p) as well as training for OD practitioners.

There is little in the way of formal training or education provision in OD in the UK, and of that which does exist, only some is related to behavioral sciences. Cheung-Judge's consultancy organization, Quality and Equality (2014), provide NTL accredited programs for OD practitioners. Roffey Park (2014) provide training programs for OD practitioners, and also a program aimed at leaders improving their relationships at work which includes feedback, and the Program Director is listed as having a Certificate in Gestalt. Whilst neither of these programs use either of the original labels, they appear to borrow some features from the forebears of sensitivity, T-group and laboratory training.

There had been an interest in organizational culture as a feature in OD in the last twenty years of the twentieth century (Woodman, 1989). However, its mention in OD literature was less than might have been expected: for example, it was not mentioned in Table 3.1 (containing themes of definitions of OD and key authors) above. Nevertheless, given the focus of OD on system-wide change the 'construct of organizational culture gives us another, possible useful, way to talk about changing whole systems' (Woodman, 1989: 218). Although the OD community recognized organizational culture as part of the field, there had been no development of thinking on organizational culture and much of the scholarly work on it had come from elsewhere (Beer and Walton, 1987).

With regard to people and culture in organizations there is a recurrence of interest in employee engagement (Cheung-Judge and Holbeche, 2015). In the second edition of their text, the chapter on culture change (in Cheung-Judge and Holbeche, 2011) was removed and chapters were added on employee engagement and building organizational agility and resilience, including reference to the cultural aspect of this (Cheung-Judge and Holbeche, 2015). This suggested that the subject of organizational culture itself was not of interest except for it being embedded in the purpose of OD.

Organizational Effectiveness

In the area of organizational effectiveness, practice was leading research and theory (Woodman, 1989). Organizational effectiveness had featured as an OD goal from early on, as 'improved effectiveness in performance and improved organizational health with the ability to remain effective' (Beckhard, 1969: 100). In the 1980s the focus on effectiveness continued, with OD considered as continuing to contribute to the field of high performance and high commitment work systems (Woodman, 1989).

In the post millennium period, Rainey Tolbert and Hanafin (2006: 70) state that 'The goal of OD is to enhance organizational effectiveness by attending to both human and organizational needs'. The commitment to effectiveness is at the core of OD practice, as important as the assumptions, values and ethics that accentuate its 'humanistic orientation' (Burnes, 2004a: 267). Effectiveness takes center stage in a recent UK text, with a title of *Organisational Effectiveness: A New Agenda for Organisational Development and Human Resource Management* (Francis et al., 2012). Although effectiveness has long been a focus for OD (e.g. Golembiewski, 1989), it is claimed that this is a new form of organizational effectiveness which 'reflects a powerful ethic of mutuality . . . is eclectic' and ' (re)regenerative' (Francis et al., 2012: 336).

However, there is an inherent tension as there has always been a strain between *effectiveness* and *the wellbeing of the employees*, and managing this paradox is a difficult but key skill for OD practitioners (Beer and Walton, 1987). Planned change originally focused on resolving 'social conflict in society, including conflict within organisations' (Burnes, 2004a: 279), with the argument being that this would, in turn, lead to improvement in the effective operation of the organization. Although planned change within OD has developed, the emphasis on effectiveness has remained (Burnes, 2004a).

Taking a Strategic Approach in OD

Taking a strategic approach is discussed at length in the mainstream HR academic community (e.g. Boxall, 1996; Paauwe and Boselie, 2005; Wright et al., 2005). In HR, the focus should be on strategy implementation rather than on strategic positioning. Differentiation should be made to HR architecture according to the business processes, and priority focus should be on the performance of those who are in strategic job roles (Becker and Huselid, 2006).

A workforce strategy mindset is far more likely to provide success than a focus on HR architecture (Becker and Huselid, 2006). By the very nature of seeking to become more strategic, such closely aligned fields such as HR and OD have to work together (Yaeger and Sorenson, 2009). Indeed, 'True organization development, by definition, is strategic' (Head, 2009: 23). Operating strategically should not negate the need for OD practitioners to perform well tactically and at group and individual levels in the organization (Anderson, 2009). In addition, alternative drivers may be used for implementing strategy at different organization levels (Holst-Mikkelson and Poulfelt, 2009).

Whilst the original focus of OD was on work groups, some argued that there had been a major shift in from the team-level perspective, to an organization-level focus and impact (Burnes, 2004a). Furthermore OD must strengthen its strategic perspective (Anderson, 2000; Burnes, 2004a). There were three reasons for this change in emphasis (Burnes, 2004a):

1   With regards to job design and socio-technical systems, OD practitioners realized that there was more to do than simply work within groups, they therefore developed into using an open systems perspective.
2   This in turn led to being involved in the management of organization culture and OD practitioners became interested in organizational learning.

3   The increasing turmoil in the environment and growing use of organization-wide perspectives led to awareness amongst OD practitioners of the importance of viewing the transformation of organizations in their totality, rather than simply focusing on individual constituents.

OD had traditionally focused on micro rather than macro issues, but as the field developed, a more strategic, system-wide and external environment approach was required if OD was to survive: especially when it was to operate in a multi-national environment (Woodman, 1989). Not only was this important to the OD profession but organizations were increasingly going through changes, such as: a change in strategy due to expansion; change in business process; restructuring; and acquisition and/or merger. Whilst organization design interventions are first required in these instances, these should be accompanied by OD initiatives to achieve the cultural change which would successfully embed strategic change (Cheung-Judge and Holbeche, 2011).

In addition to being used to facilitate culture change, strategic OD has been utilized to integrate strategic change, network and alliance interventions, organizational transformation, mergers and acquisitions, learning and self-designing organizations and knowledge management (Yaeger and Sorenson, 2009). It has also been used to strategically orient global, multinational, international and transnational management (Yaeger and Sorenson, 2009). Increasingly, organizations have been siting parts of their operations offshore, with team members situated in different countries (Anderson, 2010). All of these contexts have an impact on where and how OD operates, and a primary role for strategic OD has been to ensure the alignment of the competence of the organization with the mission of the organization (Yaeger and Sorenson, 2009).

A more recent focus for strategic OD has been in the use of positive change interventions and in particular the adoption of AI (Yaeger and Sorenson, 2009). Use of rhetoric such as 'OD Value Cycle' and 'creative organisational change' also implies a more positive approach (Anderson, 2000: 9, 31). However, it could be claimed that this has been simply spin, as might have been concluded from the use of language such as *Lead With a Need for Speed*, although arguably, there was a fundamental *Need for Speed*, since it led to competitive advantage (Anderson, 2000: 121).

Whilst OD practitioners may seek to be strategic, the term itself is ambiguous (Anderson, 2009). Common in definitions of strategy is that success varies according to the nature of the context (Anderson, 2009). Therefore, this implies that for OD practitioners to be strategic, they must have an understanding of the world external to the organization (Anderson, 2009). As the external context of any strategic approach is a rapidly changing environment, at times the nature of change may threaten the very survival of an organization. In order to be considered of relevance, OD practitioners have to be aware of external threats to organization performance and survival, and proactively operate to provide appropriate contextual support (Anderson, 2009).

It has been proposed that the integration of OD and strategy could lead to them becoming a formidable force in delivering transformational change (Palmer et al., 2009). Top down change combined with bottom up change is arguably the most effective approach. Top management have to be absolutely committed to the process of bottom up change, using OD principles and practice, for it to be effective (Palmer et al., 2009).

The Context of the Environment of OD

A myriad of background circumstances play a part in the practice of OD. This section will explore the general context of OD, its relationship with HR and HRD and discuss the role of relevant professional associations. The literature on values and ethics in OD will be examined, highlighting criticisms including the failure of OD to address issues of power and politics and to follow sound evaluation processes. It will also discuss why those criticisms are amongst the reasons why OD is often dismissed as being a fad or fashion.

Social Change Context

The ambition of OD to humanize workplaces in the 1950s took place in the context of routine and repetitive employment where initiative was punished and compliance was assumed to be required. However, routine and repetitive work environments became increasingly rare (Beer and Huse, 1972). The nature of work was changing and as such, OD was increasingly seen as having a key contribution to make to the performance of organizations where there was an increasing reliance on a scarcity of skilled knowledge workers (Purser and Pasmore, 1992).

National Context

The national context was another relevant circumstance at the root of assumptions being made. Whilst OD was seen as being desirable as an approach outside of the US and UK, people in other cultures with different learning styles, reasoning preferences and value systems were not currently equipped to cope with it in the form it was practiced in the US and the UK (Wigglesworth, 1987).

There was a need to challenge the assumption that OD could be in the same way in all national cultures (Palmer et al., 2006). US-centric traditional OD assumptions did not match Confucian/Taoist beliefs across a range of measures with respect to perceptions of change (Marshak, 1993). With reference to the theories of Geert Hofstede and Fons Tompenaars on national culture, applying OD in other countries required consideration of the national culture environment (Rothwell et al., 1995; Fagenson-Eland et al., 2004). However, a study conducted in Hong Kong found that there was no simple choice of OD interventions which would work, or not, in different national cultural contexts, and as such, it seemed that national culture affected the effectiveness of some OD interventions, but not all (Lau and Ngo, 2001). System-level interventions with significant HR focus were found to affect organization performance, but it was less clear whether interventions at individual level did (Lau and Ngo, 2001).

An example of the difficulty in importing OD approaches from the US to another national context was seen in Poland after it moved to a market-based economy (Yaeger et al., 2006). Using US-centric OD approaches as though there was no influence from deeply embedded national political and historical experiences, a team of experienced and credible OD professionals completely failed in their endeavor to assist in the development of commercial enterprises in Poland (Yaeger et al., 2006). There were a variety of issues which had to be taken into account in working in different national contexts: national, cross national and the convergence/divergence of organizational culture as well as the compatibility of the national culture with OD values (Yaeger et al., 2006). The national economic environment had an influence on OD work, as did the national and international legal framework (Yaeger et al., 2006).

Organizational Context

Another aspect of context for consideration is concerned with where OD might sit in an organization and who might be the best to *own* it. This issue will be explored further, but the organizational circumstances in which an OD approach is needed should be the first issue to be reviewed. The conditions which often create a need for OD are: rapid and unexpected change, growth in size, increasing diversity and change in managerial behavior (Bennis, 1969).

There are ten additional situations in which OD should be applied, where there is a need to: change the managerial strategy; improve the consistency of the match between organization climate, the changing external environment and individual employee needs; address cultural norms and re-design roles and structures; improve intergroup relations and collaboration; open communications channels; advance planning processes; attend to problems which have arisen from a merger; increase the motivation of the workforce and finally to adapt to a new environment (Beckhard, 1969, 2006). The spaces in which OD can work are described as: business strategy; organization design; the structure of work; workspace design; organizational culture; workforce development; team development; and leadership development (Gallos, 2006).

The level of the organization at which OD practice sits and who leads on OD issues is also of importance. There is a view that 'The primary practitioners of OD are the organization's managers, not HR/OD professionals' (Cheung-Judge and Holbeche, 2011: 11). OD practitioners are not those responsible for leading change and that the term *change managers* related to senior managers and Chief Executive Officers (CEOs) (Beckhard, 1969). OD practice fits better with the terminology of *change agent*, who could be externally or internally placed and provide consulting or technical support in the Change Management process (Beckhard, 1969). What is key is that the OD practitioner is not the person in charge, they are the third-party change agent assisting the person in charge (Cheung-Judge and Holbeche, 2011 citing Marshak, 2006).

OD's Relationship to HR(M) and HRD

As OD, HRM and HRD are all professions that concentrate on issues of people in employment there can be fuzzy boundaries between them, and all have faced their own evolutionary challenges. At this point it would normally be useful to provide definitions of HRM and HRD. However, just as OD has blurred boundaries and has developed in form over time and contextual difference, these issues which lead to difficulty in definition also extend to HRM (see Boxall, 1996) and HRD (see McLean and McLean, 2001).

In the case of HRM, HR and OD have very different agendas. HR is content driven whereas OD practitioners are process specialists involved in assisting people to derive benefit for themselves. They are also experts in change and apply their skills to business and group issues (Stanford, 2012). Challenging senior leaders and asking difficult questions is also inherent within the role of OD (Stanford, 2012). In contrast, HR is more involved with content which is what differentiates it in its contribution to the success of the organization (Stanford, 2012).

HR has had its own change journey: from Personnel to HR, the re-engineering of HR in the adoption of the Ulrich Model and the challenges of this re-engineering and the imperative to add strategic value (Cheung-Judge and Holbeche, 2011). US-based Anderson (2009: 105) described the change in HR to have been so extreme that he called it a 'metamorphosis'.

The expanding HR agenda requires an OD frame, so it is important for HR and OD to explore how they might work together (Cheung-Judge and Holbeche, 2011). Furthermore both OD and HR powers 'can wax and wane' (Cheung-Judge and Holbeche, 2011: 210). HR professionals are generally embedded in organizations as *business partners* whereas OD practitioners can be either internal or external to the system. Internal OD practitioners often have to operate as though they are external consultants, as this is essential to enable effective challenge (Cheung-Judge and Holbeche, 2011: 210).

OD has a long-term focus, whereas HRD improvements concentrated on 'individual and team performance improvement and/or personal growth' and HR works by 'aligning HR practices and people processes to the requirements of the short-term business agenda' (Cheung-Judge and Holbeche, 2011: 209). In the case of HR and HRD it could be argued that HR and HRD have been joined as professions in the UK for decades. In 1994 the professional bodies for Personnel Management (The Institute of Personnel Development [later the CIPD] {IPD}) and Training and Development (The Institute of Training and Development {ITD}) merged (CIPD, 2014b). This converged model of the three professions (HRM, OD and HRD) is not found in the US (Ruona and Gibson, 2004).

Since HR are increasingly expected to take the lead in organizational change (Cheung-Judge and Holbeche, 2011), there is increasing demand for HR professionals to have OD skills (Sharkey, 2009), and it is natural for HR and OD to be more frequently compared. A challenge for HR is to consider to what extent they are capable of OD, or if they should 'bring/buy' in these skills and experience (Cheung-Judge and Holbeche, 2011: 197). Senior Business Leaders need change agent HR professionals who can advise on matters of Change Management and culture change, in addition to advising on organization design and redesign: all of which required at least an understanding of OD (Cheung-Judge and Holbeche, 2011).

Furthermore, there is an increasing expectation that HR professionals should be capable organizational architects: designing and enabling organizational agility through self-renewing and flexible organization cultures, and using HR processes to alter behavior (Cheung-Judge and Holbeche, 2011). Working in partnership, it is proposed that HR and OD can add to an organization's competitive advantage sustainability by designing organizations which are 'built-to-change' (Sweem, 2009: 155).

In order to be seen as being effective, HR needs to assist clients through major change: to take responsibility for determining organization design and improving the wellbeing and health of both organizations and individuals (Stanford, 2012). HR also needs to apply HR approaches in order to develop future capability and address short-term business requirements (Stanford, 2012). Another area where HR and OD should act together strategically is in the development and implementation of approaches to talent management (Sweem, 2009), taking into account that within the Resource-Based View of organizations, consideration of culture is critical to its success (Sweem, 2009).

To be effective, OD and HR professions have to act in tandem within organizations. OD is successful as a result of considering the needs and reactions of employees(Cheung-Judge and Holbeche, 2011). HR policies and practices can be used to create 'great places to work' that are both affordable to the business and attractive to the "right employees" . . . 'This mutuality of interest is at the root of sustainable high performance, HR's strategic mission' (Cheung-Judge and Holbeche, 2011: 201). OD has played a key role in supporting the development of social work systems, including at the whole system level, to enhance sustainability (Docherty et al. 2009). Ruona and Gibson (2004) contend that the way forward for success in the twenty-first century is for OD, HRM and HRD to converge.

From a functional point of view, HR focuses on the management of people in an organization, and the links between this HR function and OD have been the subject of debate (Francis et al. 2012). The question of whether OD should come within the personnel function is contingent on power relationships (Beer, 1976) and if the personnel function is powerful in the organization then OD should be placed within that function. However, if personnel is not a powerful function, then the OD function should seek to be placed elsewhere.

In a more specific view on the extent of the relationship between OD and the HR function, there are five models of how OD might be situated in an organization:

1   A traditional model: where OD is situated within the HR function
2   An internal model: where OD is not situated within HR, but reports to another function, such as senior management in strategy/administration
3   A decentralized model: where OD reports within business units to either a business unit head or the HR Director
4   A fully integrated model: where OD is integrated directly within all aspects of the HR function
5   Integral to CEO-level model: OD is involved in strategy setting, reporting in a strategy function that reports direct to the CEO

(Burke, 2004)

A small-scale UK empirical study (responses n=106) was conducted between late 2010 and early 2011 to test the application of these models (Francis et al., 2012). The first set of data was collected from attendees at a CIPD Conference, the second set from respondents in the National Health Service (NHS) in England. It was found that in approximately a quarter of cases, the preferred option was for OD to be situated within the HR function (Francis et al., 2012). Organizational effectiveness was considered to be strongest if the decentralized model (type 3) of OD was adopted, and the traditional form of organization (type 1) was considered to be the least successful (Francis et al., 2012).

A linked issue is where OD was best situated, in relation to who was accountable for OD activity, and how this might properly vary depending on the organizational level of the OD issue. For example, if an issue is a corporate-level OD issue, then the responsibility/accountability and work flow, may be different from an OD issue at a divisional or department level (Anderson, 2009). It was also argued that HR and HRD are not the only disciplines that OD should be aligned with, and that there was the possibility of working fruitfully with, for example, IT and engineering professionals (Dunn, 2009).

Despite difference in the history, mode of operation or values of HR and OD functions, they have been pushed to work together (Stanford, 2012). US-based Ruona and Gibson (2004: 51) considered that OD had not been subsumed within HR, at least 'not yet'. However, it is viewed as being achievable and desirable that by 'working together HR and OD' can produce an innovative form of organizational effectiveness(Stanford, 2012: 211).

Professional Associations

This section will focus on the literature on the professional status of OD. Professionalization is a key factor in the conceptual development of a field, yet Bradford and Burke (2004: 372) were emphatic that 'OD is not a profession' in the same way as the legal, accountancy and medical professions. Weidner, II and Kulick (1999) defined OD as an occupation rather than a profession, but OD should nevertheless operate professionally (Bradford and Burke, 2004). As these authors are US-based, it should be noted that, as with other elements of OD, the denomination of professional status may differ both across and within national contexts.

Arguments for and against the professionalization of OD are based on the understanding that it provides a form of occupational control (Weidner, II and Kulick, 1999). Those against argue that professionalization inhibits the free market practice of OD and opens up the possibility for regulation (including who can practice) from within OD and from outside, in the form of state or government control (Weidner, II and Kulick, 1999). Those in favor argue that professionalization would lead to a higher level of quality control of practice and the potential for monitoring of practice, which could mitigate against ethical abuse (Weidner, II and Kulick, 1999).

Other arguments in relation to the professional status of OD are based on the creation of a body of knowledge and the opportunities it would provide for the development of an OD community of practice, and for the development of a public identity (Weidner, II and Kulick, 1999). The primary objective of forming associations is not to promote the interests of others (e.g. society), but is for the good of the members of the profession (Weidner, II and Kulick, 1999). However, professional associations do generally promote ethical conduct and their members seek to act professionally (Weidner, II and Kulick, 1999). Professional associations also provide a vehicle to minimize competition for work, which enhances the economic prospects of their members and allows practitioners a level of independence of judgement through reference to professional norms and regulations (Weidner, II and Kulick, 1999). A sequential route to OD becoming a profession has been proposed, which would involve: being recognized by the state; training and university education; forming as a professional association; seeking license from the state; and establishing a code of ethics (Weidner, II and Kulick, 1999).

In the US, the NTL raised the issue of accreditation, but found their membership did not want this. The OD Institute introduced an accrediting process and a code of ethics, but to little avail (Bradford and Burke, 2004). So, what of the position of other professional communities in the development of OD as a profession? The bodies considered to operate in the professional domain of people in employment are the CIPD in the UK; the US-founded OD Network and the European OD Network, which was founded in 2012 (OD Network Europe, 2014), and the US-based SHRM.

In the US the OD Network was founded by Burke in 1971 (Stanford, 2012), and no current membership numbers are available. In the UK the CIPD was founded in 1913 and has a current membership of 130,000 professionals (CIPD2014a). In the US, SHRM was founded in 1948 and has a current membership of 250,000 (SHRM, 2014). The CIPD has a much longer history (CIPD2014a, SHRM, 2014), and it has more than half the number of members of the US bodies which covers much larger and more highly populated geographical areas. As such, the saturation of membership amongst the UK HR professional grouping appears to be much denser.

In the US, OD established itself as a profession with its own professional body and code of practice, with membership of the profession made up of consultants from academics, consultancy practice or public- and private-sector organizations acting as consultants (Burnes, 2004a). There is currently no UK-based OD professional organization and no qualifications are required to be a member of the OD Network. Conversely, the CIPD has, for decades, had stringent standards, levels of qualifications and validated experience linked to its membership levels (CIPD, 2015).

As demonstrated earlier, the CIPD has encapsulated OD within its professional map as one of the core specialist areas of HR (CIPD, 2014a). In this regard, one could argue that in the UK the CIPD has been making a 'land grab' to own the profession of OD. The ethos of the CIPD and SHRM is that HR should ' be seen to step up to the mark' and make a tangible difference to the future of organizations (Cheung-Judge and Holbeche, 2011: 200).

A driving factor for the OD profession has been that, as with any profession or trade, customers are required for what you provide. In order that the profession can be viable, customers must receive what they perceived to need. If not, the profession will go out of business (Burnes, 2004a). Although the fiduciary character of professional work is that there is an implicit contract for ethical and competent services and client needs should take priority over a practitioner's 'need to make a living' (Weidner, II and Kulick, 1999: 335).

Values and Ethics for the OD Profession

A regularly recurring theme in the literature was that of values and their integral nature to the field of OD. The 'OD approach to change is, above all, an approach that cares about people' at all levels, and that change can only truly happen when people consider that they have a good Quality of Working Life (QWL) (Senior and Swailes, 2010: 317). Not only are values the scaffolding of OD, they are also the reason that many practitioners first choose OD as a career (Anderson, 2009).

Ethical and humanistic values, such as social justice and democracy, formed part of OD from the outset. OD focuses on choice, fairness, human development, and openness with constraint balanced by autonomy (Cummings and Feyerherm, 2003). Values are linked to organizational effectiveness: 'Underpinning OD is a set of values, assumptions and ethics that emphasise humanistic orientation and its commitment to organisational effectiveness' (Burnes, 2004a: 267). Hayes (2014: 281) also emphasizes the implicit nature of values from the origins of OD with:

> a series of studies on autocratic and democratic leadership produced findings suggesting that participation and involvement led to improved outcomes, which stimulated the development of a new approach to managing change, known as organization development (OD), based on these values.
>
> Hayes (2014: 281)

The importance placed on ethics continues with Cheung-Judge and Holbeche (2011) who situate OD as having humanistic democratic values, in that people have to be given a voice in changes that affect them. When they emerged in the 1950s, OD values were considered revolutionary although they became accepted as a mainstream view (French and Bell, 1999). They followed scientific management, the:

> humanistic approach of OD began to replace the machine metaphor of organisations with natural images of body and health and drew on the behavioural sciences to suggest how people, systems and technology could be organised in more effective and humane way. The key strands of work that form the core of classical OD relate to humanistic values, training and development, employee feedback, systems thinking and action research.
>
> (Garrow, 2009: 2)

In 1969, Beckhard laid out six principles on these revolutionary values in relation to how a workplace should be viewed by OD practitioners: 1) People are more autonomous and independent—as it should be. 2) They have choices in their work and leisure, and should have these choices. 3) Employees shouldn't be concerned with basic security needs, but able to concentrate on realizing their potential and their self-worth. 4) If there is a conflict or tension between the organization's needs and the person needs, they can and should put their needs first. 5) The organization should provide work which is organized in such a way as to make it meaningful/interesting as well as providing sufficient monetary rewards, and 6) Managers should no longer retain the level of power they have had in the past. Instead of using coercive measures to manage, including the withholding of financial rewards, employees should have choice in leisure and in work, so managers should use other methods to influence and motivate employees (Beckhard, 1969).

Issues of ethics and values form part of the landscape of professions which are 'built around strong norms and values about how one is to conduct oneself . . . yet it is clear that norms and values relating to professional conduct are at best loosely held and agreed upon' (Church et al., 1992: 22). The construct of ethics is often accompanied by the issue of clarity through declarations of the need for professional codes of practice, in order for OD practitioners to have a moral baseline against which to measure their actions (Cummings and Feyerherm, 2003).

However, it is not easy to regulate OD and since it cannot be defined easily, set rules are not appropriate and situational approaches are instead necessary (DeVogel et al., 1995). There is though, an issue on the ethical decision making principles and values of its practitioners (DeVogel et al., 1995). There are no definite standards or qualifications set in OD nor is there a professional association which represents the community with authority (DeVogel et al., 1995). What should take the place of regulation is the application of individual professional ethics, which take into account society's legitimate interests and concerns specific to that area of professional practice (DeVogel et al., 1995).

The OD Network (2014) published *Principles of Practice* where 'The practice of OD is grounded in a distinctive set of core values and principles that guide behavior and actions'. This outlines the key areas of respect and inclusion, collaboration, authenticity and self-awareness. The focus on adherence to values is also demonstrated by their publication of an *Organization and Human Systems Development Credo* (OD Network, 1996). Even the Network's definition of OD is saturated with their pervading approach to values, noting that: 'Organization Development is a dynamic values-based approach to systems change in organizations and communities; it strives to build the capacity to achieve and sustain a new desired state that benefits the organization or community and the world around them' (OD Network, 2014).

With DeVogel et al.'s (1995) view that one set of rules for OD does not work, self-regulation and audit is an alternative approach to ethics (DeVogel et al., 1995). This could be achieved by, for example, the use of a Values-Clarification Instrument, which allows the consultant to self-evaluate their value preferences on the topics of: Client Autonomy, Informed Consent, Collaboration, Objectivity and Independence, Confidentiality, Truth Telling, Professional Development, Social Justice and Recognizing Limits (DeVogel et al. (1995).

Interestingly, in the UK the CIPD do not mention values with specific reference to OD in its professional map, but have an overarching Code of Professional Conduct which includes five points on integrity and ethical standards (CIPD, 2014c). However, there is a view that there is a fundamental difference between OD and HR which 'may have lost sight of its original values.' In HR 'the people champion' role is now seen as 'soft', and no longer 'relevant to the needs of business' (Cheung-Judge and Holbeche (2011: 208). Although 'HR is more firmly identified with business needs', they should have rebalanced and reclaimed the 'people champion' emphasis in at least equal balance with 'organizational champion' (Cheung-Judge and Holbeche, 2011: 208).

However, a question arose for the author in relation to the numerous short statement references to humanistic values and ethical concerns. Are authors applying the same meaning and using the same yard stick? If these terms are not qualified, are scholars using the same meaning or lifting and applying labels without much conscious thought? Cummings and Feyerherm (2003: 99) cited Tannenbaum and Davis (1969) as the original source for outlining the humanistic values of OD, and noted that 'For a long time, this list represented the de facto statement in the field'. There had been a definitive list, but since this was rarely referenced, we cannot assume that all authors used this list as their baseline.

Tannenbaum and Davis (1969) consider their values to be consistent with working in the field of behavioral sciences, which is 'deeply rooted in the nature of man and therefore basically humanistic' (Tannenbaum and Davis, 1969: 69). With thirteen statements, although there was a breadth of topic, these issues are usually wrapped simply under the labels *humanistic* and/ or *democratic* values by others. However the original list had more variety than might be covered by those terms e.g. *Away from Avoidance of Risk-Taking toward Willingness to Risk* (Tannenbaum and Davis, 1969: 69). In addition, there have been changes in values over time as OD scholars in the early 1990s reviewed the lists of values and 'noted that the practice of OD had become more "results" and "bottom line" oriented' (Cummings and Feyerherm, 2003: 99)

The usefulness of OD values is a much-debated topic in the context of a changing world. In transformational change, what might be good for senior managers and the organization does not necessarily match what is right for society or for individuals (Underwood Stephens and Cobb, 1999). Executive groups are the decision makers and the choices they made are unlikely to be governed by moral fairness and equity (Underwood Stephens and Cobb, 1999). However, van Nistelrooij and Sminia (2010) argue that through dialogue, shared perceptions between the various parties affected can be achieved.

Moreover, OD values were developed primarily in the US, and to assume that, for instance, democratic values could be applied in the same way in different national contexts is inherently flawed (Yaeger et al., 2006). There is duplicity within OD adherence to values (Palmer et al., 2009): with OD practitioners criticizing the Change Management camp as being a faddist panacea provided by management consultants for commercial gain, whilst arguing that as a discipline, OD had become more strategic and holistic in approach (Palmer et al., 2009). OD practitioners were concerned about being identified as part of the Change Management community, but for the OD community to suggest that they could keep their values intact whilst increasingly having their practice driven by the needs of business leaders, was hypocritical (Palmer et al., 2009).

Over time, OD moved considerably from its roots in planned and group-based change and developed into a much greater focus on OD's organization-wide transformational approaches. However, the organization-wide approaches were less refined, less clear and less well established (Burnes, 2004a). Ironically the more OD focused on organization-wide issues, the less closely connected it was to teams and individuals, and lost its core democratic/humanist values (Burnes, 2004a). However, Anderson (2009) argued, that in concentrating on core humanistic values, OD had lost sight of the *organization* part of its name. In continuing to adapt and maintain its currency and relevance, OD was losing touch with the core values which had always been its distinguishing feature: the paradox being that, in the postmodern world, these values which support empowerment, consensus-building, equality and horizontal relationships are exactly what is required (Burnes, 2004a).

Another inconsistency is identified in that if OD is concerned with changing behavior, to what extent can that be considered as an ethical and values-based objective (Stanford, 2012)? Stanford (2012) argue that to aim to change the behavior of others is in itself a manipulative and question-able act. That an OD practitioner might prescribe the behavior which they consider to be in others' interests, is arguably riddled with assumption and value judgement, and also contrary to the humanistic value set lauded by OD professionals (Stanford, 2012). In addition, the application of demo-cratic principles and consultation mean that if the views of stakeholders are not put into practice, they may disengage: judging that if meaningfully solicited, they have the right to expect changes to be fully aligned with their views (Bradford and Burke, 2006).

Nevertheless, the call to 'Return to Lewinian Values' (Burnes, 2009: 359) is strong. The late 1970s marked the end of the post-war approach to eco-nomics and politics, which had emphasized 'common good' over gain for the individual and state regulation was loosened in the interests of mar-ket forces (Burnes, 2009: 374). However, this ethos was and continues to change: with the financial crisis; the increasing awareness of environmental issues; organizations becoming more interested in putting social responsi-bility over profit; and the influence of President Barack Obama (Burnes, 2009). An emergent approach to change may have fitted with the previous political and economic era, but in a world where there was more support for ethical approaches to business 'an ethically-based approach to change' was more pertinent, the only way to successfully deliver the changes required (Burnes, 2009).

Critiques of OD

OD has been subject to criticism in the UK and in the US; with particular questions as to whether it has outlived its time (e.g. Legge, 1995, 2005; Bradford and Burke, 2006). It was thought that the OD community should have changed their label since the term OD had gone out of fashion, and that this should have also been accompanied by updating traditional OD thinking (Porras and Bradford, 2004). The primary criticisms of OD were that it lacked definition; having single/multiple interventions over time made measurement and evaluation difficult; and internal validity was difficult, in relation to the extent to which the intervention created change, or there was another factor of influence (Palmer et al., 2009: 192). External validity was also difficult; the extent to which OD techniques were suitable to all settings was questionable; there was a problem with generalizing on the application of OD in different settings; and there was a lack of theory, with no thorough account of the theory of change (Palmer et al., 2009). It did not seem an appropriate single method for such a pluralistic field of practice, but Svyantek et al. (1992) proposed a *Bayesian* approach as the solution to the evaluation of OD interventions.

Additionally, critiques have highlighted the lack of clarity on cost/benefit analysis and contribution to organization performance. There were also deficiencies in distinctiveness or definition and a need for more quality control of practitioners. Moreover, critiques have also highlighted the lack of concern for customers' needs and insufficient business acumen (amongst OD practitioners) (Wirtenberg, et al., 2004). Some OD campaigners sought clarification of the field or identified a need to reshape the field, whilst others believed that there was a lack of interest in OD from students of business, and from executives. It was believed that OD no longer had relevance and that its practitioners were woefully inadequate across the range of business knowledge and skills (Palmer et al., 2009). Additionally, OD practitioners were often considered to be naïve in devaluing organizational politics (Bradford and Burke, 2006).

One weakness of OD was that it did not always face up to the harsh realities of change, for example the need to speed up the unfreezing process through unpleasant means (Senior and Swailes, 2010). OD did not sufficiently adopt the perspective of the general manager: it needed to be far more cognizant of the context and adopt stronger situational perspectives and practice (Beer and Walton 1987). Given that over recent decades many organizational change initiatives have involved downsizing, it was rare to find references to this form of change in OD publications (e.g. Legatski, II, 1998).

OD was also highlighted as being limited when the change situation was constrained: for example, if the need for change has been created by a legal, regulatory or financial crisis issue which means that the design of the change is not completely open (Senior and Swailes, 2010). It has also been criticized as not being strategic in approach (e.g. Worren et al., 1999). It has 'failed glaringly in developing models, approaches, and strategies for gaining power in organizations' (Beer, 1976: 47).

Additionally, OD requires 'out of the ordinary' leadership (Senior and Swailes, 2010: 356). Few leaders have the persistence or personality to stick with involving others to achieve long-term change, especially when under pressure within the organizational cultural context or dealing with the tension of competing goals. It takes persistence to achieve 'frame-breaking change' (Senior and Swailes, 2010: 357). In addition, OD fits uneasily with the structures and culture of the public sector, due to the bureaucratic nature of the organizational environment not being best suited to OD. The public sector involves multiple decision makers, and system-wide effort is very difficult, with decision making tending to be driven upwards (Senior and Swailes, 2010).

Whilst OD tools and techniques have been favored for teaching in universities, there is a need for more use of theory and alternative methods of change should be taught, since no one approach is the answer (Dawson, 2003). When people have been on the receiving end of ill designed tools and techniques, and in particular where there have been a series of these, they become cynical and jaded (King and Anderson, 2002). With tools applied badly, it was not surprising that OD was seen as being faddish (King and Anderson, 2002).

However, there is a view in defense of OD (see French and Bell, 1999: 291), that it allows the organization 'to go beyond the negative face of power and *politics*' (French and Bell, 1999: 291). However, to operate in a political environment OD needs to have: 'Competence . . . Political Access and sensitivity . . . Sponsorship . . . Stature and credibility . . . Resource management' and 'Group support'(Cheung-Judge and Holbeche, 2011: 176–177). Nonetheless, issues around the nature of the relationship between OD practitioners and their pay master should not be ignored, as this could lead them to be tempted as 'servants of power' (Golembiewski, 1989: 178) and OD practitioners who are 'simply mouthpieces for the establishments who pay their fees, which can be substantial' (Golembiewski, 1989: 43). There were specific condemnations, including issues of power, marked out against planned change itself. The main criticisms made were that:

1   planned change was suitable in an era where organizations were more stable. With turbulent change in the environment, change has become open ended and continuous rather than one discreet move from one steady state to another;

2   it was focused on incremental change and did not offer anything for transformational/radical change. However, there is a range of change requirements from transformation to fine tuning, so not all change is radical either;

3   planned change is based on the assumption that agreement between all parties can be arrived at, and that all stakeholders are devoid of

personal interest (or at least not driven by that) and will happily engage in the planned changes with one common spirit. The assumption is that if there is power and politics at play, differences can be easily identified and resolved; and

4 the assumption of one approach: suitable in all eras, to all types of organizations, in all situations.

(Burnes, 2004a)

Advocates of OD contend that it has developed as a profession, and has integrated the need for approaches to organizational transformation, power and politics (Burnes, 2004a). In any case, in Lewin's original version of OD, the importance of politics and power was not disregarded and it was recognized that change could be extreme and swift (Burnes, 2004a), and in particular, 'Lewin did not see organisations as stable and changeless entities', with his views being similar on this point to many of his critics. Neither did Lewin consider planned change to be the only approach. It was instead the variants which had emerged from Lewinian roots that were being criticized. As such, to apply the ownership of *Lewin* to the work under critique was incorrect (Burnes, 2004a). Lewin would 'be astonished at the widespread and creative ways his model has been (socially) reconstructed' (Bartunek and Woodman, 2015).

Debates on the Value of OD, Contemporary OD and the Prognosis for its Future

Although the debate on the ongoing relevance of OD has already been touched on in this chapter, it is a critical issue requiring more detailed analysis. In the UK, in 1995 and 2005 Legge claimed that OD was past its heyday of the 1960s. Later, in the mid-2000s, there was significant debate amongst US-based academics and practitioners on whether OD was dead, or simply having a 'midlife crisis' (Cheung-Judge and Holbeche, 2011: 23). Burnes and Cooke (2012: 1396) also reflected the energy given to the debate about 'whether or not' OD was still alive and kicking. In 2004, a Special Issue of arguably the most prominent OD academic journal, the US-based *Journal of Applied Behavioural Science* focused entirely on reflecting on the 'relevance and continued viability of OD', in which Bradford and Burke (2004: 369) posed the question 'Is OD in Crisis?'

In 2006, US-based Bradford and Burke pessimistically reflected Legge's (1995, 2005) rhetoric and asked if OD was past its prime and if it was, should it simply be allowed to die a graceful death? There was question as to whether OD was being kept going by periodic transfusions of a new approach that rejuvenated the field for a short time, only to then to relapse into a semi-comatose state (Bradford and Burke, 2006). Greiner and Cummings (2004: 374) headlined *Wanted: OD More Alive Than Dead*. However, they outlined a route to a more fruitful future for OD through embracing content as much as process. Another view was that OD was instead already very healthy and was very much needed, given that organizations had to constantly change to adapt to rapidly changing environments (Dunn, 2009).

Worren et al. (1999: 274) were amongst those that levelled criticism that OD practitioners 'do not understand business' and that 'the field is invisible to the majority of executives'. Whilst in the founding of BPR, the people element was forgotten, so it could be said that the OD community 'forgot about markets, strategies and computers' (Worren et al. (1999: 284).

The normally accepted history of OD was that it began in the 1950s, nor was it in a terminal decline by the 1980s. However, there is an alternative view that the history of OD went back longer and is far from obsolete (Burnes and Cooke, 2012). Moreover, this view proposes that there was fight left in the OD community, and 'although there was a great deal of soul searching in the OD community, this was accompanied by an intellectual renaissance, which created the conditions for OD to reunite its academic and practitioner wings and rebuff its critics' (Burnes and Cooke, 2012: 1397).

There were three empirical studies on the nature of the difficulties faced by OD and the opportunities to overcome perceived problem areas. In 2003, Cummings and Feyerherm reported on the opinions of twenty-one OD *thought leaders* on overcoming the challenges faced by OD. In this study they looked at features which had created success in the past; what the OD community needed to do more and less of; and what they should have aimed for in the future. They found that the top three reasons given by the thought leaders for past success were:

- Broad education and training, experience (48%); their interpersonal skills (43%); and having an accurate knowledge of self (33%).

When reflecting on what those in OD needed to do more or less of, the top responses were:

- Relying less on techniques and fads (48%); increasing collaboration within the field (43%); selecting context relevant approaches to change (43%); and addressing group and individual development (43%).

Finally, with regards to future competencies, the following were the areas most referred to:

- Competence in understanding and working with large systems (43%); being able to challenge and say give the tough messages to senior managers (28%); competence in design (24%); able to exert influence and power (24%); commercial acumen (24%); to have a broad understanding of the world (24%); and systems thinking (24%).

In a survey of 1201 respondents of self-identified OD practitioners Shull et al. (2013) compared results with an earlier 1995 study. The 1995 study found that OD practitioners should have focused on business-related and system issues rather than on the traditional territory of 'interpersonal, group process and human relations' (Church and Burke, 1995: 11). There was a need for OD professionals to be more 'self-aware of their own behaviour and internal states' (Church and Burke, 1995: 19), the importance of OD values was on the wane, and this trend would continue (Church and Burke, 1995).

Any conclusions drawn from the later study reported by Shull et al. (2013) are arguably limited by the method (for example the use of self-identifying participants) used for issuing the questionnaire. Nevertheless, the results gave a broad indication of where the US OD community saw themselves in terms of their professional association membership (Shull et al., 2013). The findings, when compared with the 1995 study, highlight a perceived weakening in the professional values and grounding in social sciences, particularly amongst newer members of the field; an increasing focus on business effectiveness outcomes: less of a touchy feely orientation (see Sharkey, 2009); and an increased importance of challenging misuse of power within organizations (Shull et al., 2013). Further findings were concerned with a growing commitment (from OD practitioners) to their employing organization, the view that coaching was integral to OD and that there was generally optimism about the future of OD (Shull et al., 2013).

In comparing the results, Shull et al. (2013) notes a transition from *Old Guard* to the *New Practitioner* from the 1995 study, and a subsequent transition to the *2012 Practitioner*. The results from these studies appear to be less geared towards strategic-level competency than those outlined from the Cummings and Feyerherm (2003) study of *thought leaders* outlined above. In reviewing the future of strategic human resources, as opposed to traditional HRM, Becker and Huselid (2006) appear to find views closer to those given by the OD *thought leaders*, in explaining a new emphasis on the link to organizational performance, rather than individual performance; and at systems rather than individual HRM practice level. Also in line with the OD *thought leaders* they argue that Strategic Human Resources (SHR) needed to be differentiated in line with the organizational context.

Sharkey (2009) outlines three areas of importance in the future of organizations, all requiring OD skills. First, HR and OD should move from a business partner role into driving business strategy through shaping culture and leadership: the rhetoric of business partners and seeking a 'seat at the table' was history (Sharkey, 2009: 16). Second, they highlight the importance of the need to have talented leaders who can operate successfully in a global economy, and understand how important their behavior is in driving culture. Finally, having the best of top talent is critical to company performance Sharkey (2009).

OD must first address the following three problems in order to remain relevant: It must put more O in OD; be less exclusive on the emphasis of human processes; and remedy the harm of having adhered so dogmatically to humanistic values (Bradford and Burke, 2006). With regards to the first problem, very few people who have labelled themselves as OD are true OD people, as working effectively in OD means working at a system-wide, strategic level. It is not just a case of applying OD techniques to clear up the mess, nor is it simply about changing individuals, for example through executive coaching (Bradford and Burke, 2006). To be effective, change needs to be system-wide and it therefore follows that OD practitioners cannot operate without a thorough knowledge of the business. Nor can they operate in a socio-technical change context whilst ignoring the technical aspect issues due to it being outside the core competence of OD (Bradford and Burke, 2006).

To combat the second problem area, OD practitioners must fully understand the problem or opportunity. This is not always, or exclusively, about the way people interact and the setting of ground rules for interactions (Bradford and Burke, 2006). If OD practitioners always resort to a default setting of *it is the norms of behavior that need addressing*, **or** *we need to revisit the mission and objectives so that we are all agreed on the objectives*, then credibility will be quickly lost (Bradford and Burke, 2006).

With the third problem area, whilst democratic values had been strength and underpinned achievements for OD, a dictatorial emphasis on them can be harmful. Research has found that commitment can be developed without employee participation in the decision-making processes. However, when challenged, OD practitioners often seem to let the humanistic values predominate over behavioral science research findings (Bradford and Burke, 2006). Furthermore, there is a paradox in that OD practitioners have strongly advocated and imposed humanistic values, when in taking what was in effect a dictatorial approach to this they were themselves being anti-democratic! Within the OD population there has been too strong an emphasis on the client as the enemy, with a strong anti-leadership streak running through much of the OD community (Bradford and Burke, 2006). Moreover, OD has had an unexplored dark side in that it has not been open to objective evaluation (Bradford and Burke, 2006).

Every organization has a history which means that some approaches may be inappropriate for that organization (Bradford and Burke, 2006). So, for example, in an organization that had previously used TQM, if it was used to manipulate the outcome of goals, then TQM might thereafter be perceived as negatively (as a tainted process) by some stakeholders. In this case, assuming that TQM could be applied afresh and received without prejudice could be foolish. There may be sacrosanct positions which must be considered, or change will not happen. There may be individuals who have more or less power than an organisational position chart suggests; some individuals who must be included; others for whom inclusion does not matter; and those who influence others (Bradford and Burke, 2006).

Several scholars have explored the trials and tribulations of OD and between them presented a disparate range of advice on where opportunities lie. Woodman (1989: 206) published a review article that examines developments, offering the following areas for examination: 'refinement of change theories, developments in research methodologies, developments at the level of firm strategy, OD in multinational firms, development of the organizational culture construct, development of high performance, high-commitment work systems, and OD in social movements'.

A more recent school of thought has been emerging since the early 2000s. Under the label of *Positive Organizational Scholarship*, along with fields like AI and *Positive Psychology*, it promotes that the focus of OD should not have been dominated by negative issues and addressing problems only, but should also focus on building on strengths (Palmer et al., 2009). However, any agreement on what was positive should not have been assumed, nor should behavior have been judged, in that *correct* behavior was a situational issue (Palmer et al., 2009). Furthermore, if positive and negative aspects could have been separated, they were just flip sides of the same coin and change for the positive could come out of experience of adversity. Besides, a criticism of mass positivity was that it assumed a unitarist perspective (Palmer et al., 2009).

OD is still in its adolescence, searching for its identity and uniqueness, and is still relevant. However, there are many areas where it needs to do better: in particular maintaining integrity while demonstrating capability of dealing with commercial concerns (Cheung-Judge and Holbeche, 2011). It would be useful for OD to revisit its identity and boundary, identifying the core of OD that should be preserved whilst other parts evolve (Cheung-Judge and Holbeche, 2011). In a global environment where complex and ongoing changes are normal, OD is at a defining moment in its history, with OD skills in higher demand than ever (Gallos, 2006). They are rarely identified as valuable and necessary, though ascending:

> fully to this challenge, however, takes the field towards new theories, practices, markets and applications. Doing this well requires (1) differentiating OD's core from its peripheral trappings and (2) creating a proactive strategy for identifying possibilities for OD's future.
>
> (Gallos, 2006: 829)

There may be a positive prognosis for the future of OD. There is still an important role to release 'human potential within organisations', indeed at a time when the lack of moral rigor had presented us with various business catastrophes, a community that has held on to its values when they were considered out of date, should have something to offer (Bradford and

Burke, 2004: 372). However, in order to survive, OD needs to express more clearly 'what it is and what it is not' (Bradford and Burke, 2004: 372).

Furthermore OD needs to identify itself as a profession which has 'clear boundaries that define the field, rules that govern entrance, a code of ethics, and a way of disciplining members who violate those ethics' and at the moment, OD has none of this (Bradford and Burke, 2004: 372). In the UK, though, if OD is to be considered to be within HR, it does have all of these features under the umbrella of the CIPD.

Additionally, OD can achieve a better understanding of itself as a field, through looking at its practice as developed in the *Strategy as Practice* academic community (Hutton and Liefooghe, 2011). There is an argument 'for a concept of unity of theory and practice that places primacy on practice and in which OD as a pragmatic reconstruction draws on the multiple perspectives of participant, observer, and critic' (Hutton and Liefooghe, 2011: 92). In the founding of OD, this process was applied (Hutton and Liefooghe, 2011).

A major strength of OD is that its processes were essentially well founded, but its future will depend upon numerous connected circumstances (French and Bell, 1999). In the main conditions are favorable to OD, but there are ambiguities and countertrends that require attention: 'The conditions and contingencies have to do with leadership and values; diffusion of technique; integrative practice; mergers, acquisitions, and alliances; rediscovering and recording history; and the search for community' (French and Bell, 1999: 324).

Amongst the ideas for improving OD are that the design sciences were brought to OD and Change Management to see what could be learned from them, and there are examples of academics who have successfully used design science in disciplines such as engineering, architecture and medicine (Bate, 2007). Design science is suitable for use in OD since it sits 'within a discipline aimed at developing general substantive and procedural design science to solve to solve the field problems of that discipline' (Van Aken, 2007: 71).

French and Bell (1999: 323) argue that

> The future of OD is bright as long as the high-quality, hard work of the past continues, and providing it does not become fashionable for top leaders to revert to autocratic or capricious practices in times of high turbulence or crises.

There are some CEOs, Finance, and HR leads who are committed to dual objectives of organization performance and humanistic values, whether they are correlated or not (French and Bell, 1999). In the US some CEOs are committed to this duality, whilst others are only interested in the bottom line (French and Bell, 1999). However, there is unfinished business in OD and in particular change efforts have failed, so the OD community has to continue to search for innovative solutions that work (Burke, 2011). Furthermore, whilst OD has been adept at 'tightening loose systems', it has to become equally skilled in loosening tight systems (Burke, 2011: 163).

The barriers that OD needs to overcome to be successful in the future (Bradford and Burke, 2006) are: it must be able to reinvent itself; practitioners must develop new competencies (e.g. commercial acumen and knowledge of business components); OD consultants should be capable of evaluating which needs are crucial in any situation (i.e. improvements in the human process, or business improvements); and OD practitioners should consider that not only have they lost their values, but must equally address that they had lost their relevance (Bradford and Burke, 2006). There is also a need to critically revisit the supporting system for OD practice, through books, articles and networks, as there is a requirement for strong leadership in the development of the profession, or in the evolution/revolution that will make that happen in the future (Bradford and Burke, 2006).

On the question of the existence of revolution or evolution in OD (e.g. Mirvis, 2006), an evolution generates fresh content which produces quantitative change, whereas revolution 'involves a change in context' that is more fundamental and has more significant impact (Mirvis, 2006: 48). OD is undergoing both, in particular where stakeholders take on new roles, for example, from clients to co-creators (Mirvis, 2006). OD initiatives have been designed around getting the whole system in the room, through using the open space format, and there has also been new theory, complex adaptive systems, new processes and the move towards using positive perspectives and action (Mirvis, 2006). OD has a role in creating a new purpose, which is a better world (Mirvis, 2006).

Many academics argue that a primary issue facing OD is in the lack of academic theory, rigor and research. Pettigrew (1985) describes how OD was considered as a fad, preoccupied with the people perspective of organizations to the exclusion of other factors, and not sufficiently informed by rigorous research. OD must be 'driven by the twin forces of academic rigour and practical relevance' (Burnes and Cooke, 2012: 1414). In the 1970s and 1980s, practitioners developed approaches to change by responding to client needs. Since the 1990s academics have been shaping the way forward 'as they seek to develop theoretically strong and rigorous approaches to change' (Burnes and Cooke, 2012: 1414). The call for better research and theory was also made by Beer and Walton (1987) who advocated a longitudinal approach, returning to action research, but over a much longer time frame; and Cummings and Feyerherm's (2003: 107) conclusion on the future was that 'the field of OD will continue to rely on a theory of change and research'.

A shared research agenda is key to OD's 'scholarly development' (Cummings and Feyerherm (2003: 107) with a need to bridge the research gap between academics and practitioners (Bunker et al. (2004). Bunker et al. (2004) suggested that areas which came from social and organizational psychology were ripe for the application of research, including virtual teams; conflict resolution through mediation and negotiation; work group effectiveness (in terms of effective output rather than measured by improved process and interpersonal relationships); and analysis of social networks. These are more fitting for practical application than the other areas of intractable conflict and trust (Bunker et al., 2004). OD needs to have more coherent links between theory, research and practice. This is not concerned with whether the research methodology used is quantitative or qualitative, but that the standard of the research has been questionable and some has been of poor quality (Woodman, 1989).

OD needs to earn credibility through evaluating the effectiveness of the models deployed (Francis et al., 2012. This sentiment is not new, with Beer commenting in 1976 (1976: 50) that 'OD suffers from an inability to demonstrate the relevance of its interventions' and 'developing a method for measuring . . . can not only increase the effectiveness and professional responsibility of OD but it can increase the power of OD within organizations'. Beer (1976) also called for robust theories and archetypes to increase the power and influence of OD.

Additionally, whilst there is much rhetoric on the failure of change, there is little valid and reliable evidence on which to base judgement of the reason for failures (Burnes and Cooke, 2012). Lack of consistency in study methods between 'types of OD', and differences in methodologies and organizational contexts, makes comparison difficult (Burnes and Cooke, 2012: 1415). Conclusions could be over generalized and lead to invalid suppositions. For academics and practitioners to work on the scale and over the time span necessary to be able to make more generalizable claims is a vast endeavor (Burnes and Cooke, 2012).

Not only did Hutton and Liefooghe (2011) emphasize that there was much that was right in the early field of OD, but in a stronger vein, Burnes and Cooke (2012) advised that it was crucial to pay attention to OD's Lewinian roots in order to add to its rigor. Despite the four common criticisms of Lewin, his approach was neither simplistic nor outmoded (Burnes, 2006). The appropriateness of emergent change faded, with complexity theory proving to be more fitting (Burnes and Cooke, 2012). The importance of values and ethics which had been considered old fashioned, were restored to vibrant life following the 'various organisational and financial scandals of the past decade' (Burnes and Cooke, 2012: 1415) with the consequence that OD values became relevant again.

There are 'two fundamental issues that OD needs to address' the first is 'rigour and relevance' and 'what is needed is a genuine commitment by both academics and practitioners to restoring Lewinian rigour and relevance to OD' (Burnes and Cooke, 2012: 1415). The second issue is the willingness and ability of OD to address the most significant questions facing global society (Burnes and Cooke, 2012: 1415).

Organizational effectiveness (OE) has been put forward as the vehicle for future OD success: new 'OE is eclectic since it involves practitioners' embracing humanist and business values'. Moreover, in seeking to 'build healthy and effective organisations characterised by learning, innovation, improvement and self-renewal' as well as building 'sustainable high performance through people', it meets the goals of OD and HR (Francis et al., 2012: 336) and HR's role should be central in fueling this shift.

The compelling motivation for the founders of the discipline was to improve the human condition and to wipe out totalitarianism. It could be argued that OD narrowed its driving goal to be that of achieving organizational effectiveness, which opens it to criticism of being 'merely a vehicle for managerialist co-optation' (Burnes and Cooke, 2012: 1416). In the current global, economic, environmental and ethical context the 'big questions' have never been so important (Burnes and Cooke, 2012: 1416).

Only leaders and organizations with a strong moral compass are likely to be able to resist the siren call of short-term expediency in order to promote long-term sustainability. People have a choice to behave ethically or otherwise; they cannot be manipulated or tricked into it (Burnes and Cooke (2012). To achieve an embedded long-term approach to change, OD approaches are required and OD should lead the move to a more sustainable and ethical way forward (Burnes and Cooke, 2012).

It should be remembered that one circumstance of Lewin as a founder of OD was that he 'lost many of his family in the holocaust' (Burnes and Cooke, 2012: 1416). In this context, his powerful motivation to resolve social conflict, extend democracy and root out totalitarianism was simple to understand. In contemporary OD the challenges may be different, 'but the need to promote ethics and democracy in order to build a better, more sustainable, world remains' (Burnes and Cooke, 2012: 1416).

Summary of Key Themes

The review of literature on OD has revealed that there are several key themes which take priority of focus in the literature on OD:

1   One of the strongest themes is that of the difficulty of definition and the fuzzy boundaries of OD.
2   Much has been written on the history of OD and on its founding years, on these topics discrepancies were, in the main, minor. However, one key difference is in the challenge to the perspective of the sole US influence in OD's founding. A further issue is the continuing domination of influence on OD by US-based scholars, in terms of what is written with regards to OD.
3   In terms of core OD, the traditional approach to OD has been outlined, with information on how this original form of OD has evolved.

However, there is also variation from this traditional form of OD in terms of what else has been described by the scholars.

4 Although the majority of accounts of the practices, skills and competence required to be an OD practitioner emanate from US-based scholars, the CIPD also provides information on this in their professional model map. There is much discussion on, and general agreement that OD practitioners should be capable of challenging organizational orthodoxy.

5 The relationship of OD to *Change Management* is blurred and there is variation on views as to how they fit with each other.

6 In the main, in the literature, there seems to be an assumption that OD is provided through a *Consultancy Orientation*.

7 OD as an application of *Behavioral Science* is still prevalent in the literature. However, the need to have *Behavioral Science knowledge and skills* is less prominent. In addition, there is not much provision in the way of formal OD education in *Behavioral Science* in the UK.

8 *Organizational Effectiveness* has been a goal of OD from its early years, and the emphasis placed on effectiveness has recently become stronger.

9 A *Strategic Approach* was less prevalent in early OD, but has also become a strong focus for contemporary OD.

10 There is little in the way of acknowledgement of the national, social or organizational context of OD practice from academic authors.

11 OD's relationship to HR and HRD has been almost ignored by the US-based scholars, and where it has received attention it has been primarily from UK-based authors.

12 The extent to which OD has, or should, follow a professional regulation route is debated.

13 The requirement to adhere to traditional OD values and ethics is a prominent feature within the scholarly community. However, there is debate on the extent to which OD should prioritize business concerns over adopting these values.

14 Critiques of OD are a focus for scholars, and a pool of US-based scholars have questioned whether the OD profession will survive. They have reflected on what OD must do to flourish in practice and in academia.

15 A tendency has emerged towards a divorce/separation between academia and practice. The lack of rigorous research to underpin OD practice has been identified as an issue.

The main themes from this chapter will be revisited and used to shape the structure of the comparison of the literature with the evidence in Chapter 6.

In consideration of the main areas of consensus in literature, the following working definition of OD was developed: **OD involves planned change (at whole or sub) system level, with the goal of organizational effectiveness achieved through the application of OD—processes, tools and techniques** *and delivered by adhering to humanistic values.* This definition includes *planned change,* since there continues to be consensus from the scholars that change in OD is specifically *planned change.* It has been clarified that in terms of the level of system change this is at system **and** sub-system level, since both are evidently important from the academic presentation of OD. *Organizational c effectiveness* and *processes, tools and techniques* have been and remain within the remit of OD, and the scholars continue to place emphasis on *humanistic values.*

As this review has demonstrated, much of the literature on OD is prescriptive in tone and at least in part, there are unfounded assumptions about the nature of OD practice. It is to an exploration of that practice that we now turn.

References

Academy of Management (2015) *Organization Development and Change Division* accessed online at: http://aom.org/Divisions-and-Interest-Groups/Organization-Development-and-Change/Organization-Development-and-Change.aspx (30th August, 2015)

Anderson, D. (2010) *Organization Development The Process of Leading Organizational Change.* Sage Publications: Thousand Oaks, CA.

Anderson, M. (2000) *Fast Cycle Organization Development.* South Western College Publishing: Toronto: Canada.

Anderson, P. (2009) 'Strategic Organization Development: An Invitation to the Table' in Yaeger, T., and Sorenson, P. (eds.) *Strategic Organization Development—Managing Change for Success.* A Volume in Contemporary Trends in Organization Development and Change. Information Age Publishing: USA. Pp. 97–114.

Austin, J., and Bartunek, J. (2006) 'Theories and Practices of Organizational Development' in Gallos, J. (ed.) *Organization Development—A Jossey-Bass Reader* John Wiley & Sons: San Francisco, CA. Pp. 89–128.

Bartunek, J., and Woodman, R. (2015) 'Beyond Lewin: Toward a Temporal Approximation of Organization Development and Change' *Annual Review of Organizational Psychology and Organizational Behaviour* (2) 157–182.

Bate, P. (2007) 'Bringing the Design Sciences to Organization Development and Change Management: Introduction to the Special Issue' *Journal of Applied Behavioral Science* 43 (1) 8–11.

Bazigos, M., and Burke, W. (1997) 'Theory Orientations of Organization Development (OD) Practitioners' *Group and Organization Management* 22 (3) 384–408.

Becker, B., and Huselid, M. (2006) 'Strategic Human Resource Management: Where Do We Go From Here?' *Journal of Management* 32 (6) 898–925.

Beckhard, R. (1969) *Organization Development Strategies and Models.* Addison-Wesley Publishing Company: Boston, MA.

Beckhard, R. (2006) 'The OD Field, Setting the Context, Understanding the Legacy' in Gallos, J. (ed) *Organization Development—A Jossey-Bass Reader* John Wiley & Sons: San Francisco, CA. Pp. 3–12.

Beer, M. (1976) 'On Gaining Influence and Power for OD' *Journal of Applied Behavioural Science* 12 (1) 44–51.

Beer, M., and Huse, E. (1972) 'A Systems Approach to Organization Development' *Journal of Applied Behavioural Science* 8 (1) 79–101.

Beer, M., and Walton, A. E. (1987) 'Organization Change and Development' *Annual Review Psychology* 38 339–367.

Bennis, W. (1969) *Organization Development: Its Nature, Origins and Prospects.* Addison-Wesley Publishing Company: Boston, MA.

Boxall, P. (1996) 'The Strategic HRM Debate and the Resource-Based View of the Firm' *Human Resource Management Journal* 6 (30) 59–75.

Bradford, D., and Burke, W. (2004) 'Introduction: Is OD in Crisis?' *Journal of Applied Behavioural Science* 40 (4) 369–373.

Bradford, D., and Burke, W. (2006) 'The Future of OD?' in Gallos, J. (ed.) *Organization Development—A Jossey-Bass Reader* John Wiley & Sons: San Francisco, CA. Pp. 842–857.

Bryant, M., and Wolfram Cox, J. (2014) 'Beyond Authenticity? Humanism, Post-humanism and New Organization Development' *British Journal of Management* 25 (4) 706–723.

Bunker, B., Alban, B., and Lewicki, R. (2004) 'Ideas in Currency and OD Practice: Has the Well Gone Dry?' *Journal of Applied Behavioral Science* 40 (4) 403–422.

Burke, W. (1971) 'A Comparison of Management Development and Organization Development' *Journal of Applied Behavioural Science* 7 (5) 569–579.

Burke, W. (1976) 'Organization Development in Transition' *Journal of Applied Behavioral Science* 12 22–43.

Burke, W. (2004) 'Internal Organization Development Practitioners: Where Do They Belong?' *Journal of Applied Behavioural Science* 40 (4) 423–431.

Burke, W. (2006) 'Where Did OD Come From' in Gallos, J. (ed.) *Organization Development—A Jossey-Bass Reader* John Wiley & Sons: San Francisco, CA. Pp. 13–37.

Burke, W. (2011) 'A Perspective on the Field of Organization Development and Change: The Zeigarnik Effect' *Journal of Applied Behavioural Science* 47 (2) 143–167.

Burnes, B. (2004a) *Managing Change* (4th edn.). FT Prentice Hall: Harlow.

Burnes, B. (2004b) 'Kurt Lewin and the Planned Approach to Change-A Reappraisal' *Journal of Management Studies* 41 (6) 977–998.

Burnes, B. (2004c) 'Kurt Lewin and Complexity Theories: Back to the Future?' *Journal of Change Management* 4 (4) 309–325.

Burnes, B. (2006) 'Theories and Practices of Organizational Development' in Gallos, J. (ed.) *Organization Development—A Jossey-Bass Reader* John Wiley & Sons: San Francisco, CA. p. 129.

Burnes, B. (2009) 'Reflections: Ethics and Organizational Change-Time for a Return to Lewinian Values?' *Journal of Change Management* 9 (4) 359–381.

Burnes, B., and Cooke, B. (2012) 'Review Article: The Past, Present and Future of Organization Development: Taking the Long View' *Human Relations* 65 (11) 1395–1429.

Burnes, B., and Cooke, B. (2013) 'The Tavistock's 1945 Invention of Organisation Development: Early British Business and Management Applications of Social Psychiatry' *Business History* 55 (5) 768–789.

Bushe, G., and Marshak, R. (2009) 'Revisioning Organization Development Diagnostic and Dialogic Premises and Patterns of Practice' *Journal of Applied Behavioral Science* 45 (3) 348–368.

Cheung-Judge, M. Y. (2001) 'The Self as an Instrument-A Cornerstone for the Future of OD' *OD Practitioner*. 33 (3) 11–16.

Cheung-Judge, M. Y., and Holbeche, L. (2011) *Organization Development— A Practitioner's Guide for OD and HR*. Kogan Page; London.

Cheung-Judge, M. Y., and Holbeche, L. (2015) *Organization Development— A Practitioner's Guide for OD and HR* (2nd edn.). Kogan Page: London.

Church, A., and Burke, W. (1995) 'Practitioner Attitudes about the Field of Organization Development' *Research in Organizational Change and Development* (8) 1–46.

Church, A., Hurley, R., and Burke, W. (1992) 'Evolution or Revolution in the Values of Organization Development: Commentary on the State of the Field' *Journal of Organizational Change* 5 (4) 6–23.

CIPD. (2009) *HR-Jobs People Management* accessed online at: http://hr-jobs.peoplemanagement.co.uk/ (2nd Dec 2009)

CIPD. (2014a) *Professional map* accessed online at: www.cipd.co.uk/cipd-hr-profession/profession-map/default.aspx (25th June 2014)

CIPD. (2014b) *History of HR and the CIPD* accessed online at: www.cipd.co.uk/hr-resources/factsheets/history-hr-cipd.aspx (17th July 2014)

CIPD. (2014c) *About us* accessed online at: www.cipd.co.uk/cipd-hr-profession/about-us/code-professional-conduct.aspx (25th June 2014)

CIPD. (2015) *About Professional Membership* accessed online at: www.cipd.co.uk/membership/professional/default.aspx (24th August 2015)

Collins, D. (2000) *Management Fads and Buzzwords Critical-Practical Perspectives* Routledge: Abingdon.

Colwill, D. (2012) *Educating the Scholar Practitioner*. A Volume in Contemporary Trends in Organization Development and Change. Information Age Publishing: Charlotte, NC.

Cooke, B. (1999) 'Writing the Left Out of Management Theory: The Historiography of the Management of Change' *Organization* 6 (1) 81–105.

Cummings, T. (2004) 'Organisation development and change: foundations and applications' in Boonstra J.J (ed.) *Dynamics of Organizational Change and Learning*. (Pp. 25–42) John Wiley and Sons: San Francisco

Cummings, T. and Feyerham, A. (2003) 'Reflections on the Future of Organization Development' *The Journal of Applied Behavioral Science* 39 (1) 97–115

Cummings, T., and Worley, C. (2005) *Organization Development and Change* (8th edn.). Thomson South-Western: Mason, OH.

Cummings, T., and Worley, C. (2014) Organization Development and Change (9th edn.). Cengage Learning: Stamford, CT.

Cummings, T., and Worley, C. (2015) *Organization Development and Change* (10th edn.). Cengage Learning: Stamford, CT.

Dawson, P. (2003) *Reshaping change: a Processual Perspective*: Routledge: London.

DeVogel, A. (1995) 'Exhibit 14.2: 'OD Values-Clarification Instrument' in Rothwell, W., Sullivan, R., and McLean, G. (eds.) *Practicing Organization Development— A Guide for Consultants*. Pfeiffer & Company: San Diego. Pp. 476–487.

DeVogel, A., Sullivan, R., McLean, G., and Rothwell, R. (1995) 'Ethics in OD' in Rothwell, W., Sullivan, R., and McLean, G. (eds.) *Practicing Organization Development— A Guide for Consultants*. Pfeiffer & Company, San Diego. Pp. 445–488.

Docherty, P., Kira, M., and Abraham, B. (2009) 'Organization Development for Social Sustainability in Work Systems' *Research in Organizational Change and Development*. (17) 77–144.

Dunn, J. (2009) 'Strategic Human Resources and Organization Development: Managing Change for Success' in Yaeger, T., and Sorenson, P. (eds.) *Strategic Organization Development—Managing Change for Success*. A Volume in Contemporary Trends in Organization Development and Change. Information Age Publishing: Charlotte, NC Pp. 131–142.

Eisen, S., Steele, H., and Cherbeneau, J. (1995) 'Developing OD Competence for the Future' in Rothwell, W., Sullivan, R., and McLean, G. (eds.) *Practicing Organization Development—A Guide for Consultants*. Pfeiffer & Company: San Diego. Pp. 493–530.

Fagenson-Eland, E., Ensher, E., and Burke, W. (2004) 'Organisation Development and Change Interventions A Seven-Nation Comparison' *Journal of Applied Behavioural Science* 40 (4) 432–464.

Farias, G., and Johnson, H. (2000) 'Organizational Development and Change Management: Setting the Record Straight' *Journal of Applied Behavioral Science* 36 (3) 376–379.

Francis, H., Holbeche, L., and Reddington, M. (2012) 'Organisational Effectiveness: A New Agenda for Organisational Development and Human Resource Management' in Francis, H., Holbeche, L., and Reddington, M. (eds.) *People and Organisational Development: a New Agenda for Organisational Effectiveness*. CIPD: London. Pp. 1–19, 335–345.

French, W., and Bell, C. (1999) *Organization Development Behavioural Science Interventions for Organization Improvement* (6th edn.). Prentice Hall: Saddle River.

Gallos, J. (2006a) in Gallos, J. (ed.) *Organization Development—A Jossey-Bass Reader* John Wiley & Sons: San Francisco, CA.

Garrow, V. (2009) 'OD: Past, Present and Future' *IES Working Paper WP22*.

Gillon, A. C. (2011) 'Does OD Practice Within the HR Profession in the UK Reflect the Academic Rhetoric?' *Leadership and Organization Development Journal* 32 (2) 150–169.

Golembiewski, R. (1989) *Organization Development Ideas and Issues* Transaction Publishers: New Brunswick, NJ.

Gottlieb, J. (1998) 'Understanding the Role of OD Practitioners' *Research in Organizational Change and Development* (11) 117–158.

Grant, D., and Marshak, R. (2011) 'Towards a Discourse-Centred Understanding of Organizational Change' *Journal of Applied Behavioural Science* 47 (2) 204–235.

Greiner, L., and Cummings, T. (2004) 'Wanted: OD More Alive Than Dead' *Journal of Applied Behavioral Science* 40 (4) 374–391.

Grieves, J. (2000) 'Introduction: The Origins of Organizational Development' *Journal of Management Development* 19 (5) 345–447.

Hayes, J. (2014) *The Theory and Practice of Change Management* (4th edn.). Palgrave Macmillan: Hampshire.

Head, T. (2009) 'Strategic Organization Development: A Failure of True Organization Development? Part Two' in Yaeger, T., and Sorenson, P. (eds.) *Strategic Organization Development—Managing Change for Success*. A Volume in Contemporary Trends in Organization Development and Change. Information Age Publishing: Charlotte, NC. Pp. 23–44.

Holst-Mikkelson, M., and Poulfelt, F. (2009) 'Getting Strategy to Work: Achieving Effectiveness in Practice' in Yaeger, T., and Sorenson, P. (eds.) *Strategic Organization Development—Managing Change for Success*. A Volume in Contemporary

Trends in Organization Development and Change. Information Age Publishing: Charlotte, NC. Pp. 115–130.

Hornstein, H. (2001) 'Organizational Development and Change Management: Don't Throw the Baby Out With the Bath Water' *Journal of Applied Behavioral Science* 37 (2) 223–226.

Hughes, M. (2006) *Change Management: A Critical Perspective.* CIPD: London.

Hutton, C., and Liefooghe, A. (2011) 'Mind the Gap: Revisioning Organization Development as Pragmatic Reconstruction' *Journal of Applied Behavioral Science* 47 (1) 76–97.

Jacobs, C., and Heracleous. L. (2006) 'Constructing Shared Understanding: The Role of Embodied Metaphors in Organization Development' *Journal of Applied Behavioral Science* 42 (2) 207–226.

King, N., Anderson, N. (2002) *Managing Innovation and Change – a critical guide for organizations* (2nd edn.) Thomson Learning: Mitcham Surrey.

Kotter, J. (2006) 'Relations With Superiors The Challenge of "Managing" a Boss' in Gallos, J. (ed.) *Organization Development—A Jossey-Bass Reader* John Wiley & Sons: San Francisco, CA. Pp. 501–517.

Lau, C-M., and Ngo, H-Y. (2001) 'Organization Development and Firm Performance: A Comparison of Multinational and Local Firms *'Journal of International Business Studies'* 32 (1) 95–114.

Legatski, II. T. (1998) 'Downsizing, Downscoping, and Restructuring Classifying Organizational Change' *Research in Organizational Change and Development* (11) 253–270.

Legge, K. (1995) *Human Resource Management: Rhetorics and Realities.* Palgrave MacMillan: Basingstoke.

Legge, K. (2005) *Human Resource Management: Rhetorics and Realities* (Anniversary Edition). Palgrave MacMillan: Basingstoke.

Livne-Tarandache, R., and Bartonek, J. (2009) 'A New Horizon for Organizational Change and Development Scholarship' *Research in Organizational Change and Development* (17) 1–35.

Mabey, C., and Mayon-White, B. (eds.) (1993) *Managing Change* (2nd edn.). Sage: London.

Marshak, R. (1993) 'Lewin Meets Confucius: A Review of the OD Model of Change' *Journal of Applied Behavioral Science* 29 (4) 393–415.

Marshak, R. (2006) 'Emerging Directions: Is There a New OD?' in Gallos, J. (ed.) *Organization Development—A Jossey-Bass Reader* John Wiley & Sons: San Francisco, CA. Pp. 833–841.

Marshak, R., and Bushe, G. (2009) 'Further Reflections on Diagnostic and Dialogic Forms of Organization Development *Journal of Applied Behavioral Science* 45 (3) 369–374.

Marshak, R., and Grant, D. (2008) 'Organizational Discourse and New Organization Development Practices' *British Journal of Management* 19 S7–S19.

Maurer, M., and Githens, R. (2009) 'Toward a Reframing of Action Research for Human Resource and Organization Development' *Action Research* 8 (3) 267–292.

McLean, G., and McLean, L. (2001) 'If We Can't Define HRD in One Country, How Can We Define It in An International Context?' *Human Resource Development International* 4 (3) 313–326.

Mirvis, P. (2006) 'Revolutions in OD The New and the New, New Things' in Gallos, J. (ed.) *Organization Development—A Jossey-Bass Reader* John Wiley & Sons: San Francisco, CA. Pp. 39–88.

Neilson, E. (1984) *Become An OD Practitioner*. Prentice Hall Inc: Trenton, NJ.

Neumann, J., Lau, C., and Worley, T. (2009) 'Ready for Consideration: International Organizational Development and Change as an Emerging Field of Practice' *Journal of Applied Behavioral Science* 45 (2) 171–185.

NTL. (2014) *NTL Institute* accessed online at: www.ntl.org/ (23rd June 2014)

OD Network. (1996) *Organization and Human Systems Development Credo* accessed online at: www.odnetwork.org/?page=ODCredo (3rd May 2014)

OD Network. (2014) *Principles of OD Practice* accessed online at: www.odnetwork.org/?page=PrinciplesOfODPracti (3rd may 2014)

OD Network Europe. (2014) *Board* accessed online at: www.odneurope.org/about-us/board/ (25th June 2014)

Oswick, C. (2009) 'Revisioning or Re-Versioning? A Commentary on Diagnostic and Dialogic Forms of Organization Development' *Journal of Applied Behavioral Science* 45 (3) 369–374.

Oswick, C., Grant, D., Marshak, R., and Wolfram Cox, J. (2010) 'Organizational Discourse and Change: Positions, Perspectives, Progress and Prospects' *Journal of Applied Behavioral Science* 46 (1) 8–15.

Paauwe, J., and Boselie, P. (2005) 'HRM and Performance: What's Next?' *(CAHRS Working Paper 05–09)*. Cornell University, School of Industrial and Labor Relations, Center for Advanced Human Resource Studies: Ithaca, NY accessed online at: http://digitalcommons.ilr.cornell.edu/cahrswp/476 (24th February 2014)

Palmer, I., Dunford, R., and Akin, G. (2009) *Managing Organizational Change a Multiple Perspectives Approach* (2nd edn., International edn.). McGraw Hill: New York.

Patching, K. (1999) *Management and Organisation Development Beyond Arrows, Boxes and Circles*. Macmillan Business: Basingstoke, Hampshire.

Pettigrew, A. M., (1979) 'On Studying Organizational Cultures' *Administrative Science Quarterly* 24 (4) 570–581.

Pettigrew, A. M. (1985) *The Awakening Giant: Continuity and Change in ICI*. Blackwell: Oxford.

Pettigrew, A. M., (1997) 'What is a Processual Analysis?' *Scandinavian Journal of Management* 13 (4) 337–348.

Porras, J., and Bradford, D. (2004) 'A Historical View of the Future of OD: An Interview With Jerry Porras' *Journal of Applied Behavioral Science* 40 (4) 392–402.

Purser, R., and Pasmore, W. (1992) 'Organizing for Learning' *Research in Organizational Change and Development* (6) 37–114.

Quality and Equality (2014) *NTL* accessed online at: www.quality-equality.com/ntl/what-is-the-ntlqe-organisation-development-certificate-programme/ (23rd June 2014)

Rainey Tolbert, M., and Hanafin, J. (2006) 'Use of Self in OD Consulting: What Matters is Presence' *The NTL Handbook of Organization Development and Change* accessed online at: http://gestaltcoachingworks.com/pdf/Presencearticle Jonno.pdf (17th June 2006)

Roffey Park. (2014) *Getting the Most Out of Your Relationships at Work* accessed online at: www.roffeypark.com/executive-education/training-courses-skills-devel opment/interpersonal-relationships-in-organisations (23rd June 2014)

Rothwell, W., Sullivan, R., and McLean, G. (1995). 'Introduction' in Rothwell, W., Sullivan, R., McLean, G. (eds.) *Practicing Organization Development—A Guide for Consultants*. Pfeiffer & Company: San Diego. Pp. 3–40.

Ruona, W., and Gibson, S. (2004) The Making of Twenty-First Century HR: An Analysis of the Convergence of HRM, HRD and OD. *Human Resource Management* 43 (1) 49–63.

Schein, E. (1969) 'Foreword' in Beckhard, R. (1969) *Organization Development Strategies and Models*. Addison-Wesley Publishing Company: Boston, MA. Pp. iii—iv.

Schein, E. (1988) *Process Consultation Volume 1 Its Role in Organization Development* (2nd edn.). Addison-Wesley Publishing Company: Reading, MA.

Schein, E. (2006) 'Foreword' in Gallos, J. (ed.) *Organization Development—A Jossey-Bass Reader*. John Wiley & Sons: San Francisco, CA. Pp. xv—xix.

Schein, E., and Beckhard, R. (1998) 'Foreword' in *Process Consultation Volume 1 Its Role in Organization Development* (2nd edn.). Addison-Wesley Publishing Company: Reading, MA. Pp. v—vi.

Schein, Edgar H. (1987) *Process Consultation Volume 11: Lessons for Managers and Consultants*. Addison-Wesley Publishing Company: Reading, MA.

Schein, Edgar H. (1999) *Process Consultation Revisited Building the Helping Relationship*. Addison-Wesley Publishing Company: Reading, MA.

Schmidt Weber, P., and Manning, R. (1998) 'Large Group Organizational Change Interventions' *Research in Organizational Change and Development* (11) 225–252.

Senior, B., and Swailes, S. (2010) *Organizational Change* (4th edn.). FT Prentice Hall: Harlow.

Sharkey, L. (2009) 'The Future of Organization Development and Its Alignment to the Business Strategy' in Yaeger, T., and Sorenson, P. (eds.) *Strategic Organization Development—Managing Change for Success*. A Volume in Contemporary Trends in Organization Development and Change. Information Age Publishing: Charlotte, NC. Pp. 9–22.

SHRM (2014) *History* accessed online at: http (25th June 2014)

SHRM (2015a) *Membership Options* accessed online at: www.shrm.org/about/infokit/pages/membershipoptions.aspx (24th August June 2015)

SHRM (2015b) *SHRM HR Jobs* accessed online at: http://jobs.shrm.org/ (24th August June 2015)

Shull, A., Church, A., and Burke, W. (2013) 'Attitudes About the Field of Organization Development 20 Years Later: The More Things Change, the More They Stay the Same' *Research in Organizational Change and Development* 21 1–28.

Smith, M., Van Oosten, E., and Boyatzis, T. (2009) 'Coaching for Sustained Desired Change' *Research in Organizational Change and Development*. 17 145–173.

Smither, R., Houston, J., and McIntire, S. (1996) *Organization Development Strategies for Changing Environments*. HarperCollins College Publishers: New York.

Stanford, N. (2012) 'The Historical and Theoretical Background to Organisation Development' in Francis, H., Hobeche, L., and Reddington, M. (eds.) *People and Organisational Development: A New Agenda for Organisational Effectiveness*. CIPD: London. Pp. 42–64.

Sullivan, R., Rothwell, B., and Worley, C. (2001) *OD Competences 'in Organization Change and Development Competency Effort* (20th edn.) accessed online at: www.odnetwork.org/?page=ODCompetencies (15th June 2015)

Svyantek, D., O'Connell, S., and Baumgardner, T. (1992) 'A Bayesian Approach to Evaluation of Organizational Development Efforts' *Research in Organizational Change and Development* 6 235–266.

Sweem, S. (2009) 'Talent Management. The Strategic Partnership of Human Resources and Organization Development' in Yaeger, T., and Sorenson, P. (eds.) *Strategic Organization Development—Managing Change for Success*. A Volume in Contemporary Trends in Organization Development and Change. Information Age Publishing: Charlotte, NC. Pp. 143–164.

Tannenbaum, R., and Davis, S. (1969) 'Values, Man and Organizations' *Industrial Management Review* 10 (2) 67–83.

Underwood Stephens, C., and Cobb, A. (1999) 'A Habermasian Approach to Justice in Organizational Change: Synthesizing the Technical and Philosophical Perspectives' *Journal of Organizational Change Management* 12 (1) 21–34.

van Aken, J. (2007) 'Design Science and Organization Development Interventions: Aligning Business and Humanistic Values' *Journal of Applied Behavioral Science* 43 (1) 67–88.

van Nistelrooij, A., and Sminia, H. (2010) 'Organization Development: What's Actually Happening?' *Journal of Change Management* 10 (4) 407–420.

Watkins K., and Golembiewski, R. (1995) 'Rethinking Organization Development for the Learning Organization' *InternationalJournal of Organizational Analysis* 3 (1) 86–99.

Weidner, II. C. K., and Kulick, O. (1999) 'The Professionalization of Organization Development A Status Report and a Look to the Future' *Research in Organizational Change and Development* 12 319–371.

Weiss, A. (2006) 'What Constitutes an Effective Internal Consultant' in Gallos, J. (ed.) *Organization Development—A Jossey-Bass Reader* John Wiley & Sons: San Francisco, CA. Pp. 470–484.

Werkman, R. (2010) 'Reinventing Organization Development: How a Sensemaking Perspective Can Enrich OD Theories and Interventions' *Journal of Change Management* 10 (4) 421–438.

Wigglesworth, D. (1987) 'Is OD Basically Anglo-Saxon? Some Potentially Controversial Thoughts on Applying OD in Other Cultures' *Leadership & Organization Development Journal* 8 (2) 29–31.

Wigglesworth, D. (1995) 'International OD' in Rothwell, W., Sullivan, R., and McLean, G. (eds.) *Practicing Organization Development—A Guide for Consultants*. Pfeiffer & Company: San Diego. Pp. 421–444.

Wirtenberg, J., Abrams, L., and Ott, C. (2004) 'Assessing the Field of Organisation Development' *Journal of Applied Behavioural Science* 40 (4) 465–479.

Wolfram Cox, J. (2009) 'Safe Talk Revisioning, Repositioning or Representing Organization Development' *Journal of Applied Behavioral Science* 45 (3) 369–374.

Woodman, R. (1989) 'Organizational Change and Development: New Arenas for Inquiry and Action' *Journal of Management* 15 (2) 205–228.

Worren, N., Ruddle, K., and Moore, K. (1999) 'From Organizational Development to Change Management: The Emergence of a New Profession' *Journal of Applied Behavioral Science* 35 (3) 273–286.

Wright, P., Snell, S., Dyer, L. (2005) 'New models of strategic HRM in a global context' *The International Journal of Human Resource Management* 16 (6) 875–881

Yaeger, T., Head, T., and Sorenson, P. (2006) *Global Organization Development Managing Unprecedented Change.* A Volume in Contemporary Trends in Organization Development and Change. Information Age Publishing: Charlotte, NC.

Yaeger, T., and Sorenson, P. (2009) 'A Brief Look at the Past, Present and Future of Strategic Organization Development' in Yaeger, T., and Sorenson, P. (eds.) *Strategic Organization Development—Managing Change for Success.* A Volume in Contemporary Trends in Organization Development and Change. Information Age Publishing: Charlotte, NC. Pp. 3–8.

3 Evidence on the Nature of Practitioner OD

Having examined the literature on OD in the last chapter, what is there in the way of evidence in terms of practice? In seeking to understand the perspective of practitioners on the development of OD, the operationalization of requirements though the medium of job advertisements was examined. This chapter therefore presents the findings from content analysis of job advertisements from a forty-year period (1970–2010) together with the bibliometric searches presented in Chapter 4, this addresses the research study's first research question, which was to establish to what extent there is a difference between the academic literature and practitioner perspective of the development of the OD profession in the UK. The data presented in this chapter will also relate to the second research question, which focuses on the evidence on development of the form, magnitude and perceived importance of the OD profession.

The content analysis data will detail the change in volume of roles advertised between 1970 and 2010, and the development of the content of roles, as portrayed in the wording of job advertisements, will also be presented. The findings presented here will be discussed in Chapter 6.

Content Analysis Findings

Change in the Volume of OD Job Roles Over the Four Decades

In order to understand the extent of difference between the academic literature and practitioners' perspective of the development of the OD profession in the UK, an examination of the evidence on the development of the profession in terms of size, status and content is required. As such, changes in the number of OD job roles advertised, and the nature the development of OD roles over time will be presented as a measure of this development. Trends in academic publishing on the subject of OD are then compared with this data.

A count was conducted of advertised job roles in the publication *People Management* and its predecessors, with OD and its specified variations in the job title (hereafter referred to as OD job roles), over the four decades from 1970 to 2010. In order to source every copy of the publication since job advertisements began, it was necessary to visit six libraries: The University of The West of Scotland, The Mitchell in Glasgow, Glasgow University, Strathclyde University, Glasgow Caledonian and the CIPD Library in London. The title and frequency of the publication issued to CIPD, and its predecessors' members changed over the period of this study and the details of change in publication name are noted in the table descriptions. No OD job roles were published between 1967, when job advertisements first appeared in the CIPD press, and 1971. The first job advertisement for an OD job role was identified in the September 1972 issue. Table 3.1 shows the number of OD job roles in the 1970s. The volume number given in the second top row relates to the publication sequencing for each year. **The bottom row,** *Total* **is the number of OD job roles per year.**

The number of OD job roles advertised was low throughout the 1970s. Similarly, low levels were advertised in the first half of the 1980s. However, there was then a rise in the advertisement of OD job roles, as can be seen in Table 3.2.The bimonthly publications up until the end of the 1980s were stored offsite from the London CIPD library. Publications were bimonthly until the end of 1994, and then moved to twenty-four issues a year between 1995 and 2010. With anticipated small numbers of OD job roles in the 1980s publications based on data already collected, and the difficulties and cost involved in accessing the publications, it was decided not to include this source in the sample.

As a result, post-1990 advertisements could not be compared *like with like* in terms of the raw numbers, but the change in trend was distinguishable nonetheless. Table 3.3 below shows the number of OD job roles advertised in the 1990s. From July 1990 to December 1994 there was a second

Table 3.1 Number of OD Job Role Advertisements in the 1970s (from Personnel Management: the magazine for Human Resource Professionals)

VOLUME	1970	1971	1972	1973	1974	1975	1976	1977	1978	1979
	2	3	4	5	6	7	8	9	10	11
Jan	0	0	0	0	0	0	0	0	0	0
Feb	0	0	0	1	0	0	0	0	0	0
Mar	0	0	0	0	0	0	0	0	0	1
Apr	0	0	0	0	0	0	0	0	0	1
May	0	0	0	0	0	0	0	0	0	0
Jun	0	0	0	1	1	0	0	0	1	0
Jul	0	0	0	0	0	0	0	0	0	0
Aug	0	0	0	0	0	0	0	0	0	0
Sep	0	0	1	0	0	0	0	1	0	0
Oct	0	0	0	0	0	0	0	0	0	0
Nov	0	0	0	0	0	0	0	0	0	0
Dec	0	0	0	0	1	0	0	1	0	0
Total	0	0	1	2	2	0	0	2	1	2

Table 3.2 Number of OD Job Role Advertisements in the 1980s (in Personnel Management: the magazine for Human Resource Professionals)

VOLUME	1980	1981	1982	1983	1984	1985	1986	1987	1988	1989
	12	13	14	15	16	17	18	19	20	21
Jan	1	0	0	0	0	0	0	0	0	1
Feb	0	0	0	0	0	0	1	0	0	2
Mar	0	0	1	0	0	1	0	1	0	1
Apr	0	0	0	0	0	0	0	0	0	0
May	0	0	0	0	0	0	0	0	1	0
Jun	0	0	0	0	0	0	0	0	1	0
Jul	0	0	0	0	0	0	0	0	2	1
Aug	0	1	1	0	0	2	1	1	1	0
Sep	0	0	0	0	0	1	0	2	0	0
Oct	0	0	0	1	0	0	0	0	1	1
Nov	0	0	0	0	0	0	2	0	0	0
Dec	0	0	0	0	0	0	1	0	1	1
Total	1	1	2	1	0	4	5	4	7	7

Table 3.3 Number of OD Job Roles Advertised in the 1990s (in Personnel Management: the magazine for Human Resource Professionals, and the bimonthly PM Plus and Personnel Management Plus between 1990 and the end of 1994 and in People Management since January 1995)

VOLUME	1990	1991	1992	1993	1994	1995	1996	1997	1998	1999
	22	23	24	25	26	1	2	3	4	5
Jan	0	0	0	0	0	3	1	0	2	1
Feb	3	0	0	0	0	0	0	1	0	3
Mar	0	0	0	0	1	0	3	4	1	5
Apr	1	1	0	1	1	1	0	2	5	3
May	2	0	0	0	0	3	2	2	2	3
Jun	0	1	1	0	0	2	1	0	2	4
Jul	3	1	0	0	5	1	1	2	4	6
Aug	0	0	1	3	0	1	0	3	0	1
Sep	0	0	0	0	2	1	1	1	3	2
Oct	1	1	1	0	2	0	0	2	3	5
Nov	2	0	0	2	0	1	4	4	2	2
Dec	0	0	0	0	2	0	1	1	1	2
Total	12	4	3	6	13	13	14	22	25	37

monthly publication, the results from those are included in the columns for each year.

There was a fall in the number of OD job roles advertised between 1991 and 1993, prior to an increase towards the end of the 1990s: from 1994 onwards. The number of OD job roles advertised continued to grow significantly between 2000 and 2010, as can be seen in Table 3.4.

Table 3.4 Number of OD Job Role Advertisements, 2000–2010 (in People Management)

VOLUME	2000	2001	2002	2003	2004	2005	2006	2007	2008	2009	2010
	6	*7*	*8*	*9*	*10*	*11*	*12*	*13*	*14*	*15*	*16*
Jan	5	2	8	5	11	8	7	11	6	10	7
Feb	3	7	5	2	6	10	3	3	10	5	5
Mar	8	7	6	0	7	12	4	2	3	5	3
Apr	7	10	4	3	6	6	4	3	5	5	5
May	6	7	9	10	12	2	9	10	9	8	1
Jun	0	3	4	6	10	15	6	9	12	7	4
Jul	2	2	2	3	3	4	6	3	7	6	3
Aug	6	4	3	4	0	2	3	6	3	0	1
Sep	5	5	7	10	7	10	7	3	11	9	4
Oct	6	4	4	11	8	2	7	6	11	0	2
Nov	3	1	4	5	9	6	6	9	2	6	1
Dec	3	3	3	5	3	2	0	2	1	1	1
Total	54	55	59	64	82	79	62	67	80	62	37

Although there was a decrease in the number of OD job roles advertised at the end of the 2000s, there were still a relatively high number of OD jobs being advertised in print publications, bearing in mind the increasing use of the internet for recruitment. One of the interviewees with extensive experience in the UK recruitment industry (BUSINESS LEADER 2) recounted that 'the biggest change from hard copy advertisements to online attraction mechanisms happened 2008'. In assessing how the numbers of OD job roles advertised compares with other job roles in the paper copy of the same publication, a count was conducted in the job advertisement section of the March and September issues for each five-year period under study. The data from this exercise is detailed in Table 3.5.

The number of pages in the job advertisements section in the CIPD hard copy publications peaked at 353 advertisements in 2000. However, this had fallen to a total of twenty-two adverts by 2010. This is a significant downward trend in advertising of job roles in the paper publication of *People Management* and its predecessor publications; this trend is displayed in Gillon et al. (2014).

According to interviewee BUSINESS LEADER 2, the significant decrease in the job advertisements was due to the increased use of online methods for recruitment. However, despite the decrease in advertising of all vacancies in the CIPD paper publication post-2000, the number of OD job roles advertised continued to grow, and therefore the share of advertisements in comparison to other HR specialist areas also grew. As such, the data shows that there was a clear growth in the number of OD job roles advertised between 1970 and 2010. A visual representation of this exponential growth trend generated from the data in Tables 3.1 to 3.4 above, is set out in Gillon et al. (2014).

Table 3.5 Numbers of Pages in the Job Advertisement Section in the Hard Copy of the CIPD Publication between 1970 and 2010

Year	March Advertisement Section Page Count	September Advertisement Section Page Count	Total
1970	31	23	54
1975	28	20	48
1980	35	26	61
1985	40	40	80
1990	87	75	162
1995	71	80	151
2000	171	182	353
2005	81	122	203
2010	9	13	22

Table 3.6 Percentage Ratio of Jobs Advertised by Sector 1995–2010

	Public Sector	Private Sector	Other (e.g. social enterprise)
1995	53.8	30.8	15.4
1996	35.7	57.1	7.1
1997	40.9	54.5	4.5
1998	40.0	44.0	16.0
1999	51.4	40.5	8.1
2000	48.1	42.6	9.3
2001	52.9	35.3	11.8
2002	73.2	16.1	10.7
2003	73.4	12.5	14.1
2004	60.8	16.5	22.8
2005	72.2	20.3	7.6
2006	56.5	22.6	21.0
2007	65.2	12.1	22.7
2008	76.3	11.3	12.5
2009	87.1	6.5	6.5
2010	74.3	0.0	25.7

Despite the difficulties and limitations in the application of a precisely reliable and valid method for collecting this type of data, there is an apparent and significant growth trend in the number of OD job roles advertised.

OD's Presence in the Private, Public and Other Sectors

The distribution of OD job roles across the public, private and other sectors advertised was also examined (post-1995). The percentage ratios of total OD job advertisements by sector are presented in Table 3.6.

Although this data provides a general indicator, a level of caution should be applied in interpretation, particularly in relation to the later years. Private-sector organizations have, in particular, progressed to using online and headhunting methods of recruitment. With the onus on the public sector to demonstrate transparency in recruitment processes, they continued to use hard copy as a media for advertising job roles. So although the proportion of private-sector job roles, for example post-2007, is very small, this may be more because they were faster to transfer to using online methods of recruitment.

Salary data as an Indicator of Perceived Importance of OD

Another indicator of perceived importance of the field of OD in practice is the level of salary of OD roles in comparison to other HR roles. Gathering data on salary levels was particularly difficult as not all OD or HR job role advertisements cited a salary. Those advertisements that did, often presented it within a range alongside other elements of an employment package such as a company car or performance-related pay, which were not easily quantifiable. In addition, comparing salary levels over a forty-year period would be a nigh on impossible task to carry out with any level of validity. In short, making comparisons of the perceived importance of a profession by comparing remuneration packages had substantial potential for misinterpretation.

However, this study examines an area that eminent mainstream HR academics ardently ignored or considered to be an out of date fashion. Whilst it is understood that salary data must be approached with considerable caution, it can be useful in providing a general indicator of status. For this purpose, data from a 2012 HR specialism salary survey carried out by a global resourcing company (Company Name Witheld, 2012) will be used. The data collection method was not transparent, but it might reasonably be assumed that the data provided for *The South* used the same data collection method and all the data for *Scotland* used the same internal method. Therefore, even if it is invalid to compare them with each other, we could treat them as two separate samples: as independent tendencies.

The Company Name Witheld (2012) data covers a range of six sectors, for two geographical areas so the sectoral split of the data as documented was followed. Salaries for *Manager* and *Head of* roles in each of the HR specialism areas are represented in Table 3.6 below. In order to compare these OD job role salaries with other HR specialisms, an arithmetic mean of salaries was calculated and compared with the arithmetic mean of OD specialty salaries.

The difference between the average salaries of the other HR specialisms and OD are provided in a £ pa and a % difference format in the bottom two rows of Table 3.7. In *The South* only, the *Not for Profit* salary differential was small (£1k pa or 2%) with the percentage difference in all other sectors being at least 34% higher. In *Scotland* the salary differentials were less extreme (with 32% as the highest difference), but again all were higher. *Not for Profit* OD salaries in *Scotland* had a higher differential than in *The South*. *Professional Services* OD practitioners in *Scotland* did not have such

Table 3.7 Salary Data: Comparison of OD Salaries with other HR Specialisms

		The South						Scotland					
		Banking & Finance	Energy & Utilities	Media & Technology	Not for Profit & Charity	Profes-sional Services	Retail, Leisure & FMCG	Banking & Finance	Energy & Utilities	Media & Technology	Not for Profit & Charity	Profes-sional Services	Retail, Leisure & FMCG
Generalist	Manager	50	55	55	38	48	45	45	40	35	32	45	36
	Head of	75	70	70	55	65	65	85	70	70	55	70	70
L&D/Talent	Manager	50	52	50	38	50	50	43	40	42	30	43	42
	Head of	70	68	65	50	65	60	75	70	55	40	75	55
Recruitment/ Resourcing	Manager	55	60	55	38	45	50	43	43	42	42	43	42
	Head of	70	90	66	48	65	68	75	60	60	60	75	60
HR Reporting/ MIS	Manager	50	52	38	36	50	52	38	30	30	42	43	30
	Head of	70	80	56	55	70	75	50	45	45	60	75	45
ER/IR	Manager	55	60	50	40	55	50	45	40	40	42	43	40
	Head of	75	80	70	47	75	80	65	63	63	60	75	63
Reward (or C&B if no 'Reward')	Manager	50	55	50	45	60	53	40	35	35	42	43	35
	Head of	90	80	70	52	85	70	65	50	50	60	85	50
The above averaged:		760	802	695	542	733	718	669	586	567	565	715	568
		63	67	58	45	61	60	56	49	47	47	60	47
OD	Manager	75	96	75	40	75	75	50	50	50	42	53	50
	Head of	95	100	90	52	90	95	75	75	75	60	70	75
	Total	170	196	165	92	165	170	125	125	125	102	123	125
OD average of Mgr & Head of		85	98	83	46	83	85	63	63	63	51	62	63
Difference in £		22	31	25	1	21	25	7	14	15	4	2	15
Difference as a %		34	47	42	2	35	42	12	28	32	8	3	32

a high differential than they did in *The South*. Overall, it was of note that this data shows that in all instances, OD salaries are consistently higher than the other HR specialisms.

Changes in the Content of Job Roles Each of the Four Decades

The findings on the development in the volume of OD job roles over the four decades, sectoral differences and salary differentials, have been presented above. In this next section the nature of change in the content of OD job roles will now be reviewed. A sampling mechanism was applied to select job advertisements to which the coding dictionary would be applied. It was assumed jobs advertised in the CIPD publication would be UK-based, and roles based outside the UK would be an exception. The coding exercise resulted in the identification of twelve main elements of OD:

- *Change Management*
- *Consultancy Orientation*
- *Behavior and Cultural Issues*
- *HR, Learning and Development (HRD)*
- *OD*
- *Effectiveness*
- *Learning Organization*
- *Partnership*
- *Strategic Approach*
- *Leadership and*
- *Not just HR (Organization-wide Orientation)*

A code of **Change** was applied to all advertisement words where change was explicitly mentioned, and also where other words were used which implied that change was expected, planned or underway. Words used in advertisements which were coded in this category included: *vision, growth, new direction, future, development, transformation* and *innovation*. Advertisements coded in the category of **Consultancy** were those that included words and phrases such as *project(s), intervention, program, action research* and *clients*. Advertisements coded in the category of **Behavioral and Cultural** were those that included words and phrases such as *values, inspire, motivate, hearts and minds, psychology, team building* and *personal change*. Advertisements coded in the category of **HR** included words and phrases relating to traditional HR, such as *recruitment, manpower planning, pay and grading, employment law* and *equal opportunities*. Advertisements coded in the category of **HRD (L&D)** included words and phrases such as *learning, coaching, training, succession planning, competence* and *360-degree feedback*. Advertisements coded in the category of **OD** included words and phrases such as *organization development, organizational development, organization analysis, organization design* and *job design*.

Advertisements coded in the category of *Effectiveness* included words and phrases from a large list of available in the coding dictionary including: *organizational capability, business objectives, performance, improvements, productivity, value* and *fully exploit*. Advertisements coded in the category of *Learning Organization* included terms such *as continuous learning, change capability, continuous improvement, resilient* and *agile*. Advertisements were coded in the *Partnership* category when they suggested a spirit of active inclusion and concern for people. Words and phrases in this category included: *engagement, wellbeing, best employer* and *joint working*. Advertisements were coded in the category of *Strategy* if they indicated a strategic orientation through the use of a relatively small range of words and phrases including: *overall direction, big picture* and *executive and board level*. Advertisements coded in the category of *Leadership* were also classified by the use of a small range of words and phrases: *leaders, leadership, management, head up* and *shaping*. Advertisements coded in the final category of *Not Just HR* included words and phrases that referred to the wider context of an organization, including: *corporate, wider influence, business needs, commercial awareness, entrepreneurial* and *building business*. Further detailed findings from the coding exercise are presented in Gillon (2014).

Developments in the emphasis of each of the twelve themes identified in OD job role advertisements between 1970 and 2010 are discussed in turn below. In relation to the (or any change in) importance of *Change* in OD, *Change* was not as noticeable in the OD of the 1970s despite the early traditions of OD in planned change, but grew in importance with each decade. By the 1990s only *HRD (L&D)* was a more prominent feature of OD than *Change,* and in the period 2000–2010, *Change* had become by far the most important feature in OD job advertisements.

The importance of *Consultancy* in OD job roles remained almost constant between 1970 and 2010, with only a marginal increase in its profile post 1990.

In 1970s OD, *Behavioral and Cultural* issues were central to OD and it was the highest-ranking category in job role advertisements during this time. This decreased significantly in the 1980s and 1990s, with a slight rise post 2000.

HR had grown from having some presence in the 1970s to being the foremost feature of 1980s OD job role advertisements. Its importance waned in the 1990s but was referred to more often in OD job advertisements again after 2000.

In 1970s OD, *HRD (L&D)* was no more important than HR, and there was a moderate occurrence of both in OD job roles advertised in this era. This was in keeping with the US traditional model of OD. However, its presence grew in 1980s OD and in the 1990s *HRD* in OD flourished, becoming the leading feature in OD. It remained as a significant aspect after 2000, second only to OD, and continued to be more prominent in OD job role advertisements than *HR*.

Specific mention of **OD** within OD job advertisements was high in the 1970s, coming second only to mention of **behavioral and cultural** characteristics. In the 1980s it was second only to **HR**, but had fallen back to 5th place in the 1990s. Post-2000, **OD** was second to **Change**, and equitably placed with **HRD**.

Effectiveness was one of the seven features of OD which was worthy of note in the 1970s, found in a moderate number of advertisements, but as frequently as **HR** and **HRD**. In the 1980s, frequency of mention of **Effectiveness** remained in a similar proportion. However, other features of OD had become more important. There was a moderate increase in the use of **Effectiveness** words and phrases in OD job role adverts in the 1990s, and a significant increase after 2000, when it ranked equal to **Strategy**, and only slightly behind **OD** and **HRD**.

There was no mention of **Learning Organization** terms in OD job advertisements until after 2000, when the level of occurrence was low.

Mention of **Partnership** occurred first in the 1990s at a very low level, and after 2000 it was mentioned only slightly more often than **Behavior and Culture** and **Learning Organization.**

The incidence of **Strategy** was low in the 1970s job advertisements, grew slightly in the 1980s and doubled its presence in the 1990s, remaining at the level after 2000.

Leadership was barely referred to in the 1970s, not mentioned at all in the 1980s, was of low to moderate status in the 1990s. However, mention of it increased significantly after 2000.

Not just HR was a minor characteristic in 1970s OD, potentially reflecting the systems orientation of traditional OD at that time. OD job role advertisements in the 1980s made no mention of words in this category, although they appeared with increasing frequency during the 1990s and 2000s, when it grew to become of moderate significance.

Summary of the Development of the Content Profile of UK OD over the Four Decades

The profile of characteristics featured in OD job advertisements in the 1970s was not unsurprising when compared with the US traditional form of OD. The application of **Behavioral Science**, in terms of its appearance in job advertisements of that era, was of primary importance, followed by **OD, Change** and **Consultancy**. The profile of OD in the 1980s suggested a very different beast. **HR, OD** and **Change** lead, with **Behavioral Science** falling much further down the agenda. In consideration of the economic and business climate of that decade, it was perhaps to be expected to find what looked like a much harder hitting approach to OD and change.

In the **1990s** the importance of **HR** in OD had fallen back, **HRD** became the leading characteristic, the status of **Change** remained very important, having a **Strategic** approach had become prominent and organizational

Effectiveness reared its head. There were not significant differences in the profile of OD **post-2000**, *Change* had taken over from **HRD** as the foremost feature of OD. *Strategy* had remained important and the position of *Effectiveness* was much stronger. The presence of **HR** had increased since the **1990s** and *Organization-wide* and *Leadership* were now also features of the shape of **post-2000 OD**.

Conclusion

The most significant finding in this chapter is the extent of growth of OD job roles in the UK and the high status of OD as a specialism within the HR field. The growth in OD job roles appears to have been exponential in nature. Also of note is how the content of the UK job roles developed over each of the four decades OD practice in the UK has clearly changed with the decades, reflecting changes in business trends in each decade. An examination of how these findings compare with the key themes identified in the literature review will be conducted in the Chapter 6.

References

Beckhard, R. (1969) *Organization Development Strategies and Models.* Addison-Wesley Publishing Company: Reading, MA.

Bennis, W. (1969) *Organization Development: Its Nature, Origins and Prospects.* Addison-Wesley Publishing Company: Reading, MA.

Blake, R., and Mouton, J. (1969) *Building a Dynamic Corporation Through Grid Organization Development.* Addison-Wesley Publishing Company: Reading, MA.

Company Name Withheld (2012) *Comparison of HR Specialism Salaries in the UK.* Publisher Identity Withheld.

Gillon, A. C., Braganza, A., Williams, S., and McCauley-Smith, C. (2014) 'Organisation Development in HRM: A Longitudinal Study Contrasting Evolutionary Trends Between the UK and USA' *International Journal of Human Resource Management* 25 (7) 1002–1023.

Schein, E. (1969) *Process Consultation: Its Role in Organization Development.* Addison-Wesley Publishing Company: Reading, MA.

4 The Evolution of Published Work on OD

Who has influenced us on what OD is? In this chapter who has previously determined what OD is, when and where were they based will be identified? Having explored the development of OD in the practitioner world through the analysis of OD job role advertisements, the study then examined the focus of OD in the academic world and is explored below.

Findings from the Bibliometric Searches: Understanding the Academic Perspective of OD

To establish how OD was perceived and presented by academics between 1970 and 2010 a series of bibliometric searches were carried out. The bibliometric search data provides information on the trends in writing on OD over the decades under study, in terms of volume and country of origin. The purpose of this is to investigate the main sources of influence in shaping the perception of the features that make up OD. Searches were conducted using The Web of Science, Copac, Google Scholar and the CIPD practitioner library catalogue. The findings presented here will be discussed in Chapter 6.

Web of Science Search Findings

The first part of the bibliometric search involved using The Web of Science to search for journal articles in quality academic publications. The journals where three or more articles with OD in the title (hereafter referred to as OD articles) were published between 1960 and 2010, and into the 2010s, are listed in Table 4.1.

The data shows that the US-based *Journal of Applied Behavioural Science* published the highest number of OD articles (articles with "Organization* Development" in the title) (n = 64) in the time frame examined. Given the history, nature and community for this journal, which is the official journal of the NTL, this result was not a surprise. *Personnel Psychology* published the next highest number of OD articles (n = 48), again reflecting the *Behavioral Science* orientation of traditional US-based OD. The *Training*

Table 4.1 Journals with Three or more OD Articles 1960–2010, and into the 2010s

Journal	Number	1960s	1970s	1980s	1990s	2000s	2010s
Academy of Management Journal	4		2	1	1		
Academy of Management Review	4			4			
Administration in Mental Health	3		1	2			
Administration in Social Work	4			2	1	1	
Administrative Science Quarterly	7		5	2			
African Journal of Business Management	4					3	1
Annual Review of Psychology	4		2	1	1		
Applied Ergonomics	3			1		2	
Australasian Journal on Ageing	5					5	
Australian Psychologist	4		4				
Betriebswirt	3		3				
California Management Review	3		3				
Contemporary Psychology	12		7	5			
Education and Urban Society	5		5				
Educational Technology	8		8				
Ekonomiska Samfundets Tidskrift	3		2		1		
Exchange-Organizational Behavior Teaching Journal	8		4	4			
Futures	3				1	1	1
Gesundheitswesen	3					2	1
Group & Organization Management	4		1		3		
Group & Organization Studies	6			4	2		
Gruppendynamik Forschung Und Praxis	7		7				
Gruppendynamik Und Organisationsberatung	16					14	2
Gruppendynamik-Zeitschrift Fur Angewandte Sozialpsychologie	22			15	7		
Gruppenpsychotherapie Und Gruppendynamik	3		1		2		
Harvard Business Review	4		3	1			
Health Care Management Review	4		2	1		1	
The Health service journal	5					5	

Journal					
Hospital administration	3		3			
Hospital progress	5	1	4			
Human Relations	8		4			1
Interfaces	3		2			4
International Journal of Psychology	17			2	11	
International Journal of Public Administration	3		1	2	1	
International Journal of Technology Management	3			2	1	
Interpersonal Development	3		3			
Journal of Academic Librarianship	5		2	1	1	1
Journal of Applied Behavioral Science	64		31	19	8	5
Journal of Applied Psychology	5		3	1	1	
Journal of Business Ethics	3		1	2	1	
Journal of College Student Development	3		1	1		
Journal of Educational Administration	3		3			
Journal of Educational and Psychological Consultation	3			3		
Journal of health and human resources administration	4			4		
Journal of Management Studies	8		3	4	1	
Journal of Occupational Behaviour	4			4		
Journal of Occupational Psychology	7			7		
Journal of Organizational Change Management	3				3	
Journal of prevention & intervention in the community	4					4
Library Trends	6				6	
Long Range Planning	3			3		
Maintenance Management International	3			3		
Management Learning	5			2	1	2
Nordisk Psykologi	3		3	5		
Organization Studies	5		5			
Organizational Dynamics	9			3	3	1
Personnel	9		5	3	3	
Personnel and Guidance Journal	4		3	1		
Personnel Journal	13		12	1		

(Continued)

Table 4.1 (Continued)

Journal	Number	1960s	1970s	1980s	1990s	2000s	2010s
Personnel Psychology	48		18	14	11	4	1
Personnel Review	11		4	5	2		
Professional Psychology	6		6				
Psychology	5		1	1	3		
Psychology in the Schools	3		2			1	
Public Administration and Development	4			2		2	
Public Administration Review	4		3	1			
Public Personnel Management	9		5	3	1		
Quality & Safety in Health Care	3					1	2
Relations Industrielles-Industrial Relations	7		6		1		
Revista De Cercetare Si Interventie Sociala	3						3
Sykepleien	4		2	2			
Systems Practice	4		1		3		
Thrust-for Educational Leadership	3		3				
Training and Development Journal	34		17	17			
Unternehmung-Schweizerische Zeitschrift Fur Betriebswirtschaft	4		1	3			
Zeitschrift Fur Padagogik	4					3	1

and Development Journal published the next highest number of OD articles (n = 34). A German-based journal *Gruppendynamik-Zeitschrift Fur Ange-wandte Sozialpsychologie* was published the next highest number of OD articles (n = 22). This finding was surprising as German-based scholars are not referred to in writing on OD nor mentioned by any of the interviewees. Following on from this, and linked to the focus of this study on the development of OD in the UK, the country of origin was examined for journals with six or more OD articles between 1960 and 2010. The results of this analysis are outlined in Table 4.2.

The data shows that the country with the greatest number (n = 15) of journals with six or more OD articles was the US and with one other from North America (Canada), reflecting the US origins of OD. The country with the second largest number of journals with six or more OD articles, was the UK (n = 4). Again, Germany featured in the data, with three publications which had published six or more OD articles, with a total of forty-five OD articles, the German-based journals outnumbered the OD articles published in UK journals (n = 32).

A key focus of this study compares academic and practitioner perspectives and it is therefore important to understand trends in the interest level in OD by examining changes in volume of publishing over the decades. Table 4.3 shows the total number of articles published in journals with three or more OD articles published in them.

Table 4.3 shows the total number of OD articles published in journals which had published three or more OD articles, was at its highest in the 1970s, declined from the 1980s, and rose slightly after 2000. The number of publications for post 2010 is given, but since this decade is still underway, the figure of 29 relates only to part of the decade.

Looking at the profile of ALL OD articles published, including those in journals which had published less than three OD articles, a similar trend can be found. The results from in overall numbers from this search are detailed in Table 4.4.

Overall, the data shows that a small number of academic OD articles were published in the 1960s, with a large increase from the 1970s, followed by a gradual decline until 2000, when there was resurgence in OD academic publication. This trend was therefore evident in publications with both fewer than and more than 3 OD articles published between 1960 and 2010.

Identifying whether this trend in publication over the decades is similar for the three main countries of publication (the US, the UK and Germany) is also of interest. Table 4.5 shows the trends in the US, the UK and Germany, between 1970 and 2010.

The number of OD articles published in the UK and Germany followed a similar trend, with a small number of articles published in the 1970s; an increase in publications in the 1980s; a decrease in the 1990s, albeit with a more dramatic drop in the UK; and then an increase in publications from 2000. However, the trend differs in the US with the number of publication

Table 4.2 Country of Origin of Journals Publishing Six or more OD Articles between 1960 and 2010 and into the 2010s.

Country of Publication	Journal	No.	1960s	1970s	1980s	1990s	2000s	2010s
USA	Administrative Science Quarterly	7		5	2			
USA	Contemporary Psychology	12		7	5			
USA	Educational Technology	8		8				
USA	Exchange-Organizational Behavior Teaching Journal	8		4	4			
USA	Group & Organization Studies	6			4	2		
Germany	Gruppendynamik Forschung Und Praxis	7		7				
Germany	Gruppendynamik Und Organisationsberatung	16					14	2
Germany	Gruppendynamik-Zeitschrift Fur Angewandte Sozialpsychologie	22			15	7		1
USA	Human Relations	8		4	3			
UK	International Journal of Psychology	17				2	11	4
USA	Journal of Applied Behavioral Science	64		31	19	1	8	5
UK	Journal of Management Studies	8		3	4		1	
UK	Journal of Occupational Psychology	7			7			
USA	Library Trends	6					6	
USA	Organizational Dynamics	9		5		3	1	
USA	Personnel	9		6	3			
USA	Personnel Journal	13		12	1			
USA	Personnel Psychology	48		18	14	11	4	
UK	Personnel Review	11		4	5	2		
USA	Professional Psychology	6		6				
USA	Public Personnel Management	9		5	3	1		
Canada	Relations Industrielles-Industrial Relations	7		6		1		
USA	Training and Development Journal	34		17	17			1

Table 4.3 The Profile of Journal Article Publications over the Decades (Taken from the total number of articles published in journals with three or more OD articles published in them—data extracted from Table 4.1).

Decades	1960s	1970s	1980s	1990s	2000	Since 2010
Total Numbers	1	212	159	60	77	29

Table 4.4 The Profile of the Number of All OD Articles Published.

1960s	1970s	1980s	1990s	2000	Since 2010
3	311	262	168	180	97

Table 4.5 OD Articles Published in the US, the UK and Germany between 1970 and 2010

	1970s	1980s	1990s	2000s
USA	128	75	18	19
UK	7	16	4	12
Germany	7	15	7	14

at its highest in the 1970s; dropping dramatically in the 1980s and again in the 1990s; and with a negligible rise in publication through the 1990s and 2000s.

What then of the trends in the *Human Relations* journal notable for its link to those who founded the field of OD? In the eight publications published in *Human Relations*, in terms of volume, the trend matched with that found in the wider publication list. There were three articles in the 1970s, and there were also three in the 1980s, but these were all in the earliest part of that decade (i.e. by 1983). There was one publication in the early 1990s and finally one in 2012. Two of the articles focused on the evaluation of OD but in the main, as one might have expected for a high-ranking journal, they were, with the exception of the last review article, all driven by theoretical rather than by practice concerns.

Findings from the Copac search

The Copac search was restricted to books and the initial intention was to collate the findings in a similar manner than for the Web of Science and practitioner search findings. However, it became apparent that presenting trends in volume across the decades, country of origin and key authors would be problematic.

The publication identified as being the first text with OD in the title (hereafter referred to as OD text) was the Harvard Business School series in 1964. Authors on OD in the 1960s included Richard Beckhard (1969), Warren Bennis (1969), Robert Blake and Jane Mouton (1969) and Edgar Schein (1969).

The Copac search data was used to identify authors who published several OD texts. Table 4.6 contains authors who have four or more OD texts. This data includes publications which may have been republished in later editions.

In terms of number of OD texts published, French (mainly with Bell) has been the most prolific author, with Cummings (mainly with Worley) being the next most published and Burke also being highly published. With regards to the range of dates, most of the authors had a date range publication exceeding at least one decade. Golembiewski published texts over three decades, with Burke, French, Harvey and Schmuck all publishing OD text over a period of more than two decades.

In terms of location, although some OD texts had UK publication details, all but one had US editions and were written by US-based authors. The one exception was the UK-based author Dr. Charles Margerison, whose text was published in Bradford, UK. Dr. Margerison's text focused on management development as OD, whereas the US texts tended to be based on the traditional US OD.

Whilst volume and time span of presence in publishing were indicators of importance, they did not account for authors who may have published OD texts less frequently, but whose work was nevertheless highly influential.

A Google Scholar search was conducted, identifying thousands of cited texts. The most cited works, with 3905 citations, were the editions of Cummings and Worley's text *Organisation Development and Change*. French and Bell's 1973 *Organization development: Behavioral science interventions for organization improvement* was listed as having been cited 2894 times; Schein's 1969 *Process consultation: Its role in organization development* was reported had 2367 citations; Beckhard's *Organization Development: Strategies and Models* had 1404 citations; *Organization Development: Its Nature, Origins, and Prospects* by Bennis (1969) had 947 citations. However, caution about citation data is required as newer publications, which might become more influential, have not had sufficient time to build their citation count.

Practitioner Library Search

Given the focus on comparing academic and practitioner perspectives, resources selected for collection in the CIPD practitioner library catalogue were also examined. Year and type of publication were counted and categorized as academic book, academic journal, practitioner book, practitioner journal or report. If the book was authored by a recognized academic or its

Table 4.6 Authors who have Published Four or more OD texts.

Author	Number of Texts	Year range of publication	Co-authors on any of these texts?	Other issues of note
Brown	4	2004 -2014 (10 years)	Harvey (1)	These are all on the experiential approach to OD and appear to be editions of the same text
Burke	10	1972—1994 (22 years)	Hornstein (1)	The two 1987 texts may be the same text
Cummings	10	1980—2009 (19 years)	Huse (1) Worley (7)	There are other texts which do not appear on the Copac search. Cummings' text (with Worley) 'Organisation Development and Change' is on its 10th edition (published 2015, with previous copyright in 1994, 2000, 2004—these were not included in the Copac search). There is also a 9th International Edition. So the ten listed in the number of texts column is likely to be an underestimate.
French	19	1971—2005 (24 years)	Bell (14 texts) Hellriegel (1) Zawacki (5)	From the nineteen listed, there appear to be three texts which recur and are therefore likely to be updated editions of the same text. Zawacki is only co-author on texts that Bell has also co-authored.
Golembiewski	7	1978—2008 (30 years)	Ebrary (1) Eddy (1) Varney (1)	
Harvard Business School	4	1964—1976 (12 years)		Four-part series on OD
Harvey	7	1976—2001 (25 years)	Brown (7)	These appear to be earlier editions of the three texts listed above as being authored by Brown alone.

(*Continued*)

Table 4.6 (Continued)

Author	Number of Texts	Year range of publication	Co-authors on any of these texts?	Other issues of note
Jackson	6	1987—2006 (19 years)	Manning (2)	
Margerison	4	1973—1982 (9 years)	Hunter (2)	Drake is co-author on a text which also has Hunter as a co-author.
			Drake (1)	
			Kakabadse (1)	
Margulies	4	1971—1982 (11 years)	Adams (1)	Two of the texts with Raia appear to be editions of the same text
			Raia (3)	
Rothwell	4	1995—2011 (16 years)	Ebrary (1)	McLean is co-author on a text which also has Sullivan as a co-author.
			Stavros (1)	
			Sullivan (2)	
			McLean (1)	
Schmuck	5	1971—1994 (23 years)	Miles (1)	These are all on the subject of the use of OD in Schools
			Runkel (3)	
Varney	4	1976—1994 (18 years)	Voss (1)	

description was for use as a student textbook, it was categorized as an academic book. If the book summary focused on OD being *put into practice in an organization*, it was categorized as a practitioner book.

The split between academic and practitioner journals was less clear than for the categorization of books. Therefore, a note was made as to the specific journal and how it was categorized (see Table 4.7). The classification could be allocated in a different way, but the process used in this work is noted for the purposes of transparency and replicability.

The earliest text found in the practitioner library was an academic text from 1968 by Blake and Mouton. The next oldest eight texts were also academic, and the oldest practitioner text found in the library was dated 1989. Table 4.8 summarizes the number of academic and practitioner books and journal articles found in the CIPD practitioner library holdings.

Whilst conclusions from the findings are limited by this being a comparatively minor library holding, it was the most relevant practitioner library that might provide a broad understanding of trends in practitioner literature on OD. Of interest for this research are academic and practitioner publication trends over the decades under study, which are summarized in Table 4.9.

Seven reports, five of which were post-2000, were not included in the figures in Table 4.9. Arguably, these seven reports were written with the practitioner community in mind. However, it could also be argued that they were written by quasi-academic bodies: such as The Institute of Employment Studies and Roffey Park.

Table 4.9 shows that from pre-1970 until the end of the decade, academic publications outnumbered practitioner publications. This trend changed after 2000 when practitioner publication numbers outnumbered academic publications.

As has previously been investigated in the Web of Science and Copac searches, it is important to note any national differences in recognition of

Table 4.7 Categorization of Academic/Practitioner Journals.

Journals categorized as Academic	*Journals categorized as Practitioner*
Human Resource Development International	HR Magazine
	Organization and People
Human Resource Development Quarterly	Strategic HR Review
Human Resource Management	Workspan
Human Resources Planning	
International Journal of Training and Development	
Journal of Change Management	
Long Range Planning	
Organizational Dynamics	
Personnel Review	

Table 4.8 Number of Academic and Practitioner Books and Journal Articles in the Practitioner (CIPD) Library Holdings.

	Academic Book	Academic Journal	Practitioner Book	Practitioner Journal	Reports	Total
Year						
1968	1					1
1969	2					2
1971	1					1
1982	1					1
1987	1					1
1988	2					2
1989	1		1			2
1991	1					1
1993	1					1
1994	1	1	1			3
1995			1			1
1997					1	1
1998		1	1			2
1999	2	2			1	5
2000	1		2			3
2001		3	3			6
2002	1	2	2			5
2003		1	1	1		3
2004		1				1
2005	2			1		3
2006			1			1
2007			1	2		3
2008		1	2			3
2009	1	1	2	1	2	7
2010		3			1	4
2011			2		1	3
2012	1					1
2013					1	1
Total	20	15	21	5	7	68

Table 4.9 Number of Academic and Practitioner OD Publications, 1970 to post-2010

	Academic Publication	Practitioner Publication
Pre-1970	3	0
1970–1979	1	0
1980–1989	5	1
1990–1999	9	3
2000–2009	13	20
Post-2010	4	2

OD by academics. Given that there may have been a difference in the status of OD between UK- and US-based academics, it was of note that all earlier academic books in the CIPD library, up until as late as 1998, were authored by US-based academics see Table 4.10.

Table 4.10 Authors of pre-1998 Academic Books in the CIPD Library Holdings

Pre-1998 Academic Books	Author(s)
1968	Blake and Mouton
1969	Beckhard, Bennis
1971	Argyris
1982	Lippit
1987	Burke
1988	Greiner, Schein
1989	French and Bell
1991	Glassman and Cummings
1993	Cunningham
1994	Burke

Table 4.11 Numbers of OD Publications from The Institute of Employment Studies, Roffey Park and Mainstream Academic Publishing (post-2005)

	Institute of Employment Studies	Roffey Park	Academic Book	Academic Journal
2005			2	
2006				
2007		1		
2008		1		1
2009	2	1	1	1
2010	1			3
2011	1			
2012		1		
2013	1			

Post-2000, two quasi-academic sources (The Institute of Employment Studies and Roffey Park) were found to be active in publishing on OD, often in the form of reports (presented in Table 4.11). When compared with all other academic books and journals in the CIPD library catalogue, it was notable that together, between 2005 and 2013, they had eight publications when compared with the nine from all other academic sources.

Conclusion

As with other academic disciplines within business and management the bibliometric data show that US scholars dominated the field of thinking on OD, however UK and German scholars were also prominent. At the founding of OD, and as late as 1998, leading authors were primarily US-based. Whilst there was a resurgence of OD publications in the UK and Germany, the recovery in publication levels was less strong in the US. Furthermore, some of the growth in publications in the UK was more practitioner oriented, likely this is in response to practitioner demand rather than being led by academics.

References

Beckhard, R. (1969) *Organization Development Strategies and Models*. Addison-Wesley Publishing Company: Reading, MA.

Bennis, W. (1969) *Organization Development: Its Nature, Origins and* Prospects. Addison-Wesley Publishing Company: Reading, MA.

Blake, R., and Mouton, J. (1969) *Building a Dynamic Corporation Through Grid Organization Development*. Addison-Wesley Publishing Company: Reading, MA.

French, W. L., and Bell, C. H. (1973) *Organization Development: Behavioral Science Interventions for Organization Improvement*. Prentice-Hall: Englewood Cliffs, NJ.

Schein, E. (1969) *Process Consultation: Its Role in Organization Development*. Addison-Wesley Publishing Company: Reading, MA.

5 Subject Expert Views

Introduction

Having looked at evidence on how OD has been operationalized in practice (through the content analysis on job advertisements), and at who has influenced our thoughts on OD through their writing, another tranche of this research study was to gather qualitative data from subject experts. In this chapter findings from the semi-structured interviews conducted with twenty-one subject expert participants will be provided. The aim of the study was to elicit a range of opinions across practitioner and academic communities. To this end, in-depth discussions were held with ten practitioners, eight academics and three leading influencers. These generated a rich and complex set of material which gave depth to the data examined in the previous chapter. This material is discussed according to the themes set out in the literature review. This does mean that on occasion similar topics are treated from a slightly different angle. However, this is felt to be necessary to respect the richness and diversity of opinions presented. Those opinions differed based on both experience and career position, so in each section the different views emanating from the separate communities are given due consideration. The chapter concludes with a summary of the main points from the interviews, which is then carried forward for comparison with the data from other chapters in the Chapter 6.

Definition, Blurred Boundaries and Confusion

The difficulties of defining OD due to its broad nature, which were discussed in Chapter 2, were also reflected in interview responses. Responding to the question 'How would you define contemporary OD?', ten of the twenty-one interviewees described characteristics of OD as being change management (SENIOR PRACTITIONER 4, ACADEMIC 2), HRD (SENIOR PRACTITIONERS 4 and 6, ACADEMIC 2), strategic integration (SENIOR PRACTITIONER 6, ACADEMIC 3), leadership (ACADEMIC 2), culture (BUSINESS LEADER 1, ACADEMIC 3) and action research (ACADEMIC 8).

LEADING INFLUENCER 1 explained that OD projects could involve elements of strategy, consideration of context, cultural shifts, the development of constructive cultures and organizational and individual learning. ACADEMIC 7 considered OD to be involved in organizational structure, training and development and communications. All of the four business leaders (BUSINESS LEADERS 1, 2, 3 and 4) concentrated on the issue of alignment of people with the business. However, most of the interviewees found it difficult to provide a clear response to the question, with many answers not fitting well with any traditional definitions of OD.

ACADEMIC 3 proposed that the lack of clarity resulted from the blurring of boundary between OD and HR, saying that: 'I think that OD has become much more blurred as a discipline . . . The most significant is the blurring in being adopted as a part of HRM. It is no longer a separate and distinct field of study'.

SENIOR PRACTITIONER 4 explained that his recent educational experience of OD had included an exploration of 'what is OD', with course interviewees sharing experiences, discovering that they had: 'been doing OD, but had been unsure as to whether that was the right label before'.

ACADEMIC 1 further explained that she struggled to understand the difference between OD and having a strategic approach to HR. SENIOR PRACTITIONER 6 identified herself as an HR professional, but with OD as a specialism. ACADEMIC 1 and SENIOR PRACTITIONER 1 considered that in some cases OD functioned as a different title for what was effectively HRD practice. ACADEMIC 3 commented on the fuzzy margins between OD and change management in the literature. LEADING INFLU-ENCER 2 and SENIOR PRACTITIONER 6 both remarked on the confusion between OD and organization design, the extent to which, and how, they were related.

Commenting on the confusion over the definition of OD, BUSINESS LEADER 2 noted that:

> There is still a mystique with OD. Even in the mix of labels it is confusing: OD, organisation development, organisational development and organisation design—it is not clear what the differences are . . .' (in company name) 'there was an OD guru (based in America) who was spoken about in hushed tones. It took me six months to even ask what OD was.

SENIOR PRACTITIONER 1 noted that whilst those in HRM, HRD and OD might care about its definition that managers didn't give *'two hoots'* about OD 'as a name tag' and SENIOR PRACTITIONER 6 considered the OD label to have been 'used and abused'. ACADEMIC 3 judged that OD had lost any status as a separate profession by becoming 'morphed into' HR. SENIOR PRACTITIONER 4 referred to OD as being a rather nebulous term, and ACADEMIC 4explained the French and Bell OD text (a textbook often used to teach OD) had provided him with come clarity about its definition. However, ACADEMIC 4 highlighted that even after finishing an MSc program in OD he still wasn't sure what it was:

> our lecturer challenged us to agree 'what OD is' before we went off to the pub to celebrate. It took ages and delayed our visit to the pub for some time! . . . The field of OD is full of ambivalence and vagueness.

This experience was echoed by another interviewee with an MSc in OD (SENIOR PRACTITIONER 5) who stated it had taken her eight years to understand what OD was, and that she thought there was confusion about what OD was and a diversity of definitions, for example amongst HR Directors.

LEADING INFLUENCER 1, ACADEMIC 3 and SENIOR PRACTITIONER 4 referred to OD as being different things to different people in different contexts. In presenting workshops on OD, LEADING INFLUENCER 1 provided participants with sixty different definitions of OD, and asked them 'to decide which they think is the right one for them'. SENIOR PRACTITIONER 4 identified a key problem with clarity on the definition of OD when he likened it to: 'an elephant, if you are looking up close at the tail end, what you see is a very different picture than if you are looking from up close to the ears or trunk'.

Whilst many interviewees were keen for definitional confusion to be minimized, and to have definition of the activities related to being a legitimate OD practitioner, an alternative view was expressed by SENIOR PRACTITIONER 2. Highlighting that the modern business world existed in a context of ambiguity, dilemma and contradiction, he felt that it was better to accept that it was normal for that to have an impact of that on the nature of OD, rather than to waste time and energy seeking certainty and stability.

Development through History

Early OD

ACADEMIC 4 talked at length about the history of OD as it was his area of research interest. He also noted that that in addition to often documented accounts of Lewin, less often noted is that Lewin, Lippett and Likert were all Presidents of The Society for the Psychological Study of Social Issues, founded in 1936. This organization was very influential on government policy.

Through his research ACADEMIC 4 had found that the Blake and Mouton grid was instrumental in developing perspectives on OD. The use of questionnaires and surveys were important in the establishment of OD and with early OD large-scale, organizational analysis came to the fore. He also referred to the use of encounter groups/T-groups.

1960s and 1970s

None of the interviewees were in a position to have had personal work experience prior to the late 1960s. ACADEMIC 2 had the earliest experience of OD through study for his undergraduate and postgraduate subject in the domain of psychology. His earliest work experience in OD was also drawn from that subject foundation, and related to the traditional US form of OD and its roots in behavioral science. His first employment in OD in 1966 was with the US-owned company Esso, and he remarked that: 'the influence of the National Training Laboratory and the Tavistock Institute was also evident at that time'.

SENIOR PRACTITIONER 1 was involved in OD in the late 1970s, and also had a behavioral science background and oil industry first experience of OD. Trained at the Tavistock Institute, he described OD as 'seeming to be an interface between psychology and training'.

1980s

Many of the interviewees commented on the nature of OD in the 1980s, and especially the late 1980s. This increase in awareness may have resulted from knowledge of OD becoming more widespread at this time. However, the age of interviewees may have also affected this, as many would not have commenced their careers until the 1980s.

BUSINESS LEADERS 1 and 2 commenced their careers in the early 1980s by completing year-long post graduate CIPD accredited personnel management programs. BUSINESS LEADER 1 specifically remembered studying OD in the course, but BUSINESS LEADER 2 had no memory of this. Her first memory of encountering OD was when working for a large US organization based in a large manufacturing plant in the UK in 1984. As with the interviewees with OD experience in the 1960s and 1970, her first experience of OD was in a context influenced by a US company.

ACADEMIC 8 recounted his early OD teaching experience on an MBA program in the early 1980s, where he used (traditional US form of OD) 'French and Bell as the core text'. He noted that 'it didn't particularly resonate with me though'. ACADEMIC 3 also noted that when teaching the US-traditional form of OD in an MSc Occupational Psychology course, she didn't consider it to be meaningful to her at that time.

ACADEMIC 4 commented that his Master's Degree in OD in the mid-1980s: 'had a couple of Personnel Management modules, a couple of Organisation Behaviour modules, Research Methods, a couple of residential skills workshops and Group Dynamics exercises once a week'. However, he noted that: 'Change Management was not really current at that time, so there was no emphasis on that. It really was OD delivered by those who were committed to traditional OD'.

ACADEMIC 4 then described that in his second job role, after he completed his Master's program, that the OD function included Management

Development, TQM and the introduction of new major information systems. He explained that it had remained like that until there was a large-scale re-organization with decentralization (ACADEMIC 4).

ACADEMIC 5's first OD-related work assignment was in the late 1980s, whilst teaching Change Management and using a US text on Organizational Behavior. Although much of the content of the text related to traditional OD, she remembered less of a system-wide emphasis and more focus on the individual and team work.

LEADING INFLUENCER 3 had his first step into OD in the late 1980s. Transferring to consultancy from a psychoanalytic psychotherapist career, he was aware of the use the term OD. Given his base in The Tavistock Institute, combined with his professional background, one might expect some alignment in his practice to that of traditional form of OD practice.

The experiences of interviewees who had encountered OD in the 1980s were dominated by the traditional form of US-influenced OD. However, in the late 1980s interviewees' experience of OD changed somewhat, and the influence of UK economic environment factors was beginning to show. LEADING INFLUENCER 1's path to OD was driven by a quest to seek answers to her work context of the late 1980s. Working in a Management Development role for a US financial company in the UK, she reported that:

> There was a lot downsizing in the late 1980s / 90s—and it was an era when management gurus were particularly influential. (My company) did not make radical changes, they lost c200 people . . . but it was such a shock to everyone, including those who survived. It also had a significant effect on the reputation of the organisation and the way it was viewed. At that point I would not have known it as OD, but I had started to read around the work in the US and NLP.
>
> (LEADING INFLUENCER 1)

She explained that in the UK in the 1980s and early 1990s the general trend was for HR Directors to become 'more macho in style', with HR becoming more focused on business needs and with people more likely to be viewed as dispensable commodities (LEADING INFLUENCER 1).

The addition of quality initiatives was considered as being part of OD in the 1980s. ACADEMIC 4 mentioned TQM and SENIOR PRACTITIONER 2 remembered being in a quality team and being told that 'what we were doing was OD'. He added that 'OD was viewed as a hippy thing at that time . . . at the same time Investors in People, Quality Circles and EFQM were also in vogue' (SENIOR PRACTITIONER 2).

1990s

References to traditional US OD in the 1990s were made in the interviews, but diluted by other features of people management in the UK business context of the era. LEADING INFLUENCER 1 mentioned that whilst her interest in OD continued during the 1990s, the influence of the UK people and employment agenda was also present: 'HRM was really developing as a discipline, it was very much governed by the perceived need to align with the business focus and then moving forward into the Business Partner role of HR' (LEADING INFLUENCER 1).

Her perspective was that a 'planned change' approach to OD prevailed and that even though it involved short-term cost savings, planned change on its own did not 'stick'. ACADEMIC 4 remarked that the need to address cultural aspects of change resulting from large-scale privatization became more prominent in the 1980s and 1990s.

HRD was raised by many of the interviewees as having appeared as a new characteristic of OD in the UK in the 1990s. HRD was sometimes referred to in an unconscious manner, as though it had an assumed place in OD, or was even assumed to *be* OD. For example, in referring to his initial awareness of OD in the NHS in 1993, BUSINESS LEADER 4 also automatically referred to HRD activity: 'I would have been familiar with the terminology of "training/in service" department in terms of CPD . . . there was an OD function within the HR Department'. SENIOR PRACTITIONER 3 also noted that there was 'there was a mention of Learning and Development and OD then' in her post-graduate qualification in HR, although she wasn't aware of OD in practice for some time after. However, she was aware of job advertisements for OD roles at that time.

In the context of a US-owned company, HRD had become linked with OD in the 1990s, and SENIOR PRACTITIONER 4 recalled that during this time his first memory of OD was in using the terminology/label of OD to improve and upgrade the image of HRD which otherwise was 'sometimes perceived as just running training courses'. Also working in a US-owned company in the 1990s, BUSINESS LEADER 2's view of OD was that OD was not about HRD, but was about adopting a business-driven perspective. She explained that there was a practitioner in her organization who she categorized as an HR person at the time, but who she would have subsequently have classed as being in an OD role. Her view as to what differentiated this person as an OD person was that they got 'involved with the business to identify people issue related projects' (BUSINESS LEADER 2).

Post-2000

Despite LEADING INFLUENCER 2 coming from an HRD background with a nationally-recognized company, and SENIOR PRACTITIONER 6 coming from an HR role within a leading UK energy company, neither was aware of OD until after 2005. After graduation, SENIOR PRACTITIONER 3 worked in an HR role in four sizeable organizations consecutively. However, during that time she did not meet anyone who had an OD job title, although in the last organization an OD practitioner had been brought in after she left.

BUSINESS LEADER 1 reported having been aware of OD for three decades, since the 1980s, and that his fundamental view of OD had not changed in the last decade, but his understanding of it had broadened and deepened. However, when discussing OD after 2000, he noted that OD was referred to in more diverse ways.

SENIOR PRACTITIONER 3 highlighted that the application of OD was immature in her organization. Working in an SME, she thought that they didn't need a separate OD function, but instead, needed a role focused on working across a range of people management issues. In looking across sectors, BUSINESS LEADER 2 agreed that if there was OD activity in smaller organizations, it should not be serviced by a separate OD function, but might be led by an HR Director.

BUSINESS LEADER 2 highlighted the nature of adoption of OD in the public sector, noting that there was an intellectual acceptance of OD and it was more theoretically based. She was aware that there was less emphasis on delivering effective change in the public sector, whereas in the private-sector OD was required to demonstrate that effective change had been made and that value had been added (BUSINESS LEADER 2).

Reflecting Back over the Decades

Interview responses on the development of OD since the 1970s, and its development in the decades since then, highlighted the following notable perspectives from the interviewees.

The Senior Practitioner Perspective

Completing a CIPD course on OD had helped SENIOR PRACTITIONER 4 to understand OD and how it had changed over time:

> We have moved from T-groups to looking at different drivers and complexity, from individual and team issues to organisational wide issues in the context of effectiveness. By now using Models of Change Management and Organisational Culture models, we can have a more holistic approach.

He highlighted that OD practice in the last twenty years had moved away from micro focused laboratory behavioral science techniques and team functioning, to a focus where job design was less important and macro approaches were used. He also observed that more emphasis was placed on business competitiveness, expressing concern that the application of the Ulrich model to the HR function had led to HR being less of a *Champion of the People* role.

The Leading Influencer Perspective

LEADING INFLUENCER 3 was strong in his belief that HR had become an instrument to: 'enslave people through the application of legislation, rules, etc., and worked in the support of line management'. He proposed that OD should be about bringing positive and constructive change to improve the working lives of individuals. He was of the opinion that convergence had occurred between OD, HRD and HR; that the nature of HR had transformed over the last twenty to thirty years; and that many approaches to OD had developed. He noted that the development of the OD profession had necessarily been influenced by fundamental changes in the form of organizations, as they had more permeable boundaries and functional changes.

The Business Leader Perspective

BUSINESS LEADER 2 proposed that: 'In the last 30 years there is more acceptance of OD and that it has transferred . . . to the current focus of effective implementation of changes in business'. BUSINESS LEADER 1 placed a different emphasis on what OD had become. He remarked that in his current Middle East role, alongside many other former UK CEO's, he was aware of a: 'much stronger appreciation of OD, Organisational Change, Culture and Behaviours than would have been the case 30 or so years ago'.

The Academic Research Perspective

ACADEMIC 8 was particularly knowledgeable and involved in national research strategy and the development of policy and practice. Having been asked to provide feedback to HRD academics on their subject research rating after the Research Assessment Exercise in 2008, he advised that:

> as a field there is a lack of theory, that doesn't mean it doesn't have a useful place, but high ranking journals are expected to encompass theory—and that is what is holding the field/discipline back. A lot of the work is case based, and it is intrinsically more difficult to build theory from. As a field it needs to think more about how it theorises and to publish in mainstream journals, positioning itself amongst a more robust peer group. The field should be looking to publish in their own journals—but also in e.g. The Journal of Management Studies.
>
> (ACADEMIC 8)

Of particular interest is the link between publishing in journal articles and academic careers. The ranking of particular publications runs parallel with ACADEMIC 6's comments on OD and its lack of status as an academic discipline in the UK: 'I am not sure that OD is not much more of a practitioner type language than an academic language on behavioural sciences. I guess in my head it's a practitioner community subject area'.

Given the importance of the development of OD over time and the debate over definitions which reflects the debate in the literature, the next section will examine interviewees' responses in relation to the core attributes of OD identified in Chapter 2.

Core Attributes of OD

This section will report interview findings relating to the nature of traditional OD, followed by findings on the skills considered necessary to be an OD practitioner: the need to be able to challenge organizational orthodoxy; the relationship between Change Management and OD; consultancy in OD; and OD's role in behavior and culture issues. Respondents' responses on effectiveness, leadership, organization-wide and strategic perspectives, and issues of partnership and engagement will also be examined.

Traditional OD

The responses in relation to traditional OD tended to be indirect. Elements of traditional OD were referred to by mention of OD systems or processes, rather than by specific mention of traditional OD in itself. With few exceptions, interviewees' rhetoric suggested that they did not know of *traditional OD* as a core form of OD.

However, ACADEMIC 4 did use the term *traditional OD* and SENIOR PRACTITIONER 5 had attended a UK-based NTL program which included explicit elements of traditional OD, such as entering and contracting diagnosis, interventions, shifting team culture and planned change and other *conventional classic OD processes* such as having a system-wide approach.

LEADING INFLUENCER 1 mentioned that Mae-Yan Cheung-Judge was the Dean of this UK NTL program, describing her as the most eminent and rounded OD guru/practitioner in the UK, noting that she had studied 'at the feet of the masters'. Cheung-Judge did her Ph.D. in OD in the US and 'had the opportunity to learn from Edgar Schein'. She had, through the NTL program, trained many OD practitioners. LEADING INFLUENCER 1 also described Cheung-Judge as being highly visible as the foremost expert in OD in the UK, with a strong influence on the development of contemporary OD thinking in the UK.

SENIOR PRACTITIONER 4's description of the CIPD programme on OD also made mention of traditional OD which he said placed 'emphasis on the contracting/entering process'. LEADING INFLUENCER 3 noted that his consultancy organization's approach followed the 'entering and contracting, diagnosis, intervention and evaluation/feedback cycle'. ACADEMIC 5 described a shift in ontological thinking in OD, but did not include reference to practice in this development

SENIOR PRACTITIONER 1 made reference to T-groups, describing them as an approach that was widely criticized. SENIOR PRACTITIONER 5 also referred to T-groups in the NTL program which involved a T-group exercise and training on group processes, consulting and team coaching.

The concept of systems was mentioned in the interviews by LEADING INFLUENCER 3, BUSINESS LEADER 1, SENIOR PRACTITIONER 5 and ACADEMIC 5, in relation to a system-wide approach to change. BUSINESS LEADER 1 explained that the OD systems model had increasing utility for him, as he gained experience in senior executive roles.

In the main, indications of knowledge of traditional OD processes were included in responses on OD process. In what might be termed as contemporary approaches to traditional OD, three of the interviewees referred to using AI as an OD tool (SENIOR PRACTITIONERS 2, 4 and 6) and SENIOR PRACTITIONER 2's organization had applied 'positive psychology' in a review in conjunction with academic input. In the literature describing traditional form of OD, emphasis was placed on systematic in-depth *diagnosis* after the *entering and contracting* stage (as described in Chapter 2) and prior to the consideration of selecting and applying *interventions*.

SENIOR PRACTITIONER 4 and LEADING INFLUENCER 3 highlighted the importance of the traditional OD process in facilitating a challenge to organizational orthodoxy. Application of the *entering and contracting* processes, and accurate *diagnosis*, could lead to better managed expectations. SENIOR PRACTITIONER 4 noted that it was equally important to clarify what would 'not be achieved' through adopting set processes. LEADING INFLUENCER 3 outlined how defining and contracting could be a complex process, but noted that it was essential to do it well. He added that at the *entering and contracting* step in the process, the unconscious dynamics of organizations and hidden forces became apparent if only a rational mindset had been applied. In line with this, SENIOR PRACTITIONER 4 noted that the 'presenting problem' was often a symptom rather than a cause, and that there was often 'an elephant in the room that requires addressing first', meaning that further diagnosis was required before the contracting stage began.

Strong views on the accuracy of diagnosis was a feature of responses from ACADEMICS 1 and 6, and from SENIOR PRACTITIONERS 1, 2, and 4 who referred to the need for sound diagnosis and data. Three respondents, ACADEMIC 2, SENIOR PRACTITIONERS 2 and 4, reported on the importance of diagnosis in change processes. SENIOR PRACTITIONER 1 proposed that the route to persuading managers against quick fix changes was to challenge thinking as to what was required to make sustainable change. He proposed that this could only be achieved through the presentation of accurate data, arguing that that OD practitioners must to have strong analytical skills, such as those used in lean engineering where the emphasis is on applying diagnosis to identify root causes. ACADEMIC 8 also reflected this need for in-depth diagnosis:

The real prize would be to understand that what is presented as an organisational issue is often a surrogate of deeper issues which requires change. The same can be said for implementing solutions, so for example, use IIP as the frontline intervention, but the prize is to use it to change the way that organisational strategy is developed and implemented.

Although few of the respondents cited use of traditional OD, those who did suggested that this was of impact on the value of their work.

OD Skills, Attributes of Practitioners and OD Training and Qualifications

In line with existing literature, respondents were unclear on the definition and boundaries of the discipline of OD. LEADING INFLUENCER 1 noted that in his opinion, OD was a diverse field meaning that practitioners tend to come from a range of disciplinary backgrounds and applied a range of different approaches. SENIOR PRACTITIONER 3 stated that OD required diverse experience and was therefore not a role you could do as a first job after graduating from university. LEADING INFLUENCER 3 also felt that there was a lack of clarity as to what made a 'good' OD practitioner:

> What makes an OD person is fuzzy—and is made up of a number of things like suitable personality: a curious mind, a desire to learn and a passion for people. Personalities are so variable and different and that adds to the sense of fuzziness.

LEADING INFLUENCER 3 highlighted three primary components of an OD professional. First, academic study and knowledge of organization and social theory was necessary. Secondly, OD professionals should have had 'personal psychoanalysis/psychotherapy/counselling/coaching/supervision'. He felt that having had psychoanalysis was essential, academic study was not enough; and that although it was not normally taught in academic organizations, having a deep personal understanding of motives of self and human systems generally was essential. Finally, he proposed that an effective OD practitioner must have 'lots of years' of consulting practice experience (LEADING INFLUENCER 3).

SENIOR PRACTITIONER 5 proposed that the qualities required to be an OD person included: 'listening, consulting, questioning, building rapport, having the ability to challenge, getting buy in and being able to look at things from outside in'. She noted that a background in HR was useful, but that it was essential to have had serious line management experience before becoming an OD practitioner, noting that it was crucial that 'you had to have had experience of managing a difficult team yourself'. Corresponding with this perspective was BUSINESS LEADER 1's view that the most effective OD people he knew were HR Directors who had migrated to general management positions. BUSINESS LEADER 1 commented that that OD practitioners must have technical OD skills to enable the redesign of work structures.

Having *Emotional Intelligence* is an important feature for OD practitioners. LEADING INFLUENCER 2 judged that a competent OD practitioner it was more important to be able to 'get under the skin of people, to know what makes them tick' in addition to having technical skills in HR and OD. SENIOR PRACTITIONER 4 also believed that *Emotional Intelligence* was crucial to being an effective OD practitioner, noting that: 'If you haven't got an intuitive nature and a behavioural sensitivity, then you can't do OD. Having an analytical mind and the relevant skills are both important, but the Emotional Intelligence piece is indispensable'. BUSINESS LEADER 2 also believed that high levels of *Emotional Intelligence* and empathy were crucial to good OD practice, reflecting that she had:

> never seen a good/stupid OD person. To be a good OD person you have to a certain amount of 'smarts". Businesses and organisations and how they work is a complex issue, business and organisations are complex creatures, if you do OD you need to be able to understand that complexity.
>
> (BUSINESS LEADER 2)

She added that OD practitioners also had to be intellectually curious, a term also used by SENIOR PRACTITIONERs 2 and 6, and that they must be interested in how various aspects of business worked as well as having a natural interest in the people aspect of business to be useful. In addition to having natural 'smarts' she also believed that OD professionals must show a sound understanding of theory: 'Business people can be quite snooty about that—you have to have and be able to demonstrate some theoretical depth' (BUSINESS LEADER 2).

SENIOR PRACTITIONER 5 also believed that practitioners should work from a strong theoretical basis, noting that she could not 'bear people who wing it and use pop psychology. It staggers me how often experts get away with this'. She thought it was also important that OD practitioners were 'authentic'.

Despite the rhetoric from many scholars on the importance of taking a strategic approach in OD, ACADEMIC 2 argued that it was important to understand and function effectively at a micro and macro level. BUSINESS LEADER 3 noted that the skills and competencies required 'varied according to the business context e.g. start-up situations which require different technical skills'. BUSINESS LEADER 2 AND SENIOR PRACTITIONER 3 also noted that the type of skills required varied according to business size. BUSINESS LEADER 2 noted that, that in recent years, she had heard less about OD in small- to medium-sized businesses, and that they tended to focus on process, and therefore were more likely to employ operational HR people.

For smaller organizations, with more holistic, flexible and converged HR functions, they had a need for practitioners with more generalist skills, whereas in larger organizations, greater scope for specialism and separation is required (BUSINESS LEADER 3). However, based on her experience of working in large organizations, SENIOR PRACTITIONER 6 thought that HR, HRD and OD were converging as disciplines. She noted that HR professionals tended to be increasingly expected to operate in the OD space, and outlined that in her organization OD was no longer the responsibility of a small specialist team, as it had been previously.

Whatever the size of business, it was noted that OD practitioners should possess an understanding of systems and culture, good interpersonal skills and 'a helicopter mind' (ACADEMIC 2). ACADEMIC 2 stated that an OD professional must be able to relate to, and understand, 'the detail at shop floor level, as well as putting this in context of the big picture'. BUSINESS LEADER 2 also believed that OD practitioners must be able to influence senior managers, middle managers, technical professionals and the full range of employees.

Interviewees commented on specific OD training and qualifications programs (LEADING INFLUENCER 1, SENIOR PRACTITIONERS 4, 5 and 6). The practitioner responses indicated that qualifications provided professional legitimacy. However, interestingly, none of the academic respondents commented on this issue, nor on the UK-based organizations currently offering OD training and qualifications.

LEADING INFLUENCER 1 indicated that Roffey Park had played a key role in leading the development of thought on contemporary OD in the UK, and that the NTL (which she said was the 'biggest provider' of OD training), The Tavistock Institute and Ashridge were also influential. She highlighted that Roffey Park had progressed the OD agenda by disseminating its work through training and qualification provision, experimental practice, research and reference to theory, and that their approach was as much about 'mindset shifts' as it was about behavior. LEADING INFLUENCER 1 had also been involved in working closely with Mae-Yan Cheung-Judge who delivered the NTL programs in the UK.

SENIOR PRACTITIONER 4 felt uncertain about the legitimacy of his skills for his specific OD role, and gave this as the reason he had decided to complete a recognized, accredited OD qualification. He was not alone in this regard, as with regards to when she had begun to feel competent in OD SENIOR PRACTITIONER 6 replied that:

> I actually think—that if I am being totally honest—in the last 2/3 years. When I had the job title of OD—I thought—how on earth do I explain OD to others? I had a sense that I was not qualified in OD and I needed

a qualification to be able to lay claim to being an OD professional, so I started the OD practitioners programme in OD.

What was of particular note amongst the senior practitioner interviewees was that those who had moved from senior HR or general management careers (SENIOR PRACTITIONERS 4, 5 and 6) into specific OD roles, had completed OD specific post graduate qualifications. One (SENIOR PRAC-TIONER 5) moved into an OD role after completing a qualification and the others (SENIOR PRACTITIONERS 4 and 6) opted to take up a formal program of study through the CIPD and Roffey Park after being appointed into OD roles with organizational responsibility. Both commented on the perceived need for formal qualifications in order to consider themselves as being legitimate OD professionals.

SENIOR PRACTITIONER 5 highlighted that she had originally thought OD was about coaching and facilitating, but that since doing the NTL course (as mentioned by LEADING INFLUENCER 1 above), she considered OD to be concerned with system-wide change, and the use of tools as micro interventions which were part of a bigger picture. She was complimentary of the NTL program, explaining that it was founded on the principles of the traditional US model of OD. She claimed that it took her eight years after completing a Masters in OD to understand OD and that the Masters alone had not yet given her the confidence to know what OD was or how to tailor it to an organization. She clearly highly regarded the NTL program (it was apparent in her rhetoric) and commented that having done the NTL course, her understanding of OD had changed. It was as though she considered that having completed the NTL program she was now in the inner circle of the elite *bona fide* OD practitioners.

However, despite the perceived need for qualification, SENIOR PRAC-TITIONER 4 noted that there were few regulated OD education programs in the UK, and cited the CIPD and Roffey Park programs, but not the NTL program, as being the only ones he was aware of.

SENIOR PRACTITIONER 4 discussed skills in terms of putting teams of people together to tackle OD initiatives. Rather than focusing on the competence of individuals, he noted the importance of having fluid teams that were structured around particular projects. He highlighted the importance of OD project team members having different tasks and rotating duties to assist in the development of skills and provide for contingencies. He described this as being like a set of building blocks in terms of team member competencies, with the configuration of these competencies depending on the needs of the project (SENIOR PRACTITIONER 4). Given the broad and fuzzy nature of the OD discipline, considering skills on a group basis might be a more fruitful approach, rather than expecting individual practitioners to be competent across the broad range of OD practice. In a similar vein, ACADEMIC 2 noted that that OD 'could do a better to learn to from communities of practice approach'.

Experience and knowledge of self, both themes apparent in the literature, were also addressed by interviewees. BUSINESS LEADER 2 and SENIOR PRACTITIONER 6 both reported that self-awareness was important in order to be successful as an OD professional. SENIOR PRACTITIONER 4 noted the importance of first setting up a level of psychological distance in applying OD practice, advocating that the entering and contracting process was useful in this regard. SENIOR PRACTITIONER 2 highlighted the importance of tempering personal ego, noting that this was also the case for those in senior roles as 'Too much ego at senior levels is damaging to an organisation'.

Only LEADING INFLUENCER 3 referred to the experience base of the OD practitioner as having its place in developing OD competence: talking about the need to differentiate between intellectual understanding and experience as they were both important. He also believed it took great skill to challenge beliefs, assumptions, values and practices in a way that a client could see and understand. The next section will examine skills in relation to the ability to challenge organizational orthodoxy in more detail.

The Requirement to Challenge Organizational Orthodoxy

OD practitioners' ability to challenge constructively was a recurring theme in the interviews, and was viewed as being important and requiring great skill. Eleven interviewees made reference to the importance of the business context and the need for OD practitioners to 'hold their own' (BUSINESS LEADER 2) and to challenge organizational leaders, culture, norms and wisdom.

ACADEMIC 2 noted that OD practitioners must be tenacious and resilient in order to survive. BUSINESS LEADER 3 valued practitioners who could challenge organizational norms, beliefs and culture and provide information on relevant practices outside the business. SENIOR PRACTITIONER 5 echoed the need to work 'as though you are standing on the outside looking in and having clarity of your role' contributed to achieving that. LEADING INFLUENCER 1 had a similar view, highlighting that OD practitioners had to:

> function outside/inside, they are able to see and express things as though they were an outsider, doing that is a risk, it can get you sacked, but it is necessary and it takes immense and rare skill to be able to do it well.
> (LEADING INFLUENCER 1)

SENIOR PRACTITIONER 2 identified a key aspect of the OD role as being an organizational truth seeker. To play this role effectively, SENIOR PRACTITIONER 1 advised that those who were 'embedded in the organisation were not free to do OD'. He noted that 'OD people need to have the courage of their convictions' and must have analytical tools to produce reliable data for accurate diagnosis, to create a firm basis for challenge, or there could be a situation in which 'diagnostic interviews were done, but the views of many were influenced by politically placed answers rather than rational responses'.

LEADING INFLUENCER 3 provided a more detailed account of how a necessary stance of independence and objectivity described above can be achieved, with a very particular viewpoint:

> A well rounded OD person would not see themselves as omnipotent, they should be attuned to processes of projection and projective identification, introjection and introjective identification. There is a difference between intellect and experience. One can learn psychology, but that does not add to your own experience in the way that personal psychoanalysis does. To do OD effectively you need to have had psychoanalysis. I know that might be considered a bit radical—but I believe it with all my heart.

The leadership culture and character of the top leader could of course also have an influence on the ability of the OD professional to challenge organizational norms. SENIOR PRACTITIONER 4 highlighted that not all leadership cultures welcomed challenge, noting that in some situations 'holding up the mirror' to senior management behavior was the most effective thing to do, and that in one context the issue was that the senior managers had to model the roles that they expected in the rest of the organization. SENIOR PRACTITIONER 6 referred to having a new CEO, who was more open than his predecessor. This had created a context in which it was easier to challenge organizational traditions. SENIOR PRACTITIONER 3 explained that to be effective it was important to challenge the business to look at things differently, but it was also important to listen to others' views, and to be willing to accept that she was not always right.

The existence of a number of areas of tension was mentioned by three interviewees. ACADEMIC 5 advocated being open, where there were tensions (for example, in change processes), to discuss these and make them explicit. ACADEMIC 8 agreed with this approach and commented that if done well OD would lessen/remove tensions. A different type of tension was mentioned by LEADING INFLUENCER 1. She explained that there was a tension between having in mind an OD approach that would work well, but expanded that the critical OD view would be that any preconceived ideas on approaches without getting people fully involved was manipulative.

OD and the Field of Change Management

Is Change a Prominent Feature of OD?

It was evident from responses on the definition, nature and development of OD that the concept of change was considered as being a prominent feature, and was covered in the majority of interviews. Given the context of ongoing change in organizations, this is perhaps not surprising. Even though SENIOR PRACTITIONER 3 considered OD to be 'immature' in her organization, she reported a situation characterized by constant and dynamic change. In relation to the connection of OD with Change Management, LEADING INFLUENCER 3 noted that the concept of change had been part of OD from its origins: 'Kurt Lewin's founding work in OD included theory on the nature of change and resistance to change'.

Interviewees tended to refer to Change Management in terms of it being an assumed, intrinsic aspect of OD: I see it as including issues such as organisational culture, values, change, organisational fit, effectiveness, fit for future purpose. It is a change oriented role—and is involved in considering culture as part of the Change Management process' (LEADING INFLUENCER 2) and 'The focus of OD has been almost exclusively in Change Management' (SENIOR PRACTITIONER 1).

ACADEMIC 8 expressed the view that OD was linked to Change Management; it was hard to do well; and that it was easier to do well when there was a close fit between the organizational activities and its objectives. Only ACADEMIC 4 reported an incidence of Change Management not being included in OD, as his OD post-graduate qualification in the 1980s did not include Change Management in the syllabus.

ACADEMIC 3 remarked on an increased focus on Change Management, and the increasingly indistinct boundaries and confusion between OD and organizational change in the literature. ACADEMIC 8 illustrated this confusion in practice, reporting that he considered OD and Change Management to be intrinsically linked. SENIOR PRACTITIONER 1 observed that he did not refer to himself as an OD practitioner, using Change Management terminology instead.

ACADEMIC 1, a mainstream HR academic, explained that she had decided to check the bookshelf of her colleague, who was involved in teaching OD, prior to the research interview. However, she reported that all she found were books on Change Management, except for one that had OD in the title— *Management and Organisation Development*, which is an HRD text. She noted that she had the same types of Change Management books, so that, apart from that one exception, there was no difference in their text reference sources.

In comparing HR and OD, BUSINESS LEADER 1 took the view that HRM was focused on the maintenance of organizations, whereas an OD approach was what was needed for change situations. LEADING INFLUENCER 3 described this as 'HR has become a transactional activity; OD should be a transformational force'.

Hard and Soft Change and the Learning Organization

Change Management was often referred to in the context of a differentiation between *hard* and *soft* change, with an assumption that OD practitioners were more concerned with *soft* change. Those who applied only *hard* change were criticized, with LEADING INFLUENCER 1 arguing for more constructive consideration on the impact of change on employment. LEADING INFLUENCER 3reported being skeptical of big consultancies, who offer little variation in approach and who implement whole scale change programs with little concern or knowledge of the interface between people and systems. Similarly, SENIOR PRACTITIONER 4 questioned the extent to which many senior managers understood the human dimensions of change, speaking scathingly of those who hire: 'big consulting firms' (who) 'peddle BPR, but without consideration of OD. It is imposed change with no real understanding of the people element'.

Interviewees referred to the move away from the division between Change Management and OD in practice, proposing that effective and sustainable organizational change required both approaches. ACADEMIC 2 identified the main development in OD as being an integration of *soft* and *hard* approaches to change, rather than a focus on *soft* change only. He proposed using a cyclical approach, involving organization design being applied in the start-up phase of the change process; OD techniques being used in the implementation and evaluation stage; which then fed back into the organizational learning process; and into subsequent organization design. He referred to the *hard* approach as including 'a systems approach, business process re-engineering application of McKinsey and, in the UK, restructuring' (ACADEMIC 2); linking these developments to 'Keith Grint's pendulum of trends in approaches to leadership', where there was a swing back and forth between scientific management and human relations approaches over time.

As the head of an OD function, SENIOR PRACTITIONER 5 described her team as being very much on the *soft* side of OD: concerned with culture rather than *hard* change. However, despite being less concerned with structural change:

> we have made it our business to up skill our team on the design of organisational structures. We wanted to be able to ask credible questions. . . . We now lobby to get more involved in organisational structure design and to bring a more humane joined up thinking approach to this.
> (SENIOR PRACTITIONER 5)

The critical importance of line managers, as well as OD practitioners, in organizational change was highlighted by BUSINESS LEADER 1 and SENIOR PRACTITIONER 2. As a senior manager, ACADEMIC 3 noted that: 'In a rapidly changing environment . . . I seek to ensure that the people and their activities and development are clearly aligned with the strategic direction of the organisation'.

BUSINESS LEADER 2 reported a change in emphasis in OD over the last thirty years, proposing that it had shifted from a focus on theoretical pondering to focus on the effective implementation of changes in business. She argued that OD people need to understand business and business markets and to develop linking strategies in order to deliver market-led change. In relation to where change processes should begin, ACADEMIC 2 highlighted that it could be driven from the top down or from the bottom up, suggesting that this could also be subject to national differences.

Even though SENIOR PRACTITIONER 1 evaluated organizational learning as being a key factor, only two interviewees raised the topic of learning organizations in relation to OD. ACADEMIC 2 argued that as with approaches to leadership and management, a pendulum operated, and that the tradition of human relations had always been there, albeit waxing and waning over time. He added 'the soft side OD has come back with the Learning Organisation Movement' (ACADEMIC 2).

Interestingly, whilst ACADEMIC 2 linked the soft side of OD to a learning organization approach, SENIOR PRACTITIONER 1 advocated the use of 'diagnostic tools used in lean management' and proposed that 'Data driven decision making is often lacking'. Furthermore, he argued that the application of learning organization methodology assumed a rational context, which may work better in technically oriented organizations. He believed that attempting to apply learning organization principles in the public sector did not work, since those organizations were all about politics and power, rather than rational learning (SENIOR PRACTITIONER 1).

The Nature of Change Management had also Developed over Time

Interviewees indicated that Change Management was also a developing and changing subject field (LEADING INFLUENCERS 1 and 3). LEADING INFLUENCER 3 commented that OD was involved in wider system change: 'Wise organisations know they have to keep up with changing ideas on organisation structure and functioning. We need to look more at systemic/domain-wide change, and understand that, not just at organisational level change'.

LEADING INFLUENCER 1 described a case from her consultancy work that highlighted how the nature of change had evolved; where the purpose of the organization had itself changed, resulting in traditional Change Management outcomes such as a reduction in workforce numbers. More importantly, she noted that the change requirement was for 'a complete mindset shift'. Since the organization purpose had changed from having been a service provider to that of being a commissioning organization, this was particularly difficult since the organization members had previously taken great pride in quality of service. With a change in organization purpose, the organization members were forced to shift away from what they had previously taken self-respect from: the provision of excellent service (LEADING INFLUENCER 1).

A Consultancy Approach to OD

Interviewees did not place a great deal of emphasis on the topic of consultancy. However, one issue which was discussed was the differentiation between different types of consultants in the form and influence of large global consultancy firms, and smaller, more specialized consultancy operations (ACADEMICS 2 and 6). SENIOR PRACTITIONER 4 highlighted the influence of consultants in disseminating change in management practice, and ACADEMIC 4 noted that a main career destination of those from a 1980s OD Masters program was consultancy roles, and that the contracting/entering stage of consultancy process was taught as part of the CIPD post graduate program in OD (SENIOR PRACTITIONER 4).

The value of internal or external consultants in an organization was the most frequently referred to issue, with ACADEMIC 2 and 8 both taking the view that there was a case for both internal and external consultancy approaches. BUSINESS LEADER 3 valued internal practitioners who 'had the ability to observe as though they were observing from the outside'. However, SENIOR PRACTITIONER 1 and LEADING INFLUENCER 3, both in external consultancy roles, argued that OD could only be done by external consultants, with SENIOR PRACTITIONER 1 considering that internal OD practitioners self-regenerate existing culture and they could not be objective. LEADING INFLUENCER 3 proposed that what was important was the partnership between the internal change agents, whether they were within HR or not, and the external consultant and was: 'convinced you need to have external consultants since some changes cannot take place without external support'.

A Behavioral Science/Organizational Culture Focus in OD Practice

The assumption of rationality in organizational change settings was highlighted by LEADING INFLUENCER 3, who noted that: 'People are not rational, but most managers still believe and operate on the basis that they are. So managers implement rational solutions to irrational problems'.

LEADING INFLUENCER 3 considered that the most successful OD practitioners were so as a result of their ability to uncover, understand and work with the hidden forces in an organization that remain hidden if a rational mindset is applied. He viewed the capability to see and constructively challenge taken for granted organizational assumptions and values as being vital for OD success (LEADING INFLUENCER 3).

The traditional form of OD placed more emphasis on group and individual behavior, whereas contemporary OD has developed to focus predominantly on organizational culture. SENIOR PRACTITIONER 1 and ACADEMIC 2, who had the earliest personal involvement in OD of all the interviewees, came from psychology backgrounds in keeping with traditional approaches to OD. SENIOR PRACTITIONER 6, and ACADEMICS 4, 5 and 6 had studied Organizational Behavior in undergraduate or postgraduate programs, and SENIOR PRACTITIONER 4 considered the 'social psychology of behaviour' as a defining characteristic which differentiated OD from HR. SENIOR PRACTITIONER 4 noted that the program leader on the OD CIPD course he completed was a psychologist, and that the course was psychologically-oriented, acknowledging the *Behavioral Science* roots of OD.

LEADING INFLUENCER 1 noted that 'The Roffey Park approach goes beyond the application of old style behavioural science, also using NLP, transactional analysis, socio-technical systems, dialogic approaches, organisational politics and consideration of complexity and ambiguity'. Culture change was a major part of the role of SENIOR PRACTITIONER 6, who reported that she was responsible for investigating organizational culture, and to achieve this she led an OD team to sit alongside the HRD team which she also managed.

ACADEMIC 8 stated that organizations 'miss the plot' by not making organizational culture a priority, and SENIOR PRACTITIONER 1 was of the opinion that not addressing culture would result in a piecemeal approach. SENIOR PRACTITIONERS 5 and 6 had been appointed to head up organization-wide culture change projects, and the project led by SENIOR PRACTITIONER 6 was intended to align the internal organizational culture to the external brand change. In both cases the practitioners were, to an extent, independent of their HR leads, and SENIOR PRACTITIONER 1 contended that when it came to changing culture, that 'HR are not in the game'.

Given the origins of OD, one might have expected more to have been said in the interviews about behavior and organizational culture, but there was relatively little coverage of these topics. However, BUSINESS LEADER 1 provided some context in which they play a part:

> The fundamental that does not change is the quest for effectiveness and to achieve that it is essential to have the people, structures, systems, processes, culture, and behaviours aligned. Once the strategic direction is determined, the specifics follow on from that.

Organizational Effectiveness

Organizational Effectiveness was the focus of OD in a recent Francis et al. (2012) text, and was also considered as being important by many of the study interviewees. ACADEMIC 3 referred to the current emphasis in OD as being on efficiency, and effectiveness was considered the most important focus by BUSINESS LEADER 4. SENIOR PRACTITIONER 1 commented that: 'Effectiveness is ultimately all that OD is about. Organisational Effectiveness *IS* the focus of OD'.

SENIOR PRACTITIONER 6 was on an ongoing search for the 'holy grail of organisation effectiveness through people', and ACADEMIC 1 was searching for sustainable competitiveness. LEADING INFLUENCER 2 viewed effectiveness as sitting alongside culture, values, change and fitness for organizational purpose. BUSINESS LEADER 1 proposed that if business and organizational effectiveness was a focus of OD, it would not become a fad or a fashion.

The concept of effectiveness necessarily includes consideration of approaches, evaluation and measurement. If there was no yardstick to measure against, how did one know if effectiveness had been achieved? In LEADING INFLUENCER 3's organization the approach to OD consultancy included attempts to integrate evaluation from the outset; and ACADEMIC 6, and SENIOR PRACTITIONERS 2 and 4 referred to the increased emphasis on diagnosis and the use of metrics. The application of these metrics was increasingly perceived in terms of contribution to business performance (BUSINESS LEADER 2) and of OD 'to the bottom line' (SENIOR PRACTITIONER 3).

Leadership, Taking an Organization-wide and/or Strategic Approach in OD

In relation to the development of OD over time, ACADEMIC 8 was not surprised about the increase in the importance of leadership capability to OD, or that it developed into 'not just being HR': noting that OD had become, linked to organizational structure and operating at CEO/Managing Director (MD) level.

Leadership

The importance of OD to leadership and of leadership to OD was highlighted by five interviewees. Leadership capability and emotional intelligence were highlighted as ongoing themes of OD (SENIOR PRACTITIONER 6), and about getting the best out of business leaders (BUSINESS LEADER 2). It was proposed that OD practitioners should: 'facilitate getting the ideas coming out of the business leaders' heads, ideas that the business leader may not be aware of, or not have as a focused idea until they are asked' (BUSINESS LEADER 2).

Leadership was identified as being critical to OD (SENIOR PRACTITIONER 1), as was the challenge of finding a new form of leadership (ACADEMIC 2). It was emphasized that people who changed organizations were leaders, and that OD practitioners could act as supporters and enablers. However, unless they had a strong alliance with line managers, they would not have an impact on the organization (BUSINESS LEADER 1).

From a theoretical perspective, OD practice was thought to involve working across a whole organization (ACADEMIC 1). It was proposed that there was an increase in a strategic approach in practice and that there is now 'a stronger sense of OD is not just HR, but has an organisation wide perspective' (ACADEMIC 3). Interviewees expressed the need for OD to be organization-wide (SENIOR PRACTITIONERS 1 and 5) and SENIOR PRACTITIONER 1 explained that the downside of using OD techniques to solve a problem in a piecemeal way, rather than in a holistic organization-wide approach was that it will just 'pop up in another form elsewhere'. LEADING INFLUENCER 1 proposed that OD shouldn't just be theory driven, but should also be strategically oriented and 'people driven'. OD is no longer just organization-wide in the normal sense, in addition in contemporary OD a frequent organizational context was in mergers and acquisitions (LEADING INFLUENCER 1).

The Rhetoric on Strategy and Relationship of OD to Strategic HRM

In terms of reflecting on the development of *Strategic HRM*, SENIOR PRACTITIONER 6 recollected the rhetoric of 'does HR have a seat at the boardroom and also the move from Personnel Management into HR' which she placed in the 1990s. One interviewee did not perceive any discernible difference at the most strategic level, between Strategic HRM/HRD/OD, noting that: 'I think the clue is in the term strategic' (BUSINESS LEADER 1), with another perceiving that OD played only a small part in Strategic HRM (ACADEMIC 3). The prominence of strategy in the HR professional map was noted (LEADING INFLUENCER 2). However, others thought that the idea of *Strategic HRM* had dissipated, and did not consider there to be much evidence of strategic HRM: 'it is not any less important, but it is less in evidence' (ACADEMIC 8).

Reflecting on whether HR or OD should lead change initiatives, ACADEMIC 8 thought that OD should lead change given its strategic nature. Although seeing HR as playing a part in leading change, it was not viewed as being a driver of change but as a sub-system to support it and in his organization: 'HR was at the top table, but it was not about setting strategy, they took the role of a professional response and debates on issues such as pensions, in short they took on the staff responsibility function' (ACADEMIC 8). OD was reported as operating at the more senior levels of HR (SENIOR PRACTITIONER 6), and HR was not viewed as being the only stakeholder in OD: HR was influential, but the strategy function was seen as also being as important to OD (ACADEMIC 8).

Strategic HRM was not seen as being possible without OD by some interviewees (ACADEMIC 1 and SENIOR PRACTITIONER 4). BUSINESS LEADER 1 also outlined the need to have an overarching narrative, for example to help people, make sense of HR policies and why they mattered. SENIOR PRACTITIONER 5 deemed 'contemporary OD to be much more holistic, involving an integrated people plan' as part of the business plan. The need for a strategic approach was perceived as being important, but not always understood by organizations that often had very vague strategies which consisted of operational objectives (SENIOR PRACTIONER 1).

SENIOR PRACTIONER 1 noted that: 'what is important in real strategy is challenging thinking'. Additionally, his view was that a change process that was not congruent with strategic intent would be confusing and not tackle the underlying issues. SENIOR PRACTITIONER 4 echoed that OD should be strategic, have influence in order to be successful, and that not all organizations had the appetite for that. BUSINESS LEADER 1 believed that interventions must be: 'integrated and INTEGRATIVE i.e. they should not just respond to strategy but to play a part in shaping it. This is what an OD person should be doing'.

Thinking and Acting Strategically in OD

According to BUSINESS LEADER 2, the purpose of taking a strategic approach to OD is to enable the provision of efficient structures and organizations. BUSINESS LEADER 1 and SENIOR PRACTITIONERS 3 and 4 were in agreement that it is vital to understand the business, and leverage OD practice in the context of the organizational strategy.

In practice, in her role as a senior academic manager, ACADEMIC 3 reported being more involved in OD in terms of cultural change and the development of people in the context of her rapidly changing organization. As part of that role, she is responsible for ensuring that people, their activities and their development are clearly aligned with the strategic direction of the organization (ACADEMIC 3). BUSINESS LEADER 1 also stated the need for congruence in the approach to people across the board and when in place at a strategic level it should then be followed by having the right policies, procedures and practices in place.

Organization-wide or Wider Still?

LEADING INFLUENCER 3 expressed that it was no longer effective for OD practitioners to operate with a perspective which was limited to organizational boundaries, highlighting that organizations were 'much looser than they once were; they had more porous boundaries, they were more fragile and the future was less certain'.

The nature of employment had changed employees, and as customers no longer have life-long relationships with discreet organizations as they would have done in the past. As such, organizations have less control than they did in the past, as employees and customers no longer depend on them, and the way in which they are perceived has changed as a result of highly publicized organizational failures: 'the prevailing view of organisations as being unreliable and no longer trustworthy had to be part of the consideration of the context' (LEADING INFLUENCER 3).

The nature of organizations has changed, and this can have an impact on OD. SENIOR PRACTITIONER 2 explained that his organization's HR function provides services internally, and sells transactional services to similar external organizations. It also has a contract for the provision of organizational redesign services. As such, within the HR department, internal delivery is complemented by commercial business with an external client base. SENIOR PRACTITIONER 2 also advocated an argument for change in internal organization work group design: 'future leaders are about reading the environment and supporting self-forming and self-sustaining teams. Creating, disbanding, and morphing teams' (SENIOR PRACTITIONER 2).

LEADING INFLUENCER 3 recounted that he was not alone in his view of organizations and of contemporary concerns. He noted that at a recent international conference, attended by delegates from the US, there was much discussion of the shift to looking more broadly not just into: 'organisations as the unit of study, but outwardly into the broader social system. We need to look more at systemic/domain-wide change, and understand that, not just at organisational change' (LEADING INFLUENCER 3).

Issues of Partnership and Engagement

Partnership

The partnership approach was rarely mentioned by interviewees and from what was said, there was little in the way of common views. SENIOR PRAC-TITIONER 1 highlighted that that organizations employing the rhetoric of partnership were often the organizations that were the least likely to actually be 'doing it'. LEADING INFLUENCER 1 advised that without sound management practice at each level of the organization and shared leadership the organization was 'up a gum tree'.

The importance of applying a partnership approach to leading change was noted by BUSINESS LEADER 4, whilst BUSINESS LEADER 2considered that what was important in change processes was that 'it should make sense to the people who work in the business'. LEADING INFLUENCER 1 clearly advocated the partnership approach, and in referring to organizations that rely on knowledge workers, she proposed that 'leadership practice should be about energising and connecting employees with the organisation'. However, she noted that this approach was rare and despite the growing awareness of the need for it, there was little in the way of understanding and application of appropriate practice. However, she also stated that there was some 'effective work being done in the professional services sector', driven by the business imperative to retain professionals with skills and experience, since these were in short supply (LEADING INFLUENCER 1).

Engagement

Partnership and engagement were often mentioned by interviewees as being interlinked. SENIOR PRACTITIONER 2 was skeptical when referring to OD initiatives on employee engagement:

> My understanding of OD is that people often used it as a manipulation and designed initiatives to suit themselves. OD needs to be lead from the top but you want emotional engagement, not just compliance. The process needs to be from an honest endeavour, not just to suit the egos of those at the top.

He also referred to his organization's increasing use of employee surveys to measure employee satisfaction or engagement. His organization was not the only organization to use this approach, and SENIOR PRACTITIONER 3 also talked about her organization using '*The Times* best company "b heard" survey' process. SENIOR PRACTITIONER 6 recounted how in previous employments she had a remit to get 'people engaged', and launched an organization-wide AI process in order to get to the 'hearts and minds' of employees. In the professional services sector, LEADING INFLUENCER 1 highlighted that 'knowledge is power' and employee engagement was of sufficient importance that senior partners led on employee engagement.

Context and Challenges

This section will explore findings in relation to the context of and challenges for OD. Data will be presented on the relationship of OD to HR and HRD, the role of professional associations, and national differences, issues of power and politics, critiques of OD and perspectives on the extent to which it is considered as being a fad or fashion. Findings in relation to interviewees' views on the future of OD will also be presented.

Relationship to HR and HRD

HR and HRD did not feature in the traditional US form of OD. However, the data collected in the content analysis exercise highlighted clear relationships between HR and OD, and HRD and OD, in the UK. As a result, interview questions were asked about the potential for connection between OD, HR and HRD. Many respondents made mention of OD's relationship to HR and HRD, both from a point of view of certainty and opinion about the existence of a relationship, or in relation to the existence of fuzzy boundaries between them.

ACADEMIC 3 viewed OD, HR and HRD as being necessarily interconnected, stressing that the development of people was central to all three. LEADING INFLUENCER 1 referred to OD having an important role in leadership development, but believed that HRD, HRM and OD also had an important role to play. LEADING INFLUENCER 3 advocated that all three 'come under an umbrella which is about the quality and efficiency of work performance in the organisation'.

ACADEMIC 1 proposed a convergence of HRM, HRD and OD, as it was essential that the areas work together. SENIOR PRACTITIONER 4 explained that in applying OD you had to look at the full range of HR topics together.

ACADEMIC 8 considered HR, HRD and OD as being separate, believing that HRM and HRD had converged to some extent, but that OD was still distinct. ACADEMIC 1 contended that a false division had been created between the three areas, noting that OD practitioners seek to distinguish themselves: 'A lot of OD people make it clear they are not HRM or HRD—it's as though they are saying I am an OD person—and I am better than you'.

ACADEMIC 6 proposed that as academic subject disciplines, HRM, HRD and OD tended to remain separate. As a mainstream HRM scholar, he believed that his knowledge base might be limited, but saw OD as being more closely aligned to HRD than to HRM. He estimated that the split between the three fields was replicated in practice (ACADEMIC 6). However, talking about the process of developing the CIPD professional map, LEADING INFLUENCER 2 noted that the extent to which the functional models of HR, HRD and OD converged or diverged was about equal.

HRM, HRD and OD draw on different theory and literature, and publish through different channels (ACADEMIC 6). Based on his experience, ACADEMIC 6 did not think that journal editorial teams or reviewers were rejecting articles from other domains, but that articles covering particular areas were only submitted to particular journals by authors (ACADEMIC 6). He noted that this stratification had not arisen from the nature of research as qualitative or quantitative in nature, as methods from 'both camps' were used successfully in HRM. In talking about factors which could act as driving forces for academics assessing the value of journal selection, he noted that:

> For HRD where they are more likely to get higher ranking journals is if they are organisation psychology oriented, more theoretical and quantitative in nature. I guess if you look at HRD and HRM academic work, the HRD work tends to be less grounded in theory. In HRM, in terms of theory lenses, Institutional Theory tends to be a fairly pervasive base.
>
> (ACADEMIC 6).

Blurred Boundaries between HR and OD

Respondents from mainstream HR backgrounds (ACADEMIC 1 and SENIOR PRACTITIONER 3) considered HR and OD to be one and the same thing. ACADEMIC 3 believed that the relationship between OD and

HR had changed over time with OD now being a subset of HR, but that this was not the case in the original form of OD. She also portrayed HR as often involved in areas which were traditionally OD activities and by embracing OD, HR had sought to increase its own status. HR had strived to make their role bigger and broader. She considered that OD was no longer a separate and distinct field of study and there were no longer OD practitioners, they had been replaced by HR practitioners who had OD within their role (ACADEMIC 3).

SENIOR PRACTITIONER 6 proposed that the HR profession had also changed and developed, and that HR practitioners were expected to operate in the OD space, with OD operating at more senior levels. Part of the shift of devolving people functions to line managers meant that HR was less transactional, so to own the strategic element of OD was important to the power and status of the HR function (SENIOR PRACTITIONER 6).

According to ACADEMIC 3 the HR community had achieved advantage over the OD community: 'Over the forty years, there has been blurring of boundaries of the disciplines of OD and HRM, with HRM coming out on top'. However ACADEMIC 8 disagreed, being of the opinion that OD and HR continue to be distinct. He considered that HRM and HRD had converged a little, but OD was still separate.

OD Should Be a Subset of HR

LEADING INFLUENCER 2, BUSINESS LEADER 2 and ACADEMIC 7 suggested that OD was a subset of HR, but even with two of these interviewees, their view as to where it should sit was not set in stone. LEADING INFLUENCER 2 expressed the view that 'OD done well is an essential part of HR, it is at the crux of HR but that HR could be a subset of OD, or OD could be a subset of HR'. BUSINESS LEADER 2 proposed that if HR was working well, OD should be within the HR function; if not, then it HR should be driven by OD.

LEADING INFLUENCER 2 noted OD was within HR in the CIPD professional map, but that she found it difficult to separate them or put them in hierarchical order, highlighting that 'at the heart of HR is good business and understanding people. You could argue that that is what OD is about'.

LEADING INFLUENCER 2 was of the opinion that where OD sat within an organization was of less importance than the extent to which it was recognized as being an important people process and strategy. As a former HR Director, BUSINESS LEADER 2 believed that OD should be situated in HR. However, she also noted that if HR function was performed 'in a perfunctory manner' she would rather that HR was situated within an OD function. BUSINESS LEADER 1 said that his experience of HR Directors over the years was that he had worked with many who had really struggled to get out of the technical/functional mindset. Also, a former HR Director, BUSINESS LEADER 1 noted that in his first board-level position in the 1980s, he considered OD and HR as dealing with the same set of organizational issues and that:

> if pushed to decide, because of the way I see strategic HRM, in that it is about facilitating the people part of the organisational jigsaw in its contribution to maximising effectiveness, I would say HR and OD is a subset of that. BUT, it is all about labels.
>
> (BUSINESS LEADER 1)

Competence was referred to by LEADING INFLUENCER 2, BUSINESS LEADER 2 and BUSINESS LEADER 1, who stated that the position of OD and HR depended on who the post holders were, and that this was true for any and all major organization disciplines. Differentiating between strategic and operational-level HR and OD he noted that:

> however what is important is how these fit within the strategic intent. In terms of the operational transactional areas and the application of policies these are separate and you need people who are competent technicians in their area whether that be OD or Resourcing; but further up the food chain, you don't need to have a depth of technical competence in all the areas of HR/OD.

His opinion was that whilst knowledge of technical skills would assist at strategic level, this was not essential, and that the individual's approach, values and mindset were more important for strategic people leadership (BUSINESS LEADER 1). This sentiment was echoed by LEADING INFLUENCER 2. SENIOR PRACTITIONER 6 proposed that 'REAL HR' was not done through the provision and operation of HR policies and procedures, but through OD, noting that OD had been 'missing in action' for the last decade but was re-emerging in a converged model with HR (SENIOR PRACTITIONER 6).

Only three interviewees advocated that OD should sit within the HR function and their views were subject to a caveat. The main issues for these three interviewees (LEADING INFLUENCER 2, BUSINESS LEADERS 1 and 2) were practitioner capability and the approach of the HR function as the contingent factors in deciding where OD should sit.

OD Should Not Be a Subset of HR

Five interviewees believed that OD should not be a subset of HR. ACADEMIC 4 that this was a question that 'used to vex him', but that he now considered HR to be a subset of OD, and ACADEMIC 2 observed that although OD often sat within HR, it should be the other way around, but that it depends on whether the HR function supports an OD approach. LEADING INFLUENCER 1 stated that OD tools and techniques could be useful for HR, and had a similar view to BUSINESS LEADER 2, who was concerned that they were often applied unthinkingly by HR. SENIOR PRACTITIONER 1 advocated a 'joined up' approach, stating that HR people would like OD to be a subset of the HR function: but that ideally, the OD function should report directly to the CEO/top management team. LEADING INFLUENCER 1 was of the opinion that HR should be a subset of OD, whilst SENIOR PRACTITIONER 1 had a strong view on OD's relationship to HR: 'OD is not simply the province of HR, and if it is, god help us! HR is a politically manipulative function . . . HR are not in the game of challenging the culture'.

ACADEMIC 8 was of the opinion that HR should be a subset of OD as: 'OD is strategy and change. HR plays a part in leading change, but it is not a driver it is a sub-system'.

LEADING INFLUENCER 3 considered OD and HR to be different and separate functions. In his view, OD and HR functions were often put together only to ensure administrative convenience, and that the underlying philosophies of HR and OD meant they often couldn't work together. However, he did propose that it would be better if HR and OD worked in a collaborative way. HR has become a transactional activity and OD should be a transformational force (LEADING INFLUENCER 3).

OD and HR Should Have a Partnership Relationship

Rather than focusing on the hierarchical relationship between HR and OD, some interviewees considered a partnership approach to be more useful. SENIOR PRACTITIONER 6 believed that an individual's view depended on when they came into HR: she had previously believed that OD was a subset of HR, but was now unsure as to which one took precedence, but did consider OD and HRM to be inter-related. ACADEMIC 1 was of the view that HR and OD were synonymous but that, in her experience, OD practitioners tried to separate themselves from HR which she was critical of as: 'they are missing a trick—there is a disconnect—they don't have the resources to do what they should'. She added that there was a need to have 'joined up thinking' (ACADEMIC 1).

SENIOR PRACTITIONER 4 was of the opinion that to judge the relationship to be hierarchical was to make an assumption, and viewed the relationship between OD and HR in terms of a Venn diagram in which HR and OD were equal partners with an area of overlap. SENIOR PRACTITIONER 6 believed that OD had originally been a subset of HR, talked of the two disciplines as being inter-related and did not know which one should take precedence. However, she did note that her previous boss considered OD to be part of HR, adding that HR professionals were being encouraged to develop more OD skills.

IN SENIOR PRACTITIONER 5's organization, OD sat separately from the main HR function, but was part of the international HR department.

Although the HR director didn't fully understand what OD did, she recognized the value added by the OD team, and talking about their relationship with HR, she noted that:

> We don't do any of the 'HR bit', the downstream HR work. That is for the directors/heads of department to implement with their HR people. We do not have anything to offer in terms of the operational HR side. Even in standard structural change we do less on that.
>
> (SENIOR PRACTITIONER 5)

SENIOR PRACTITIONER 2 defined himself as being an OD practitioner who reported to the HR Director, with a remit that included leadership of OD but also Training, Staff Engagement, Recruitment, Health and Safety and Occupational Health. As such, his role encompassed a diverse mix of functions usually considered as being part of mainstream HR. This may or may not be a reflection of BUSINESS LEADER 1's comment above: that the structural organization of OD and HR has as much to do with which people were considered most suitable, as it has to do with the simple matter of objective organization design.

SENIOR PRACTITIONER 5 viewed OD as operating on more strategic concerns such as organizational culture and power, with HR operationalizing what had been designed by OD. He described HR as servicing processes and procedures and 'managing the organisational plumbing,' while OD had a longer-term orientation, positioning the organization correctly at the right time, 'moving the organisation forward for mutual survival'.

HRD and its Relationship with OD

The content analysis data highlighted the prominent position of HRD in OD in the UK since the 1990s. In the interviews, with regards to convergence of HRD and HRM, SENIOR PRACTITIONER 4 commented on 'HRD being pulled more into HR'. Both SENIOR PRACTITIONER 4 and ACADEMIC 1 recollected the merger of the ITD with the IPM in creation of the IPD (later to become the CIPD) in the UK in the 1990s.

BUSINESS LEADER 4 demonstrated how the boundaries between HRD and OD could be blurred; noting that in the public sector, OD was originally considered to be training. SENIOR PRACTITIONER 5 noted that when applying for an HRD role: 'Management development was an aspect to the job and I thought that was what OD was'.

SENIOR PRACTITIONER 4 believed that OD was synonymous with Change Management but also the same as HRD. ACADEMIC 2 considered that when change led to changes in work organization and/or different skills requirements, this was where HRD then had its place i.e. in dealing with those. SENIOR PRACTITIONER 6 related that previously known 'related subjects such as Organisational Behaviour, group dynamics and Learning and Development—which I now think of as OD' were familiar to her. So clearly, she saw HRD as being synonymous with OD.

However, some interviewees were of the opinion that OD and HRD were separate. SENIOR PRACTITIONER 5 was of the opinion that OD differed from HRD, as OD practice included 'freedom to diagnose' and use this as a basis from which to design and deliver effective interventions.

Whilst SENIOR PRACTITIONER 3 said that she had previously thought of OD as being part of HRD she no longer did. ACADEMIC 1 contended that many who call themselves OD were actually HRD practitioners, but there were other OD practitioners who sought to divorce themselves from HRD.

OD was also seen as being an extension of HRD, in that it was simply a case of change of name (SENIOR PRACTITIONER 1). ACADEMIC 1 commented that many so-called OD practitioners were simply engaged in HRD activity. This point was picked up by SENIOR PRACTITIONER 4 who recalled that:

> Especially amongst the learning and development community, I think OD was considered more sexy, a better option than learning and development, which was sometimes perceived as just running training courses. At (company name) I managed the Head of OD, I asked him to explain what it was, it sounded to me a lot learning and development with bells on.

The extent to which some in the HRD community acted in the manner of a cuckoo chicks in the OD nest (in that they took on the OD name without changing their HRD core function) was exemplified by SENIOR PRACTITIONER 5 when she explained that she applied for an MSC in Management Development, but by the time she started the course title had been changed to People and Organisational Development. Since it was reported as a change in program title only, it would appear that it was thought that a title including OD would be more attractive to potential students, than one situated in the HRD subject area.

OD as More Strategic than HRD

One possible reason for practitioners wishing to be seen as OD experts and separate from HR and HRD, is that OD is considered as being more strategic. ACADEMIC 1 explained that there is an assumed 'hierarchy of esteem for job roles' in operation. For example: 'Management Development is more highly esteemed than training, but when it boils down to it—which is more important . . . "training" of the bulk of the employees or of the much fewer senior managers'?

This indicates that a job role which is perceived as having more influence at a senior leadership level is considered as having more impact and therefore is attributed higher status. This being the case OD would, as a more strategic function, also be perceived as having a higher professional status.

SENIOR PRACTITIONER 2 believed that the role of OD practitioners was to map: 'out where we want to be: training is about providing the practical skills needed to develop that'. BUSINESS LEADER 2 was of the opinion that OD was a higher form of HRD, sitting at a more strategic level, and therefore being 'above' HRD. BUSINESS LEADER 2 noted that: 'I think OD is about strategising to provide efficient organisations and structures, then it is for learning and development at practitioner level to implement the strategy'. However, BUSINESS LEADER 1 was of the opinion that there was no difference between HRM, HRD and OD at strategic level, but at the 'deployment level', each of these areas of practice was different.

Professional Associations

Interviewees made little mention of professional associations. SENIOR PRACTITIONER 1 had been aware of a 'grouping' of OD practitioners when he worked in the insurance sector in London, explaining that: 'my boss was in the OD network part of the Association of Management Education Developers (AMED). They had an OD network, but I don't think there was a professional grouping as such'.

Some interviewees did not think that OD was a professional grouping, and ACADEMIC 3 proposed that it was not even an independent function since it had been incorporated into HR. ACADEMIC 8 judged that as a consultancy, OD is a function and therefore not a profession.

The role of the professional associations in OD, such as the CIPD, was raised by some of the interviewees. LEADING INFLUENCER 2 thought that there was more scope for the CIPD to include subjects such as OD within its remit, since it was already a complex and wide ranging professional grouping: 'When we look at other professions through their professional bodies, their world is much more simple—HR is much more complex as a profession in terms of depth and breadth'. Conversely, SENIOR PRACTITIONER 1 was of the opinion that with regards to the CIPD putting OD onto their professional map, it was a 'bolt on'. LEADING INFLUENCER 2 explained that the map had been criticized for focusing on large organizations. As such, the dissemination of management ideas from a professional body may have included unintentional assumptions about the relationship between HR and OD, since this map is used to inform all CIPD accredited programs throughout the UK and beyond.

ACADEMIC 6 compared national groupings of HR professional bodies, referring to the SHRM in the US and the CIPD in the UK:

> There may be a bit of a power play between the CIPD and SHRM, but in terms of the ISO standards, SHRM started that initiative off. In the UK and Ireland CIPD has a monopoly. In terms of post graduate

HRM programmes, they just won't have a market unless they are CIPD accredited courses. CIPD have a very strong hold over what is taught.

SENIOR PRACTITIONER 4 was of the opinion that the status of the UK HR profession was at risk and that there is a tendency to assume that that anyone can 'now do HR'. He explained that in the era of Industrial Relations and Trade Unions in the 1960s and 1970s, HR work was considered to be more complex, not everyone could do it, with an emphasis on the psychology and sociology of work.

ACADEMIC 8 had been involved with the SRHM in the US and had an interest in the differences between the professions and professional bodies in the US and UK. As with the view presented by ACADEMIC 6 above, LEADING INFLUENCER 1 also commented on the CIPD positioning itself as a monopoly. She considered the CIPD to have been particularly acquisitive in taking OD into its fold. LEADING INFLUENCER 1 considered that the US-based SHRM had had a 'more partnership of professionals working across boundaries approach'.

National Differences

Many interviewees had no knowledge of international differences in OD. For example, when asked to compare OD in the UK and US context, LEADING INFLUENCER 3 stated he was not sure of any difference. Those interviewees who did have knowledge were of the opinion that national differences did exist, but that these differences had changed over time and context.

The primary comparison drawn on OD practice was between the UK and US. Although ACADEMIC 4 referred to similarities and connections in early OD, he added that the 'story of OD had been mainly told by the US. The danger was the US scholars were hegemonous in their approach' (ACADEMIC 4). Given the notion of US dominance of early OD and OD's core values including democracy, there was a paradox in the judgement of ACADEMIC 2. The US had a more centralist approach to management, with other countries applying a more democratic approach to change processes.

Referring to the origins of OD, ACADEMIC 4 placed Lewin, who was of European origin, in the US in relation to the period during which he was considered to be the founding father of OD. He also stated that whilst 'the Americans were innovative and *avant-garde* . . . there has also been a connected/interwoven tradition of OD in the UK' (ACADEMIC 4).

ACADEMIC 8 cited samples of the early US-based OD scholars, who visited The Tavistock Institute in London, and noted, with regret, that The Tavistock did not have the same influence it once had. He referred to another senior UK academic who advocated a return to its principles in the academic and business world. ACADEMIC 2 noted that the work of the US National Training Laboratory and the Tavistock Institute were influential in the UK from the late 1960s.

Early OD practice in the UK was considered as having been dominated by the US. From his work in the late 1960s in the oil and petro-chemical sector, ACADEMIC 2 considered that the application of OD was as a result of these companies being US owned. Talking about her career in two large US-owned corporations in the early 1980s until the late 2000s, BUSINESS LEADER 2 noted that:

> My first encounter with OD was in US corporations I think they were amongst the first to adopt OD as a critical practice. OD in (company name and company name) was typically driven from the US. The OD experts were based in the States.

Interviewees also cited sources of influence on US domination of management thinking. ACADEMIC 4 explained that 'we are influenced in our discourse on OD by the US'. ACADEMICS 2 and 6 referred to a history of Anglo-American dominance in management thought and practice. On occasion, the US-centric influence could unintentionally be given a place. For example, when asked about the country of origin of the keynote speakers commissioned by the CIPD, LEADING INFLUENCER 3 said that the 'thought leaders' were mainly from the US. ACADEMIC 6 and BUSINESS LEADER 1 referred to the dominance and therefore influence of the large US and UK consultancy companies. BUSINESS LEADER 1 stated that in the middle-east, UK influence on business practice was probably stronger than that of the US.

ACADEMIC 3 was of the opinion that contemporary OD operated very differently in the UK than in the US. This was the confusion which had led to the convergence in the UK: 'OD is neither clearly one thing nor another. It doesn't seem to know what it is in the UK context' (ACADEMIC 3). Whilst this convergence might be deemed as a threat to the OD community in the UK, the outcome might not be as expected. ACADEMIC 5 noted that, unlike the situation in the US where it was under threat, in the UK OD had flourished.

ACADEMICS 2 and 6 both also refer to the influence on the Brazil, Russia, India, China (BRIC) group of countries. Whilst there was some evidence of isomorphic pressures at work, the adoption of Anglo-American management practice was very variable (ACADEMIC 6), and it was perhaps too early to tell what its influence might be (ACADEMIC 2). ACADEMIC 6 explained that the extent of US/UK influence in the dissemination of management practices to the BRIC countries was related to historical links. For instance, Brazil was more influenced by the US, and India more influenced by the UK. There was however, a much less tenuous link between management practices in the US and UK with their take-up in China. Given that China was sealed off from Western influences for decades, this is not surprising. The context of the adoption of management ideas was embedded in the context of the historical traditions of business and management and deeply entrenched in national culture.

ACADEMIC 3 reported that there was difference between the UK and European models of HR and OD. ACADEMIC 2 considered Scandinavian countries would be fertile ground for OD since they tended to have 'a more egalitarian approach in principle'. Having operated in pan-international roles, BUSINESS LEADER 2 noted that she had found that OD functions were used less in continental European countries, such as France, Germany, Spain and Italy. SENIOR PRACTITIONER 4 noted that that people management in 'continental Europe, it is often approached from a legal perspective background and tends to be regulation and process rather than human relations/behaviour oriented'.

Power and Politics

The matter of OD and power, or the failure to address questions of power and politics, was an issue often raised in the OD literature. ACADEMIC 5, BUSINESS LEADERS 1 and 2, SENIOR PRACTITIONERS 1, 2 and 5, and LEADING INFLUENCER 3 all raised issues relating to power and politics. As such, only a third of the interviewees mentioned *power* and where they did, in the main, it was in the context of personal power and influence rather than issues of power in organizations. This would indicate that power within organizations was of less importance than considered to be by scholars, or that it was such an implicit feature of organizational life that the interviewees did not consider it explicitly or consciously.

SENIOR PRACTITIONER 2 was of the view that HR was not involved in 'shifting power' but that OD was. SENIOR PRACTITIONER 5 raised the issue of power in OD work on change, with OD's influence over decision making on the future of the organization. In particular, she commented on how people become territorial when faced with the prospect of structural change. For this reason, LEADING INFLUENCER 3 was adamant that external support, in the form of external consultants, was essential. Underlying LEADING INFLUENCER 3's response was the sentiment that external OD consultants are sufficiently free of organizational power structures and therefore more able to challenge organizational norms. Most of the responses relating to power and politics were collected under the interview topic of being capable of challenging organizational orthodoxy.

References to issues of power and influence related to the OD function and practitioners as individuals, rather than to the existence of power in the context of organizational politics. ACADEMIC 5, BUSINESS LEADER 2 and SENIOR PRACTITIONER 3 were all of the opinion that OD practitioners could source power through influencing senior managers and by making a sound business case for their practice.

SENIOR PRACTITIONER 1 observed that to be successful an OD practitioner required tacit permission from those with power in the organization, and could not operate successfully from a 'boundary' position. LEADING INFLUENCER 3 and BUSINESS LEADER 1 noted that it was not possible to work effectively in OD without the sponsorship of a senior organization leader, such as the CEO. LEADING INFLUENCER 3 added that this senior sponsor need not be intimately involved in the change process, but that there must be regular restatement of support from them as the changes in the system start to 'extrude and people begin to feel less comfortable with the change process'.

BUSINESS LEADER 1cited an example of the importance of the acquisition of a powerful position for the OD practitioner, explaining that when offered his most recent role:

> At first they wanted me to run one of the operations divisions, but she . . . (his CEO) . . . said actually what I would really like you to be is to be the Chief for OD. I said no, because I don't think you can be an effective corporate OD person unless you are one of the 'big beasts' round the table. So I run one of the three divisions AND I am the Head of OD for the overall organisation.
>
> (BUSINESS LEADER 1)

He also emphasized the fundamental importance of the OD or HRM practitioner having the complete backing of the top person and the executive team (BUSINESS LEADER 1).

A Range of Critiques of OD

The lack of evaluation of OD was discussed at some length in the literature. However, only 2 interviewees' made mention of OD evaluation in the course of interviews. The lack of evaluation of OD was mentioned by ACADEMIC 1 who complained that there was 'no link between performance and HRD/OD—that seems ridiculous that HRD and OD are not informed by data on performance'.

According to ACADEMIC 2, the 'thorny subject of evaluation of OD' needed to be raised, as whilst evaluation of OD interventions was done well at micro level, without macro level evaluation it could be argued that the change would have happened even without the OD intervention.

An issue which was already raised under the section on OD's relationship to HR and HRD raised its head again in the form of criticism of OD professionals in that they project haughtiness over HR and HRD professionals. An attack on OD practitioners from ACADEMIC 1 was that her 'comprehensive experience was that OD people considered themselves to be superior'. This was also a finding from the interview with LEADING INFLUENCER 2. Her experience was that some HR practitioners said very clearly that they considered themselves to be OD people, yet: 'you can also hear quite loudly from OD people that they are not in HR and certainly do not want to be in HR' (LEADING INFLUENCER 2). BUSINESS LEADER 2 recounted criticisms of both OD and HR. She said that OD could be seen to be overly theoretical and HR, which could be seen to be too process- and technically-oriented, rather than having a focus on the business.

BUSINESS LEADER 2 had a linked but separate criticism of OD, she recounted that some HR directors take a very OD perspective, but where this was the case, 'they couldn't be bothered with the boring HR part of the job'. LEADING INFLUENCER 2reported that she was aware of some HR people rebranding themselves as OD, but what they did had not changed. She deduced that:

> There must be a perceived value of using the OD label—I have noticed a trend in the increasing use of the term OD. There must be a real interest and perceived value in the work of OD. I don't think there is a step change in practice though.

There were a number of other varied critiques of OD. SENIOR PRACTITIONER 1 referred to T-groups, explaining that they had a very bad reputation, had often been applied in the wrong way, and could be very damaging in the wrong hands. He also reported that OD had 'been sanitised, for example, OD as it is now done in the NHS is politically manipulative' (SENIOR PRACTITIONER 1).

LEADING INFLUENCER 1 saw a primary problem for OD as being that it was often viewed as being a collection of initiatives which were not fully understood by others. She explained that OD could be good at interventions, but that: 'the risk is that they do big change projects applying techniques and not embedding the change'.

SENIOR PRACTITIONER 1 agreed that where OD interventions often failed was 'on their tail piece'. SENIOR PRACTITIONER 5 noted that OD could take up a controversial role in organizations, dealing with change where people want to protect their territory. She had found that negative power dynamics could come into play in that situation and people had 'been very badly bruised as a result'.

Fashion or Fad and the Dissemination of Management Ideas

Many interviewees commented on the extent to which they viewed OD as being a fad or a fashion. Sometimes comments were made specifically using the terms *fad* and/or *fashion*. In other instances, the reference was in terms of characteristics, such as the credibility of OD, which suggested they were reflecting on whether OD was considered it to be a *fad* or *fashion*. BUSINESS LEADER 2 reported that both OD and HR have had to justify their existence on an ongoing basis. ACADEMIC 3 stated that in its original form OD was a fad/fashion.

The adjective 'hippy' had been applied to OD four times in the interviews, by SENIOR PRACTITIONER 5, ACADEMICS 2 and 4 and by SENIOR PRACTITIONER 1, who commented that in its early days it was ' on the margins, some thought of it as hippy type stuff and not connected to the business, but some organisations thought it was great'.

ACADEMIC 3 used the term 'soft and furry' when she described the original approach to OD. When asked about his first encounter with OD, BUSINESS LEADER 1 reflected that he remembered it 'as a relatively esoteric branch of HRM'. There appeared to be elements of these opinions which have remained. SENIOR PRACTITIONER 5 recounted 'I think they see us as slightly odd people with coloured pens, post it notes and flipcharts'. SENIOR PRACTITIONER 2 thought 'slightly weird' people were good to have in OD, but that most organizations would not cope with well with that prospect. LEADING INFLUENCER 2remarked that she had previously thought OD was 'faddy', but had since heard very good samples of OD work being described. BUSINESS LEADER 1 complemented this view, in stating that there were OD fads, but it was not fundamentally a fad.

In terms of whom was driving the development of ideas and trends ACADEMIC 7 explained that, in many cases, academics follow practice but as academics then take ideas forward, practice did not catch up. SENIOR PRACTITIONER 2 considered that a driver for adoption of OD by individual practitioners was that they see it as a route to career promotion, authority, influence and being respected.

ACADEMIC 2 provided a further example of how the dissemination of management ideas happens in practice. He gave the illustration of how one large company influenced the practice adopted by another large organisation in the same geographical area: 'because the companies were fishing in the same Labour market it was natural that some of the practices from (company name) would spread to other manufacturers' (ACADEMIC 2). In other perspectives on the dissemination of ideas, SENIOR PRACTITIONER 2 proposed that the shape of OD was being driven by social networks and online communities such as Twitter, Facebook and LinkedIn, with 'a lot more conversation is taking place through these forums every day'.

ACADEMIC 6 presented the view that since 'OD had been around for a while so it was de facto not a fad', but added that the definition of 'fad' had to be considered. LEADING INFLUENCER 3noted that there were fashions and some elements of management practice become fashionable at points in time. Both ACADEMIC 6 and SENIOR PRACTITIONER 4 described the nature of fashion in applying the label of fashion to a practice but explained that applying the label fashion to an OD practice did not necessarily mean that there was a change in the underlying practice. ACADEMIC 6 referred to 'talent management' when discussing the aspect of fashions in labels and SENIOR PRACTITIONER 4 recounted that 'of course there is no longer Personnel now it is always HR. We no longer see Pay and Benefits we see Total Rewards. No longer is it Training and Development, but now it is OD'.

There were phases where 'managers can't do without' OD Professional guidance and then other phases when self-sufficiency became the fashion

(LEADING INFLUENCER 3). ACADEMIC 8 was clear that he judged OD to be an important aspect of change, an ongoing necessary competence of any organization. BUSINESS LEADER 2 was equally robust in her view that OD was a critical element in driving a business forward and added that she had '25 to 30 years of practical samples of that'.

Two of the interviewees (SENIOR PRACTITIONERS 2 and 4) concluded that OD being considered as a fashion or fad was due to the lack of a clear definition, it was unclear and misunderstood, which left it open to criticism and condemnation as a fad. SENIOR PRACTITIONER 1 argued that it was in the context of HR that OD had become a fad, since HR people didn't understand what OD was or what they were dealing with. BUSINESS LEADER 2 agreed that there remained 'a lot of mystique' around OD. SENIOR PRACTITIONER 4 advised that the way to prevent misunderstanding was to develop rigor for the practice field, and to develop a body of knowledge with a clearer construct of what OD required 'that we all need to agree on'.

BUSINESS LEADER 1 criticized the 'OD toolbox guy, who looks for a problem to solve using his/her toolbox—irrespective of the organisational context'. His view was that OD was about two core elements. Firstly, and most importantly, business was about business and OD was about ensuring that the business is fit for purpose. Second, the complexity of human behaviour remains unchanged. Furthermore: 'If you keep these two "universal truths" in your sight, then it stops you being conned by the snake oil salesmen' (BUSINESS LEADER 1). LEADING INFLUENCER 1 agreed that OD must 'not just be a box of tricks', but capable of assisting in change contexts and volatile contexts where people, on whose performance an organization depends, were treated ethically and equitably.

ACADEMIC 5 advocated the need for more transparency on what OD was about and SENIOR PRACTITIONER 4 added that without further clarity it risked being considered as a fad or fashion. His view was that there needed to be a clearer construct of what OD requires and there need to be agreement.

The Application of the OD Name as a Fashionable Label

The issue of naming of OD was perceived as subject to fashion by four interviewees. ACADEMIC 1 was very much of the view that the title 'OD' was a fad and would disappear. LEADING INFLUENCER 1 agreed that there may be an incentive for individuals to adopt the title of OD as: 'job adverts do promote practice; they are often designed to be sexy/attractive. I guess you could say they are aspirational. Hopefully there is an underlying shift in OD; it's not just a fashion'.

SENIOR PRACTITIONER 1 was of the opinion that there were instances where OD had been 'stuck on' as a label to what were essentially HRD job roles. ACADEMIC 6 viewed OD as being 'a trendy term that reared its head from time to time'. He commented that whether it was 'applied with the intention of being an impressive term that organisations used, it had been around for a while and it was distinct'. SENIOR PRACTITIONER 3 also referred to the naming issue: 'I do think there is an element of—oh god, not another change in title. If HR don't even know what OD is, then how the hell is anyone else supposed to know'?

Trends on Being in or Outside of HR

With regards to whether OD sits within or outside of HR, ACADEMIC 1 considered that OD will go out of fashion if it continues to be a separate function, distinct from HR. SENIOR PRACTITIONER 4 stated that OD was still ' zigzagging in and out a bit, where it goes depends on those in the OD profession'.

SENIOR PRACTITIONER 4 noted that part of the context is that HR needs to decide whether it will step up to the challenge. If not, it risks becoming side-lined as a simple administrative function rather than proving itself capable of being a more powerful influencer at top management level (SENIOR PRACTITIONER 4). His argument indicated that OD is likely to be more powerful and influential in the longer term if it stays separate from HR. However, SENIOR PRACTITIONER 6 took a different view, that 'Perhaps there was a shift from OD to HR which has now come the other way round, from HR to OD? However, with the recession it may be that we will go back to the hard form of HR'.

A singular perspective put forward by BUSINESS LEADER 2 was that in terms of significant changes in its development, OD had shifted its orientation away from HRM towards the business. This was contrary to the view of ACADEMICS 2 and 3: ACADEMIC 2 considered there to be a general trend of convergence between OD and HR driven by the HR community; and ACADEMIC 3 proposed that 'by mimicking OD, HRM has gained strength and strayed into the OD domain. HRM has strived to make their role bigger and broader' (ACADEMIC 3).

SENIOR PRACTITIONER 1 argued that the move of HRM into OD had led to it being viewed as a fad, since HR people didn't understand what OD was. He said that this was especially so in the public sector where OD was not understood as being a competency. LEADING INFLUENCER 1 also referred to the growing popularity of OD in the UK HR community, noting that 'In HR circles, OD is seen as a discipline that HR ought to own, but I don't think OD is a discipline within HR, if anything HR is a discipline with OD'. Another contextual trend of relevance was identified by SENIOR PRACTITIONER 4 who noted that with increased pressure on business profitability, there was more concentration on cost efficient methods such as the use of technology and outsourcing of people management processes.

Future Projection for OD in the UK (Growth or Decline?)

With regard to the future projection of OD, ACADEMIC 1 estimated that OD would experience exponential growth and then decline. ACADEMIC 5 differentiated between what would happen in the UK and in the US, noting that 'there is a decline in OD in the US and an ascendancy in the UK'. LEADING INFLUENCER 1 partly linked the resurgence to OD in the UK to the interest shown by the CIPD.

BUSINESS LEADER 2 considered market conditions, and the size and success of individual organizations, would be the predominant influence on the future of OD. She noted that when economic conditions became tighter, organizations with separate OD functions cut back the OD function. Interestingly, LEADING INFLUENCER 3 said that although economic retrenchment usually involved cuts in investment in development, OD consultancy was often busier when the economic environment was difficult. He maintained that this was due to some organizations using the time to prepare and develop in order to gain advantage for when recession ends.

Is a Change of Focus of OD Anticipated?

With respect to the future development of OD, evidence of effectiveness and tangible outcomes of OD efforts was a key theme. ACADEMIC 3 reflected that business focus was now on the bottom line, but that this did not sit easily with the original concept of OD. ACADEMIC 1 envisaged that in the future, the requirement in OD will be for 'all-rounders'. ACADEMIC 1 and BUSINESS LEADER 1 considered that a focus on organizational effectiveness would lead the OD agenda. BUSINESS LEADER 2 described this as a move to OD being required to show competence in 'value add' activity, and this would be particularly needed if OD was to succeed in the private sector.

ACADEMIC 6 predicted that OD would be affected by the general trend of increasing use of evidence-based management approaches. He highlighted the increase in the effective design and use of data analytics to provide information on how people based decisions were made. SENIOR PRACTITIONER 2 referred to instances of metrics being used in his HR Department, explaining that they made use of an HR dashboard: with data provided by 'an analytics team—so we have an economist a mathematician and a psychologist in the team. We use data mining techniques'. Diagnostic metrics were used to inform a number of activities, such as the decommissioning of services and the design of the structure of new services.

SENIOR PRACTITIONER 1 also reported greater emphasis being placed on performance and the use of metrics, and SENIOR PRACTITIONER 1 advocated learning from the use of diagnostic root cause skills from the discipline of lean engineering. He proposed that a combination of the application of diagnostic skills based on lean principles, with people and Change Management skills, would work best.

Overarching Development of OD

ACADEMIC 4 described two main views of contemporary OD in the UK. One perspective is: 'That it was of its time and has had its day. I guess this is the view you get from Karen Legge, and that it was killed in the economic and political climate of the 1980s and 90s'.

That is to say, that the OD was considered as *soft* in its approach to change and this simply did not fit well with the ethos of that business era in the UK. He added though that ACADEMIC 4 described two main views of contemporary OD in the UK. One perspective is:

> But, the other view is that OD is still very much alive—it is being researched, written about and being taught. These may not always be called OD but there is still activity: Action Research, Group Dynamics, Reflective Change, a focus on Culture, Consultancy Process and Change Management Processes.

LEADING INFLUENCER 2 remarked that change and development of OD was not a matter of changing fads, but of evolution: 'I think the trends wax and wane—but the underlying concepts never go away. Certain things have more prominence at certain times'. She also referred to OD as being considered as undergoing ongoing development, even amongst the 'US gurus such as Edgar Schein'. She proposed that OD had moved on from planned change being the focus, to process interventions. LEADING INFLUENCER 3 thought that the clue to change in Organization Development was in its very name, noting that:

> The big changes in the last 20 years come from what has happened with organisations—the change in their purpose, functioning and how the individual and public perceive them. The large hierarchically structured, stable organisations no longer exist in the way they once did.

Moreover, the extent to which organizations had 'porous boundaries' and their tasks were changing (LEADING INFLUENCER 3) required consideration. Taking the current context of organizations into account, LEADING INFLUENCER 1concluded that OD was far more than a fashion and that the applied field of thinking and practice was even more important now than in the past.

Conclusion

The interviews proved invaluable in giving life to the rather inert data supplied by the analysis of job advertisements and the bibliometric search. Although their very richness makes it challenging to tease out common themes, the data presented is all important and inter-related. For example, the sections on history and contexts and challenges contribute to understanding *how* contemporary OD has developed. Furthermore, other sections add to our understanding of the *why* OD has developed in the way it has—for example—the presence of mimetic forces at work.

The next chapter draws together the three strands of evidence, but it is helpful to summaries some key findings from the interviews. It is certainly clear that this material supports the need for a multi-attribute definition of OD. Interviewees represented a range of views, but what was clear was that the *traditional* form of OD, as *Behavioral Science* and/or the application of recognized OD processes was a minor note in contemporary practice. Although most interviewees could not provide much evidence on the early years of OD practice, they were able to reflect on developments from the 1980s onwards, in which issues of the relation between OD and aspects of HR practice, such as HRD, started to appear. The material confirms the degree to which opinions diverged based on experience and community membership, which points to the gap between academia and practice discussed below.

The interviewees shed a considerable degree of light on the core attributes of OD. As well as downplaying the *Behavioral Science* aspects, it was noticeable that there was also relatively little mention of concepts such as the *learning organization*. Instead, interviewees drew attention to the *big picture* aspects of OD—the need for systemic thought and attention to organizational culture. In this, and in other areas of discussion such as the contemporary nature of change, the question of organizational boundaries was raised. OD was seen by some to draw attention to the need to place the organization in its broader context, considering change across organizational boundaries. This challenging expansion of the scope of OD also drew attention to the need for team working within the profession (and with its boundary professions), as individuals could not be expected to encompass the broad range of skills and experience needed. The interview material was invaluable in pointing to the varied routes in to OD, all of which emphasized the need for broader thinking.

This also raised questions about the need for and capability of OD to challenge organizational orthodoxies. This raised an unresolved question about the position of consultants. For some, such a position gave the necessary independence of thought to challenge those in positions of power. Certainly, interviewees confirmed the growing importance of Change Management in conceptualizations of OD (something to be returned to when set against the job advertisements in the next chapter). Interviewees contrasted the transformative potential of OD initiatives to what they saw as the transactional nature of much HR. As discussed in some detail above, the relationship between OD and HR is a complex one, on which there were divergent opinions. It was important to rehearse these divergent opinions in some detail, as they provide understanding of common influencing forces in the development of the professions and as such form part of the concluding discussion. However, what was clear from the interviews was the growing emphasis amongst practitioners and academics on the need for evaluation of the effectiveness of OD. This could be related to the widespread discourse of strategic thinking in organizations, with an accompanying emphasis on ways of measuring performance.

It was here that there was a divergence between academics and practitioners. Perhaps unsurprisingly, it was the academics in the sample who were more likely to raise concerns found in the literature review to do with the role of professional associations and national contexts and questions of power and ethics. This points to the divergence between the two communities, one which it will be argued in the following chapter has to be related to differing standards of performance in each community. The boundaries explored between, for example, OD, HR and HRM, are as much an artifact of artificial academic boundaries, reinforced by publishing practices, as they are accurate representations of practice. These questions are taken up in the following chapters, first through a comparison of the evidence obtained through the three different methods.

Reference

Francis, H., Holbeche, L., Reddington, M. (eds.) People and Organisational Development: a New Agenda for Organisational Effectiveness. CIPD: London

6 Comparing the Literature on OD with the Evidence

The literature on OD was set out in Chapter 2, and the findings of the research study were presented in Chapters 3, 4 and 5. Part 1 of this chapter will compare these findings with the themes identified in the literature. Part 2 will analyze the findings through the lens of Institutional Theory, the Diffusion of Management Ideas and Fashions and Fads in Management. Part 3 will then present a discussion on the debate of the future of the OD profession.

Part 1. Similarities and Differences between the Literature on OD and the Data Collected in this Study

Origins of the Name of OD, Early OD, Definition, Blurred Boundaries and Confusion

The interview data did not highlight dispute about the validity of the label 'Organization Development'. However, they did support the literature in relation to OD being difficult to define and with blurred boundaries. Whilst early and US-based literature (e.g. Beckhard 1969) appeared to provide definitions with more certainty, more recent literature has presented multiple definitions (e.g. Cheung-Judge and Holbeche, 2011; Cummings and Worley, 2015; Senior and Swailes, 2010) and highlighted difficulties in providing a clear definition of contemporary OD (Garrow, 2009; Greiner and Cummings, 2004). The content analysis data suggests that the nature of UK OD changed between the 1970s and 2010, again highlighting definitional difficulties. This suggests that any definition of OD has to be multi-dimensional.

Boundaries with other linked disciplines also cause definitional uncertainty. The literature identifies these linked disciplines as being organization design, operational science and HRD (in particular Management Development). The variation found in the content of job roles over time adds to this confusion with, for example, the HR and HRD functions. The interview data highlighted HR and HRD as having blurred boundaries with OD. Change Management was also identified as proving difficult in terms of boundary clarity with OD.

Core attributes of OD

Traditional OD and its Development over the Decades

A noteworthy discrepancy between the literature and the research findings in relation to the development of OD over time was found. One academic interviewee, and the bibliometric data, highlighted that the US view of OD had dictated thinking on the nature of OD. Moreover, in describing OD, the mainly UK-based interviewees made little mention of the potential for national differences in OD form and practice.

US-based scholars (e.g. French and Bell, 1999; Cumming and Worley, 2015) provided accounts of OD that clustered around descriptions underpinned by traditional OD with a systems and process orientation and a *Behavioral Science* focus, in particular around team functioning. However, even though most US-based scholars' explanations of the development of OD were based on the traditional form of OD and its evolution, US-based scholars Ruona and Gibson (2004) advocated that OD should converge with HR and HRD,. Only in UK texts by Cheung-Judge and Holbeche (2011 and 2015) and Francis et al. (2012) was there any significant reference to the relationship between OD, HR and HRD.

More recent perspectives include AI, discourse and dialogic approaches to OD as outlined by Bartunek and Woodman (2015); Bushe and Marshak (2009); Grant and Marshak (2011); Marshak and Grant (2008); and Oswick et al. (2010). Although this range of authors are internationally based with three from the US, one from Canada, two from Australia and one from the UK, much of their debate was conducted through publications in the US-based OD *Journal of Applied Behavioral Science*. Other significant developments in OD, such as a large group focus for practice, were reported by US-based Schmidt Weber and Manning (1998). Another area of discussion, first generated by Marshak and Grant (2008: S7), focused on the eras of 'Classical OD' and 'New OD'. In the main, the differentiation of these eras of OD is recounted by others without critique, with the exception of Burnes and Cooke (2012).

Although some of these developing OD perspectives were discussed by interviewees, in general, the nature of interviewees' experiences did not match with the discourse of the literature in this area. Dialogical, discourse or large group approaches to OD practice were not mentioned, and only one interviewee made reference to 'Classical OD' or 'New OD'. The most significant difference between the literature and the content analysis and interview data was in reference to HR and HRD, where the concentration of views in the literature on OD being around traditional OD was far outweighed by rhetoric of OD and its relationship to HR and HRD. However, the interview data highlighted the presence of an assumed ongoing link to HR and HRD which was absent from the primarily US-generated literature on OD.

The interview data and content analysis findings contradicted the existing literature on the nature and form of OD. As outlined in the content analysis findings in Chapter 3, the 1970s profile of OD in the UK was found to have a resemblance to traditional OD, but changed over time. The content analysis highlighted the prominent HR presence in UK OD in the 1980s, with HRD becoming important in the 1990's. Between 2000 and 2010 UK OD evolved to include a broader range of key characteristics; including HRD, HR and the development of a *Strategic and Organization-wide Orientation.*

OD Training, Qualifications and Skills

It is apparent from the literature review that the organization of training and qualifications differs between the US and the UK. US scholars were credited with the development of the first degree and PhD programs in OD, and establishing an OD Network in the 1970s. Along with the Colwill (2012) scholar practitioner text, it would appear that there was a long-held tradition of formal training and qualification being considered integral to OD in the US. In the UK, OD was only subsumed within the CIPD professional map in 2007 and there was little else in the literature to suggest that UK training and qualifications infrastructure was as embedded as that in the US, or that it had a similar history of development. The interview data supported this, with only Sheffield Polytechnic (now Sheffield Hallam University), Edinburgh University, Roffey Park, the CIPD and NTL cited as delivering training and qualifications (at the time of writing). However, neither Edinburgh nor Sheffield Hallam Universities now offer OD programs.

In relation to skills requirements for OD practitioners, there was broad agreement between the literature and interview findings. Interview responses aligned, to a large extent, with Neilson's (1984) framework which proposes that effective OD practitioners should have conceptual, technical, interpersonal and integrative skills. The need to possess an understanding of businesses, Change Management and developing experience were also features of both the literature and the interviews. However, interview responses were more detailed in this area, highlighting that skills requirements should be related to the context, so different competences were required in different business. For example, interview responses highlighted that OD competences required for involvement in developing organization strategy were not the same as those required to implement interventions, where knowledge and experience of technical OD tools was more important. As such, any attempt to have a general model of the skills required by an OD practitioner may not be feasible or appropriate, since the competencies required depend on context. Of note in the interviews, but not mentioned in the literature, was the extent to which generalized or more specialized people management skills are required by OD practitioners, with interviewees proposing that this was linked to the size of an organization.

The extent to which knowledge of self was required by OD practitioners was a feature of the literature and the interviews. Several of the interviewees mentioned the need for self-efficacy in relation to the ability to challenge organizational orthodoxy. Whilst this was a prominent feature in the interview data, it received less coverage in the literature.

Other Core Attributes of OD: Change Management, Consultancy Orientation, Behavior and Culture, Effectiveness, Strategic, Leadership, Partnership, Engagement and Learning Organizations

The boundary between the field of OD and the field of Change Management receives little attention in existing literature: planned change is presented as being a feature of OD, with other forms of Change Management generally treated as being distinct and separate. However, interviewees' understanding of distinct boundaries between Change Management and OD was less clear. In particular, a small number of the academics expressed that there was confusion on this topic. The content analysis found that Change Management had come to prominence from a base of being a strong foundation feature of 1970s UK OD. The importance of Change Management in OD was reflected in the interview data, and almost all of the interviewees discussed the management of change in the context of OD.

A *Consultancy Orientation* was assumed as a characteristic of OD in the literature, in particular in the US, but was seldom mentioned in this study by the interviewees. In the content analysis profiles in each of the four decades, having a *Consultancy Orientation* in the role of OD practitioner held a consistent position. However, there was a mixed response from interviewees with the two OD consultant interviewees, perhaps not surprisingly, proposing that external OD consultants were essential to its success.

The importance of *Behavioral Science* in early OD is a feature of the literature amongst US-based scholars until the late 1990s, and in more recent accounts by UK authors (see Cheung-Judge and Holbeche, 2011; Stanford, 2012). It was also an element in OD training at Roffey Park and in the UK NTL program. However, the content analysis data found this facet of OD to be of importance only in the 1970s. Its importance then declined over the 1980s and 1990s, then becoming more important again between 2000 and 2010: most likely in the guise of organizational *Culture* rather than *Behavioral Science* per se. In the main, interviewees acknowledged that *Behavioral Science* is trait of OD, with a number referring to their study of organizational behavior. However, there was little discussion of organizational *Culture* in the interviews.

The quest for *Effectiveness* had been an early attribute of OD identified in the literature which increased in focus particularly in the UK with, for example, the Francis et al. (2012) text. The growth in importance of *Effectiveness* in the UK form of OD was also expressed by interviewees, both explicitly and implicitly: accounts were provided of the growing importance of performance data and the measurement of contribution to the *bottom line* across all people management disciplines. The content analysis data accorded with this focus on *Effectiveness*: it had a small but clear presence in UK in the 1970s profile of OD, became slightly more important in the 1980s and 1990s and grew to become the fourth (equal with *Strategy*) aspect of OD between 2000 and 2010.

With few exceptions, the need to take a *Strategic Approach* to OD was evident in the literature, particularly after 2000, and in the interview and content analysis data. However, there was little written, with the exception of Burnes and Cooke (2012), on the need to consider wider than organizational boundaries in terms of the system within which OD is situated. One interviewee (a leading influencer) gave the opinion that there was a requirement to understand that organizational boundaries were not as firm as they once were, and the wider business and social system must be considered.

The content analysis data identified that issues such as *Leadership, Not just HR, Partnership* and *Learning Organization* had a small to moderate presence in UK OD after 2000. Although these topics were barely mentioned in the existing literature, in one exception (Sharkey, 2009) there was a call for OD to become more involved in the selection and development of organizational leaders. There was little mention in the interviews of *Partnership* and *Learning Organization*, topics which appeared in a small number of the later advertisements. However, the trend of seeking information on and improvement in employee engagement, which was not mentioned in the literature, was reported as being of importance in the organizations of a small number of the interviewees.

Context and Challenges

Relationship to HR and HRD

With the exception of Beer (1976) and Burke (2004), few US-based authors make reference to HR and HRD. Even where OD and its relationship to HR/HRD is mentioned by US scholars, it tends to be as a tangential issue (see Sweem, 2009) on the subject of talent management, and in Sharkey (2009) in the context of alignment to the business strategy.

In contrast, UK authors such as Cheung-Judge and Holbeche (2011), Francis et al., (2012), and Stanford (2012) present a far more entrenched link. The content analysis data identifies a relationship between UK OD and HR/HRD starting in the 1980s, so this convergence has had decades to become the norm. A primary difficulty cited in the literature is that OD and HR have different functional modes, with OD being process driven, and HR being content driven. Another area of difference identified in the literature is the extent to which OD and HR are considered as being embedded within the business. HR is considered as being more aligned with hard-line business objectives and OD practitioners thought to be governed by their professional value set, and more open to challenge senior leaders. With respect to HRD, a small number of interviewees were of the opinion that OD and HRD were synonymous: a finding which matched the content analysis data from the 1990s onwards.

The findings of the content analysis data for HR and HRD in OD in the UK focused on the variation in its profile in OD over the decades. As such, it is not surprising that interviewees expressed a wide range of varied opinion on the relationship between OD and HR/HRD. Interviewees viewed the boundaries between these three functional areas as being particularly unclear, and expressed a range of views on the existence of a hierarchy between the disciplines. Some expressed that if there was a hierarchy, that OD had the higher status of the three professions. From other interviewee perspectives, OD practitioners created an impression of superiority, in that they actively distanced themselves from being identified as a form of HR/HRD. Most interviewees considered OD to be more strategic in orientation than HR or HRD, with some highlighting that OD and HR and HRD must work together (see Ruona and Gibson, 2004).

National Differences

Although there was occasional reference to national differences in the *application* of OD in the literature, OD in itself was treated as though it was a homogenous practice. The one exception is Burnes and Cooke (2013), who highlight that UK scholars had influence in the development of early OD. The bibliometric search identified a significant number of published journal articles in UK- and German-based journals. The existence of this body of work is not reflected in the writing of US-based scholars. It was also clear from the content analysis that the UK form of OD has significantly changed from the traditional form of OD which had been practiced in the UK in the 1970s. The wide range of content in contemporary UK OD, as reflected in the twelve facets which emerged in the content analysis coding exercise, was also reflected in the interviews. As stated previously, it is of particular note that the content analysis and interviews highlighted that OD in the UK is not the form of OD described by dominating US scholars.

Academic interviewees made comment on national differences in the origin and development of OD. The extent to which embedded national culture and tradition in management practice was linked to the likely adoption, or otherwise, of any developing idea was also discussed. Their views reflected the findings from the content analysis: that in the UK, OD had developed and moved away from the traditional form of OD. Nevertheless, a small number remarked on the ongoing dominance of the US on management thought and practice. The influence of the US in early UK OD practice was also noted by practitioner and business leader interviewees with experience of working in US-based companies. A more recent example of US influence was given in the impact of the employment of large US consultancies in international settings.

A particularly noteworthy difference between the literature and the content analysis data was that after 2000, there was debate amongst US-based scholars on the decline of OD, whilst during the same time period OD in the UK was thriving, as reflected by the significant growth in the number of job roles advertised.

Ethical Values, Issues of Power and Evaluation of OD

A notable difference between the literature and the data from this study was in the perceived importance of ethical and humanistic values to the OD profession. Whilst this was given prominent coverage and considered to be a core attribute of OD by scholars, there was mention of the importance of the need for an ethics by only one interviewee. With one exception, the notion of values was primarily used in the context of being able to challenge organizational values, rather than personally holding values as a practitioner. The concept of ethics was absent from the content analysis and was not allocated a code given that it did not arise as a feature in OD job advertisements.

Existing literature criticized OD for not acknowledging or dealing with organizational-level differences in power. The concept of power was mentioned in interviews in relation to the sense of increasing power and influence for the OD function and practitioner. The rhetoric was that of the OD practitioner being capable of dealing with organizational politics in order to enhance OD's influence, as opposed to power issues within organizations.

Although more prevalent in the literature, the topic of evaluation was also mentioned by a small number of interviewees, mainly in relation to criticism of OD for failing to clearly evaluate its contribution. A key concern in the literature, and from interviewees, was that OD must demonstrate a tangible contribution to organization performance. The literature focused on a range of issues, from the simple evaluation of practice at the organization level, to the need for academics and practitioners to work in partnership to develop rigorous research suitable for application. The literature also proposed that OD should become involved in the increasingly difficult business issues which impact at societal level. This sentiment was also expressed by two of the interviewees.

The Role of Professional Associations

Existing literature and interviewees made little mention of the professionalization of OD. In the instances when professionalization was mentioned, it was primarily with reference to ethics and regulation within the profession. Also apparent from the literature was that in the US, OD is a particularly scholarly area of practice and a small number of the interviewees also considered OD practitioners to be more academically inclined than their HR colleagues. This feature was arguably one that added to the perceived higher status of OD practitioners.

Although no membership numbers are available for the US-based OD Network, it was an embedded institution in that it had long founded relational links to other organizations, such as the *Journal of Applied Behavioural Science*: and a Division of The Academy of Management. There was no apparent link between the OD Network and SHRM. Whilst the US OD Network developed codes of practice, they did not regulate their membership. However, based on the extent of coverage on their website, they were particularly keen on promoting OD's values and ethical approach. In the UK, the CIPD had a code of conduct and their approach was more clearly aligned with the findings in the literature: that HR has a different value set and is more embedded in business rather than with employee concerns.

The situation with professional associations was found to be different in the UK to the US. There was no UK-based professional association for OD, although there was the comparatively new European OD Network which was linked to the US Network. In the UK, the CIPD integrated OD in its professional map, whereas in the US, SHRM appeared to have little presence in OD. The CIPD took a highly regulated approach to their chartered membership status and levels (CIPD, 2015), but anyone could become an SHRM member (SHRM, 2015a) and SHRM certification was not required to secure employment (SHRM, 2015b). In short, the professionalization and nature of professional associations in US and UK OD/HR/HRD communities was fundamentally different.

The professional status of OD was mentioned by two of the academic interviewees. Of note was the strong opinion expressed that the CIPD was more predatory in its approach than SHRM. Including OD in the CIPD professional map was considered as one example of the CIPD moving into professional territory that was not theirs to take.

Part 2. A Comparison of Insights from the Theoretical Position with the Data Collected in this Research

In the literature and interviews OD was consistently referred to as being a profession, and could therefore be viewed through the lens of Institutional Theory. A primary concept within institutional theory is the phenomenon of isomorphism (DiMaggio and Powell, 1983). OD as a profession in the UK has so far behaved in a less isomorphic way, in terms of professional association, than might be predicted. Practitioners in OD have been slow to form into professional association; although the foundation of the European OD Network in 2012 shows that the situation might be changing.

Professional Association Status for the UK OD Profession and Agency Therein

Having been late to form a specific association, OD practitioners left a vacuum in terms of professional grouping. Interview data highlighted that the CIPD is thought to have taken advantage of this by absorbing OD into their community. With such a long-held presence in the UK, the CIPD has an interest in maintaining its position and managing its boundaries. In accordance with Institutional Theory, they act as gatekeepers with tight control over membership status, although having less of a hold over dictating who can legitimately provide which services (Muzio et al., 2011). Although a normative approach was that normally taken by professions, unlike the OD Network, the CIPD appeared to apply agency in acting as regulatory agents for their professional community (Greenwood et al., 2002).

The CIPD has highly developed relational networks (Scott, 2008a), interacts with other organizations and acts as a lobbying body at national level. It is normal for professional institutions to collaborate with other institutions in networks (Greenwood and Meyer, 2008), engaging in joint discussion and development of practice. However, no evidence was found of the CIPD seeking relational networks with the OD Network, or vice versa.

Arguably, the timing of CIPD and OD practitioners becoming interested in the development of a professional association for OD may have been linked to the growth of OD job roles, as found in the content analysis. One reason why management fashions develop is in response to economic forces (Abrahamson, 1996), and as such it could be considered that the CIPD reacted to the exogenous precipitating jolt of growth in market demand for OD skills by placing OD within its professional map (Greenwood and Suddaby, 2006). However, that said, the CIPD did not include OD in its professional map until 2007.

A Greenwood et al. (2002) model of non-isomorphic change includes a de-institutionalization phase prior to re-institutionalization. If the CIPD is to be successful in integrating OD professionals within its community, according to Greenwood et al.'s (2002) model, it may have to de-institutionalize first. With respect to the union of the IPD and the ITD in 1994, one would expect there to have been extensive de-institutionalization in each of the organizations to achieve the merger. There were likely to have been extensive changes such as: agreement to a new name for the organization, revised organizational structures including in the leadership structure, office location changes, merger/alteration of membership levels criteria, revision of publication. These were both independent professional associations, therefore to have carried out deinstitutionalization on this scale, one might naturally expect that there was perceived advantage for both parties to the merger.

It is unlikely that the CIPD would be prepared to de-institutionalize in order to integrate OD as an equal partner in their professional grouping, as the OD community has not yet sufficiently institutionalized in itself as a professional association to be in a position to negotiate an advantageous integration with the CIPD. Nor would it necessarily be to the advantage of the OD profession to merge with an HR/HRD professional association. As highlighted by one interviewee, putting OD into the CIPD professional map was a 'bolt on'. Applying the Greenwood et al. (2002) model of non-isomorphic change also highlights that should OD practitioners not institutionalize themselves through, for example, forming a professional association, they may be perceived as a fad or fashion.

In Institutional Theory, the drive for change is often assumed to come from the less embedded periphery of the profession which in this case would be from the OD practitioners. According to Greenwood and Suddaby (2006) one of the reasons for the motivation for change coming from the periphery is that those are the members of the profession most likely to be disadvantaged. However, in this case the change to include OD within its remit was driven by the CIPD, from the center of the HR profession. The findings from this study will be examined for a potential explanation of this phenomenon in the section entitled *OD, HR, HRD—Perceived Importance, Mimetic Forces and Agency* below.

The US-based OD Profession, its Institutional Status and Comparative Lack of Agency

The existing literature highlights that the US OD profession rejected elements of professional convention, such as regulation, in favor of normative systems. The interview data highlighted signs of a quest for regulatory approach as a route to legitimacy in the UK through recognized qualifications. The preference in the US OD profession for a normative system appears to be at odds with their general national approach to the development of professions. Whether the lack of regulation was an element in the accounts of the decline in of OD in the US is worthy of consideration. One might argue they are neither *fish nor fowl:* the US OD profession had not actively pursued strengthening of their institutionalized status as a profession, but they have also simultaneously remained unyielding to business market forces.

Scott (2008b: 219), considered professions to be the 'Lords of the Dance'. However, although that may be the case for professions such as medicine and law, in the context of the power of global organizations it is not the case for the OD profession. This may be due to the profession of management being less established and/or less respected, meaning that legitimacy cannot be assumed (Hilmer and Donaldson, 1996). With stronger and embedded institutionalization in professions such as medicine, law and engineering, quick fix practices based on flimsy evidence from those with no recognized academic or professional credentials would be completely dismissed (Hilmer and Donaldson, 1996). However, in the less established professions within management, such as OD, new ideas tend not to be exposed to the same level of critical evaluation as they are in more established and institutionalized professions. Furthermore, in contrast to the perspective of Muzio et al. (2011), the consumers of the professional services of OD have overriding power in their relationship.

The literature provided several accounts of the US OD profession being under threat of extinction. Interview data described the US-based OD Network and SHRM as having a more partnership approach. It appears that as professional institutions they have been less active in applying an agency approach to strengthen their institutional status than the CIPD has been in the UK.

OD, HR, HRD: Perceived Importance, Mimetic Forces and Agency

The extent to which OD is advantaged or disadvantaged in comparison to HR and HRD communities, by being included in the professional CIPD community is revisited in this section. The content analysis and interview data highlighted that OD professionals are not disadvantaged in comparison to those at the center of the HR profession. Interviewees clearly stated that they perceived OD to be of higher status than HR and HRD. This may have been due to the OD profession having gained power, and therefore status, by demonstrating success in dealing with sources of uncertainty in change situations within organizations (Scott, 2005). In the illustrative salary information in Chapter 3, the OD specialism was found to attract a salary premium greater than all other areas of HR, and the interview data also confirmed that OD was viewed as a more attractive specialist area. The incentive to become an OD practitioner might therefore have been linked to a personal capitalism motivation, as identified by Thornton et al. (2012) as the economic system of professionals.

Given that individual actors have a level of partial autonomy from their social structure (Whittington, 2001), the motives of individual practitioners within HR, HRD and OD practice should be considered in addition to review of the interests of the CIPD. If there is a difference in status and earning potential between the domains of OD, HR/HRD, what might be the implication of that for individual practitioners? Would agency be exercised in order to transfer to a perceived higher status specialism within the profession? Greenwood and Suddaby (2006) outlined that changes in professions could arise from the actions of calculating and interest aware parties in the professional community. The interview data highlights that mimetic and agency forces are at work with regards to HR and HRD professionals seeking identification as OD practitioners. This was evident in the content of some job advertisements with OD in the title, yet the nature of the content primarily reflected mainstream HR responsibilities. This phenomenon was also reported in the interview data.

However, the sub-group of OD within the HR/HRD/OD professional grouping could also have competing personal capitalism and status interests in retaining their distinction, leading them to seek to control the intra-professional boundary (Greenwood et al., 2002). In the fashion perspective, Abraham (1991) outlines the phenomenon of higher reputation organizations disassociating themselves from those with a perceived lower status. When the fashions of the higher reputation groups were mimicked by lower reputation groups, in this case HR and HRD, they would adopt new fashions. Grint (1997) similarly describes how, in a social hierarchy, higher class groups engage in distancing behavior when their norms are mimicked by a lower-class group. This disassociation/distancing effect was also highlighted in the interview data, where it was noted that OD practitioners actively distance themselves from other HR professionals. There was evidence that at least some OD professionals clearly wish for a distinct boundary between themselves and other HR/HRD professionals.

With regards to professional association, what is of interest was that a half (five of the ten) interviewees who are currently or had been OD practitioners, had not come from an HR background, and were therefore unlikely to have already had CIPD membership. It was also strikingly evident that six of these interviewees did not see HR as having an automatic place in OD, and two were clear that they did not wish to be associated with HR. As such, despite their strong UK institutional presence, the CIPD may find it difficult to engage UK OD practitioners to become part of their professional association.

Nevertheless, content analysis and interview findings highlighted that the OD professions inclusion in, or self-exclusion from, the HR/HRD community is not an *all or nothing* situation. Thornton et al.'s (2012) summary of DiMaggio and Powell's 1983 propositions, found that circumstances where OD practitioners are more likely to become morphed into mimicking HR are:

- where they are placed in a highly centralized organization and dependent on resources from an HR function;
- if they are in a context where the path to goal achievement is uncertain, then it is more likely to imitate another professional grouping, such as HR, if they consider it to be successful (although the reverse appeared to have been more common);
- if it is made easier to attain HR/HRD qualifications than OD qualifications, in organizations where academic and professional qualification is the norm;
- where the organization already has a high proportion of senior managers with an HR/HRD background and/or CIPD affiliation; and
- if there are fewer alternative models to achieve professional association status (such as an active and dominant OD professional association).

In relation to the existence of individual actor agency, one trend from the interview data which is of particular note is that with the exception of the academics in the sample, responses tended to reflect interviewees' respective professional context. So, when the interviewee worked in a consulting capacity, there was a strong view that OD could only be effectively delivered by external consultants. When the interviewee was, or had been, in a generalist HR career area, their perspective was often that OD should be subsumed as a part of the HR function. Where the interviewee had no career experience in HR, the dominant view was that OD was and must remain distinct from HR. In short, the existence of agency to promote vested interests carried over into, and was therefore embedded within, the answers given in the interview process.

The Application of Agency in Achieving Legitimization

The normative approach to legitimacy for professions was given as *morally governed* (Scott, 2008a). Morality and professional values are discussed widely in the literature, but there is a marked absence in relation to the content analysis and interview data. There were signs of the development of isomorphic forces in the desire for legitimatization of professional status, specifically in OD. This was evident from the interview data: it was significant that all three Senior Practitioners who moved into OD post 2005 had sought to become qualified in OD, and their responses indicated a perceived need to legitimize their place as *bona fide* OD practitioners.

It would seem that there was perceived advantage to all three of these highly qualified interviewees in order for them to have opted, mid-career, to gain an additional professional qualification in OD. One interviewee was effusive in her praise for the NTL program she had completed. Two interviewees did not see their HR CIPD qualification as being sufficient for their OD practitioner status. This trend is aligned with the sociological view that professionals control their own work terrain and boundaries (Abbot, 1988; Muzio et al., 2011) as these individuals were actively marking themselves out as being different from HR/HRD professionals. As noted above, there may have been a significant vested interest for all three interviewees to apply agency in order to create disassociation/distance and a clear boundary between them and other HR/HRD professionals.

Who Held the Influential Position in the Diffusion of Management Ideas, Fads and Fashions on OD?

The bibliometric findings highlight that published work on OD is heavily dominated by US academics. However, in the UK practice model, OD was found to have diverged from the US form. The content analysis and interview data found that adopters varied OD by customizing it to their preferences (Rogers, 2003). The source of influence in this diffusion appears to have come from fellow OD/HR professionals and from social system networks that had already adopted OD practice (Rogers, 2003).

In terms of Abrahamson's (1991), typology of four perspectives on the adoption of innovations it might have been expected that in the increased adoption of OD in the UK the *efficient choice perspective* was in operation: that organizations were free to choose. However, rising uncertainty in the achievement of business goals as a result of a turbulent global business environment may have been an external condition which acted as driver for change. In this context, the *fashion* or the *fad perspective* (Abrahamson, 1991) might have been responsible for the growth in OD roles.

The *fad perspective* might be considered as a more secure route for managers than the *fashion perspective*, in that they can demonstrate that they have done, or mimicked, what *similar* organizations with a higher reputation have done (Abrahamson, 1991). The context for increased use of OD professionals would involve mimetic forces being in operation where there was uncertainty and ambiguity (DiMaggio and Powell, 1991), and the perceived safest route for managers would be to mimic other organizations (Abrahamson, 1991). In this way, decision makers would appear to be making rational choices by following the advice of OD professionals. Additionally, in their decision making, they would avoid the risk of being singled out from the norm (Grint, 1997).

The global business context is likely to continue to be turbulent and unpredictable, so it seems likely that there will be an ongoing need for practitioners competent in Change Management. In this context, managers will likely avoid personal career risk, by taking the option of deferring to highly institutionalized professionals for guidance. This implies a danger for OD if it does not become institutionalized, as it could be viewed as a passing fashion rather than a legitimate profession from which to seek authoritative advice.

With respect to the *forced selection* perspective in the adoption of OD, there is a level of state involvement within the public sector in the UK. As such, the possibility for a degree of forced selection/mimicking of other similar organizations, whether technically efficient or not, could be a feature in the growth of OD.

It was clear from the content analysis data that the magnitude of public-sector roles in OD was, and became more, significant. It could be said that, in this way, the public sector mimicked the private sector in its initial take-up of OD. Furthermore, the reduction in proportion of private-sector roles may have resulted from private-sector organizations actively distancing themselves from OD fashion adopted in what they perceived to be lower-status, public-sector organizations. However, interview data does not suggest that this is the case. Interviewees who would be knowledgeable on this did not report any drop off in the use of OD professionals in the private sector. The observed reduction in advertised OD job roles is more likely to have resulted from the decreased use of hard copy media for recruitment purposes in the private sector.

However, there may have been isomorphic mimicry forces at work in the increase of the 'other' social enterprise sector. These organizations are often more like public than private-sector organizations. Mimicry of public-sector organizations may have taken place in the social enterprise sector as, in these smaller organizations where the route to goal achievement is less clear (DiMaggio and Powell, 1983), security may be sought by mimicking other similar but more established institutions such as the NHS or Local Government. In addition, some *other sector* organizations may also have had established relational networks in place with public-sector organizations, which would mean they were more inclined to mimic these organizations.

Abrahamson (1991) warned of pro-innovation bias, and Meyer and Rowan (1991) highlighted that there was much rationalized myth involved in developing institutions. Was a driver in the adoption of OD as a result of pro-innovation bias (i.e. that all innovation is good and should be embraced) and if so, are there consequences for OD? With the influence on the development of what constituted OD in the UK coming from the practitioner rather than academic community, there was scope for a lack of critical evaluation in the adoption of practice. This, in turn, could lead to OD being written off as being a fad or fashion. However, the prospect of dismissal of OD as a fad or a fashion relates to common usage of these terms, rather than necessarily as they are applied in Abrahamson's (1991) typology where there is specified meaning. According to Abrahamson (1991) fashions and fads are similar and are commonly adopted in uncertain conditions. The difference being that in fads the organizations mimicked are of a similar nature.

Agency from Different Interested Parties

This chapter has discussed agency of practitioners, managers, professional associations and interviewees. However, a primary focus for this research is the comparison of academic and practitioner perspectives. It is assumed that academics are likely to take objective, evidence-based, longer-term and rigorous approaches to producing valid research findings (Blackler and Shimmin, 1984), and that they are more likely to be neutral commentators: using critical analysis to illuminate understanding of phenomena.

Abrahamson (1996) and Collins (2000) argue that academics have a role in assisting managers to critically evaluate ideas and models from managerial fashion for application in practice. However, although there is a compelling call from academics for more rigorous research and theory on OD to be developed (e.g. Bunker et al., 2004; Burnes and Cooke, 2012; Cummings and Feyerherm, 2003), this study found no evidence of UK-based academics having yet responded to this need.

With few exceptions (e.g. Burnes and Cooke, 2012; Cheung-Judge and Holbeche 2011, 2015; Francis et al., 2012; Garrow, 2009; Oswick, 2009) little has been published on OD from the UK. Even from the small sample of UK-based authors writing on OD, the Oswick (2009) article is embedded within a US OD academic community discussion. Most of the contributors to the Francis et al. (2012) text are practitioners, as are Cheung-Judge and Holbeche (2011, 2015). The bibliometric search found that other post-2005 UK publications on OD are led by the practitioner linked Institute of Employment Studies (where Garrow, 2009 was based) and Roffey Park, rather than from mainstream, university-based academic sources. Given the significant growth of UK practice and its divergence from the US OD model (highlighted in the content analysis), there is a notable absence of guidance from the academic community for the UK form of OD.

Since academics have an important role to play in assisting the OD practice world through the production of objective, rigorous research, it is notable that there is an absence of such research. It may be that there are also agency factors at work in the community of scholars. The career considerations of many academics may affect the area in which they focus their research. As Grint (1997) commented, academics publish primarily for an academic audience, with academic journal success being particularly important to career progression.

Some interviewees sought both clarity on, and convergence in OD, HR and HRD. It may be the role of academics to provide this clarity, and to advise practitioners on the convergence of these fields. However, as one academic interviewee highlighted, academics in OD, HR and HRD do not publish in the same journals as they draw from different theory bases. As such, the academic subject areas of OD, HR and HRD are significantly divergent, and potentially are so as a result of the agency of academics seeking career progression through publication rather than due to issues of change in the practice world. However, there is evidence of potential change in this situation.

The bibliometric search made comparisons on the level of publishing of academic journal articles with OD in the title between 1970 and 2010, identifying if trends in publication were similar in the three main countries of publication; US, UK and Germany. In the US, publication levels were highest in the 1970s, dropping in each subsequent decade, with a negligible increase between 2000 and 2010. In contrast, in the UK publication rates were low in the 1970s (7), more than doubled in the 1980s (16), reduced to their lowest level in the 1990s (4), and grew significantly between 2000 and 2010 (14). Perhaps the primary influence in the diffusion of management ideas in the UK OD community were the practitioners who had led the trend of growth in the take-up of OD, rather than the academics; as the literature would suggest should have been the case. Moreover, academics appeared to have responded to growing practitioner interest in OD.

Part 3. Debates on the Value of OD, Contemporary OD and the Prognosis for its Future

OD Presence and Development of OD Practice and Research

In the main, OD is absent from UK HRM literature with what few comments there are tending to note that OD was *past its heyday* (e.g. Legge,

1995, 2005). In 2004 there was a dialogue between US scholars, such as that in the special issue of the *Journal of Applied Behavioural Science*, on the terminal decline of OD. Of all the findings of this study, perhaps the most striking is the extent to which the perspective of (particularly HR) UK and (OD) US scholars varies from UK practice. With few exceptions (see Burnes and Cooke, 2012; Dunn, 2009), academic rhetoric focuses on the deterioration of the OD profession. However, in contrast to this, content analysis findings in this study highlight the significant rise OD job role advertisements in the UK.

Existing literature on contemporary challenges for OD is, to a great extent, supported by findings from this study. The perspective of a number of academic interviewees was that OD practitioners were under particular pressure to become more knowledgeable of, and competent in dealing with, global and local business matters (Bradford and Burke, 2006; Church and Burke, 1995; Cummings and Feyerherm, 2003; Sharkey, 2009; Worren et al., 1999). The focus of OD should be on the quest for organizational effectiveness and this would require better processes for measurement and evaluation (Beer, 1976, Francis et al., 2012). This emphasis on the need for measurement and evaluation is reflected in the content analysis and interview findings.

OD practitioners have been warned to rely less on tools and techniques (Cummings and Feyerherm, 2003) and traditional domains of OD, such as over-riding adherence to humanistic values, and interpersonal and group process (Bradford and Burke, 2006; Shull et al., 2013). Consistent with the literature, findings in this study suggested that OD professionals should become more flexible in response, context relevant, competent in large system orientation, and be influential (Bradford and Burke, 2006; Cummings and Feyerherm, 2003). There appeared to be a call to increase the institutional status of OD, through recommendation for more clarity on what was core OD, and what was peripheral (Cheung-Judge and Holbeche, 2011; Bradford and Burke, 2004; Gallos 2006) and appeals for greater regulation on membership and conduct (Bradford and Burke, 2004). All of these issues in the existing literature matched by what was found in the content analysis and interviews.

The content analysis and interview data indicated a weakening in the link between OD and its grounding in *Behavioural Science*. However, with the exception of Shull et al., (2013), this was rarely highlighted by scholars. The comparatively tangential references to new OD practices in the literature such as *Positive Organisational Scholarship*, *AI* and *Positive Psychology*, (Palmer et al., 2006) were given brief mention in a small number of interviews. The increased need to be more involved in shaping organizational leadership (see Sharkey, 2009) was evident in the content analysis, but less so in the interview findings. Increased commitment to employers (Shull et al., 2013), and a growing emphasis on linking work output to organizational performance for HR professionals (Becker and Huselid, 2006) was also evident in the interview data on the need for OD practitioners to be seen to contribute to the *bottom line.*

In looking to the future of OD, one area which was a feature of the literature, but absent from the content analysis and barely mentioned in interviews, was OD values and ethics. If the holy grail of OD was to achieve organizational effectiveness, it had opened itself to reproach as simply being a tool of senior managers (Burnes and Cooke, 2012). Cheung-Judge and Holbeche (2011) consider that the greatest challenge for OD professionals is the maintenance of integrity alongside business acumen. In 1999, French and Bell argued for the need for a more ethical approach to business. The call for an ethical approach has increased, and with the financial and organizational scandals of recent history, the necessity of values and ethics have come to the fore (Burnes and Cooke, 2012). However, concerns with issues of ethics and values were barely in evidence in the content analysis or interview data.

The need for more rigorous research in OD was not evident from the content analysis and seldom arose in interviews, but was of significance in the literature. Many academics argue that a primary issue facing OD is the lack of academic theory, rigor and research (Beer and Walton, 1987; Burnes and Cooke, 2012; Cummings and Feyerherm 2003). Furthermore, they argue that this research should be aligned with applicability in practice (Bunker et al., 2004; Hutton and Liefooghe, 2011; Woodman, 1989) with a return to the use of action research (Burnes and Cooke, 2012). Burnes and Cooke (2012) also recommend that there is a need to produce reliable and valid research on which to assess reasons for failure in change programs.

Given Beer's (1976) proposal that archetypes and robust theories increase the power and influence of OD, one might argue that demand for more rigorous theory from OD academics could be linked to greater institutionalization and legitimacy of OD. Any increase in institutionalism should come, in part, from improving the supporting system of knowledge of OD practice. Proactive leadership in the development of the profession is also needed (Bradford and Burke, 2006; Gallos 2006). However, the literature and interview findings from this research found little evidence of this. There has been little evidence of leadership activity from UK academics, and US-based scholars have focused on issues such as dialogical approaches to OD. Professional organizations in the UK, Europe or the US have also yet to provide a clear and positive leadership role.

Overall Prognosis

Although facilitating the optimization of the release of 'human potential within organisations', remains as an important role and focus of HR academics, (Bradford and Burke, 2004: 372), the OD community have been positioned as having lost their relevance (Bradford and Burke, 2006). However, the content analysis found that in the UK (at least) until 2010, OD skills continued to be in high demand.

The rise in demand for OD skills should be expected in a global environment where ongoing and complex changes are the norm (Gallos, 2006). Nevertheless, the way in which OD deals with the context of the failure of change efforts and becomes competent in loosening tight systems (as well as the other way round) will be important to future success (Burke, 2011).

A point highlighted in one interview was that a number of scholars have reported that the essential principles and processes of OD are well founded (e.g. Burnes and Cooke, 2012; French and Bell, 1999; Hutton and Liefooghe, 2011) and a return to core OD principles would be of use. It is thought to be particularly essential to restore *Lewinian* values of relevance and rigor in OD (Burnes and Cooke, 2012).

There have been a number of business disasters which have arisen from a lack of application of rigor in moral values by organizational leaders (Bradford and Burke, 2004). The fact that OD has retained its values at a time when they were considered to be old fashioned, should have been an advantage (Bradford and Burke, 2004). However, the issue of the behavior of top leaders in the context of turbulence or crises will be a defining factor (French and Bell, 1999). Whether the OD profession can prove capable and motivated to attend to difficult questions in a global society is important (Burnes and Cooke, 2012). Whatever the result, having an OD approach is vital in resisting short-term expediency in favor of sustainable and embedded longer-term change. Therefore, for this reason amongst others, in theory, OD is well placed for the future (Burnes and Cooke, 2012).

Conclusion

In this chapter academic perspectives on OD (as depicted in the literature) were compared with data from the study; similarities were found, however there were significant differences. The data was analyzed through reflection on the theoretical position of Institutionalism, Fashions, Fads and the Dissemination of Management Ideas. The value and the nature of contemporary OD were examined and predictions for its future were presented. In the concluding chapter, the salient points from this chapter will be summarized. The issues which have been discussed will be reviewed in relation to how they compare with the questions raised in the introduction.

References

Abbot, A. (1988) *The System of Professions: An Essay on the Division of Expert Labour*. The University of Chicago Press: Chicago.

Abrahamson, A. (1991) 'Managerial Fads and Fashions: The Diffusion and Rejection of Innovations' *Academy of Management Review* 16 (3) 586–612.

Abrahamson, A. (1996) 'Management Fashion, Academic Fashion and Enduring Truths' *Academy of Management Review* 21 (3) 616–618.

Austin, J., and Bartunek, J. (2006) 'Theories and Practices of Organizational Development' in Gallos, J. (ed.) *Organization Development—A Jossey-Bass Reader* John Wiley & Sons: San Francisco, CA. Pp. 89–128.

Bartunek, J., Woodman, R. (2015) 'Beyond Lewin: Toward a Temporal Approximation of Organization Development and Change' *Annual Review of Organizational Psychology and Organizational Behavior* (2) 157–182

Becker, B., and Huselid, M. (2006) 'Strategic Human Resource Management: Where Do We Go From Here?' *Journal of Management* 32 (6) 898–925.

Beckhard, R. (1969) *Organization Development Strategies and Models.* Addison-Wesley Publishing Company: Reading, MA.

Beer, M. (1976) 'On Gaining Influence and Power for OD' *Journal of Applied Behavioural Science* 12 (1) 44–51.

Beer, M., and Walton, A. E. (1987) 'Organization Change and Development' *Annual Review Psychology* (38) 339–367.

Blackler, F., and Shimmin, S. (1984) *Applying Psychology in Organizations.* Methuen & Co Ltd: London.

Bradford, D., and Burke, W. (2004) 'Introduction: Is OD in Crisis?' *Journal of Applied Behavioural Science* 40 (4) 369–373.

Bradford, D., and Burke, W. (2006) 'The Future of OD?' in Gallos, J. (ed.) *Organization Development—A Jossey-Bass Reader*. John Wiley & Sons: San Francisco, CA. Pp. 842–857.

Bunker, B, Alban, B., and Lewicki, R. (2004) 'Ideas in Currency and OD Practice: Has the Well Gone Dry?' *Journal of Applied Behavioral Science* 40 (4) 403–422.

Burke, W. (2004) 'Internal Organization Development Practitioners: Where Do They Belong?' *Journal of Applied Behavioural Science* 40 (4) 423–431.

Burke, W. (2011) 'A Perspective on the Field of Organization Development and Change: The Zeigarnik Effect' *Journal of Applied Behavioural Science* 47 (2) 143–167.

Burnes, B., and Cooke, B. (2012) 'Review Article: The Past, Present and Future of Organization Development: Taking the Long View' *Human Relations* 65 (11) 1395–1429.

Burnes, B., and Cooke, B. (2013) 'The Tavistock's 1945 Invention of Organisation Development: Early British Business and Management Applications of Social Psychiatry' *Business History* 55 (5) 768–789.

Bushe, G., and Marshak, R. (2009) 'Revisioning Organization Development Diagnostic and Dialogic Premises and Patterns of Practice' *Journal of Applied Behavioral Science* 45 (3) 348–368.

Cheung-Judge, M. Y., and Holbeche, L. (2011) *Organization Development—A Practitioner's Guide for OD and HR*. Kogan Page: London.

Cheung-Judge, M. Y., and Holbeche, L. (2015) *Organization Development—A Practitioner's guide for OD and HR* (2nd edn). Kogan Page: London.

Church, A., and Burke, W. (1995) 'Practitioner Attitudes about the Field of Organization Development' *Research in Organizational Change and Development* (8) 1–46.

CIPD. (2015) *About Professional Membership* accessed online at: www.cipd.co.uk/membership/professional/default.aspx (24th August 2015)

Colwill, D. (2012) *Educating the Scholar Practitioner*. A Volume in Contemporary Trends in Organization Development and Change. Information Age Publishing: Charlotte, NC.

Collins, D. (2000) Management Fads and Buzzwords Critical-Practical Perspectives Routledge: Abingdon.

Cummings, T., and Feyerherm, A. (2003) 'Reflections on Organization Development' *Journal of Applied Behavioral Science* 39 (1) 97–115.

Cummings, T., and Worley, C. (2015) *Organization Development and Change* (10th edn.). Cengage Learning: Stamford, CT.

DiMaggio, P., and Powell, W. (1983) 'The Iron Cage Revisited: Institutional Isomorphism and Collective Rationality in Organizational Fields' *American Sociological Review* 48 (2) 147–160

Dunn, J. (2009) 'Strategic Human Resources and Organization Development: Managing Change for Success' in Yaeger, T., and Sorenson, P. (eds.) *Strategic Organization Development—Managing Change for Success*. A Volume in Contemporary Trends in Organization Development and Change. Information Age Publishing: Charlotte, NC. Pp. 131–142.

Francis, H., Holbeche, L., and Reddington, M. (2012) 'Organisational Effectiveness: A New Agenda for Organisational Development and Human Resource Management' in Francis, H., Holbeche, L., and Reddington, M. (eds.) *People and Organisational Development: a New Agenda for Organisational Effectiveness*. CIPD: London. Pp. 1–19, 335–345.

French, W., and Bell, C. (1999) *Organization Development Behavioural Science Interventions for Organization Improvement* (6th edn.). Prentice Hall: Saddle River.

Gallos, J. (2006) in Gallos, J. (ed.) *Organization Development—A Jossey-Bass Reader*. John Wiley & Sons: San Francisco.

Garrow, V. (2009) 'OD: Past, Present and Future' *IES Working Paper WP22*.

Grant, D., and Marshak, R. (2011) 'Towards a Discourse-Centred Understanding of Organizational Change' *Journal of Applied Behavioural Science* 47 (2) 204–235.

Greenwood, R., and Meyer, R. (2008) 'Influencing Ideas: A Celebration of DiMaggio and Powell (1983)' *Journal of Management Inquiry* 17 (4) 258–264.

Greenwood, R., Suddaby, R. (2006) 'Institutional Entrepreneurship in Mature Fields: The Big Five Accounting Firms' *Academy of Management Journal* 49 (1) 27–48

Greenwood, R., Suddaby, R., and Hinings, C. (2002) 'Theorising Change: The Role of Professional Associations in the Transformation of Institutionalised Fields' *Academy of Management Journal* 45 (1) 58–80.

Greiner, L., and Cummings, T. (2004) 'Wanted: OD More Alive Than Dead' *Journal of Applied Behavioral Science* 40 (4) 374–391.

Grint, K. (1997) *Fuzzy Management—Contemporary Ideas and Practices at Work*. Oxford University Press: Oxford.

Hilmer, F., and Donaldson, L. (1996) *Management Redeemed*. The Free Press: New York.

Hutton, C., and Liefooghe, A. (2011) 'Mind the Gap: Revisioning Organization Development as Pragmatic Reconstruction' *Journal of Applied Behavioral Science* 47 (1) 76–97.

Legatski, II. T. (1998) 'Downsizing, Downscoping, and Restructuring Classifying Organizational Change' *Research in Organizational Change and Development* (11) 253–270.

Legge, K. (1995) *Human Resource Management: Rhetorics and Realities*. Palgrave MacMillan: Basingstoke.

Legge, K. (2005) *Human Resource Management: Rhetorics and Realities, Anniversary Edition*. Palgrave MacMillan: Basingstoke.

Marshak, R., and Grant, D. (2008) 'Organizational Discourse and New Organization Development Practices' *British Journal of Management* 19 S7–S19.

Meyer, J., and Rowan, B. (1991) 'Institutionalized Organizations: Formal Structure as Myth and Ceremony' in Powell, W., and DiMaggio, P. (eds.) *The New Institutionalism in Organizational Analysis*. The University of Chicago Press: Chicago. Pp. 41–62.

Muzio, D., Kirkpatrick, I., and Kipping, M. (2011). 'Professions, Organizations and the State: Applying the Sociology of the Professions to the Case of Management Consultancy' *Current Sociology* 59 (6) 805–824.

Neilson, E. (1984) *Become an OD Practitioner*. Prentice Hall Inc: Saddle River, NJ.

Oswick, C. (2009) 'Revisioning or Re-versioning? A Commentary on Diagnostic and Dialogic Forms of Organization Development' *Journal of Applied Behavioral Science* 45 (3) 369–374.

Oswick, C., Grant, D., Marshak, R., and Wolfram Cox, J. (2010) 'Organizational Discourse and Change: Positions, Perspectives, Progress and Prospects' *Journal of Applied Behavioral Science* 46 (1) 8–15.

Palmer, I., Dunford, R., and Akin, G. (2009) *Managing Organizational Change a Multiple Perspectives Approach* (2nd edn., International edn.). McGraw Hill: New York.

Rogers, E. (2003) *Diffusion of Innovations* (5th edn.). Free Press: New York.

Ruona, W., and Gibson, S. (2004) 'The Making of Twenty-First Century HR: An Analysis of the Convergence of HRM, HRD and OD' *Human Resource Management* 43 (1) 49–63.

Schmidt Weber, P., and Manning, R. (1998) 'Large Group Organizational Change Interventions' *Research in Organizational Change and Development* (11) 225–252.

Scott, W. R. (2005) 'Evolving Professions: An Institutional Field Approach) in Klatetzki, T., and Tacke, V. (eds.) *Organisation und Profession VS Verlag für Sozialwissenschaften*. Wiesbaden. Pp. 119–141.

Scott, W. R., (2008a) *Institutions and Organizations* (3rd edn.). Sage: Thousand Oaks, CA.

Scott, W. R., (2008b). 'Lords of the Dance: Professionals as Institutional Agents' *Organization Studies* 29 (02) 219–238.

Senior, B., and Swailes, S. (2010) *Organizational Change* (4th edn.). FT Prentice Hall: Harlow.

Sharkey, L. (2009) 'The Future of Organization Development and Its Alignment to the Business Strategy' in Yaeger, T., and Sorenson, P. (eds.) *Strategic Organization Development—Managing Change for Success*. A Volume in Contemporary Trends in Organization Development and Change. Information Age Publishing: Charlotte, NC. Pp. 9–22.

SHRM. (2015a) *Membership Options* accessed online at: www.shrm.org/about/infokit/pages/membershipoptions.aspx (24th August June 2015)

SHRM. (2015b) *SHRM HR Jobs* accessed online at: http://jobs.shrm.org/ (24th August June 2015)

Shull, A., Church, A., and Burke, W. (2013) 'Attitudes About the Field of Organization Development 20 Years Later: The More Things Change, the More They Stay the Same' *Research in Organizational Change and Development* 21 1–28.

Stanford, N. (2012) 'The Historical and Theoretical Background to Organisation Development' in Francis, H., Hobeche, L., and Reddington, M. (eds.) *People and Organisational Development: A New Agenda for Organisational Effectiveness*. CIPD: London. Pp. 42–64.

Sweem, S. (2009) 'Talent Management. The Strategic Partnership of Human Resources and Organization Development' in Yaeger, T., and Sorenson, P. (eds.) *Strategic Organization Development—Managing Change for Success*. A Volume in Contemporary Trends in Organization Development and Change. Information Age Publishing: Charlotte, NC. Pp. 143–164.

Thornton, P., Ocasio, W., and Lounsbury, M. (2012) *The Institutional Logics Perspective. A New Approach to Culture, Structure, and Process.* Oxford University Press: Oxford.

Whittington, R. (2001) 'Putting Giddens into Action: Social Systems and Managerial Agency' *Journal of Management Studies* 29 (6) 693–710.

Woodman, R. (1989) 'Organizational Change and Development: New Arenas for Inquiry and Action' *Journal of Management* 15 (2) 205–228.

Worren, N., Ruddle, K., and Moore, K. (1999) 'From Organizational Development to Change Management: The Emergence of a New Profession' *Journal of Applied Behavioral Science* 35 (3) 273–286.

7 A Puzzle Solved but not Resolved

Having discussed the literature and compared with the evidence collected in the research study, and analyzed this through theory lenses, this chapter presents a summary of the key findings. Each of the three research questions set out in Chapter 1 will be answered in turn. A working definition of OD was presented in Chapter 2 and in this chapter, this is revisited with a revised definition proposed. How this study has added to knowledge on the nature of contemporary OD will be considered. The implications of the findings for OD practice, professional associations and academics will be addressed and areas for further research will be identified. It will conclude with a return to the puzzle set out at the start of the book.

Summary of Key Findings and Return to the Research Questions

Findings

A summary of the most significant findings from this research are shown below.

The research identified broad agreement that:

- OD is difficult to define and has blurred disciplinary boundaries.
- Its early history was perceived as being dominated by US-based scholars.
- The CIPD has attempted to subsume OD practice within its professional association.
- OD skills will continue to be in demand in an increasingly complex global business world, where there is an ongoing quest to optimize the realization of human potential.
- In the future, OD needs to be business competent, focused on large systems and context relevant.
- There is an increased emphasis on evaluating OD practice and identifying the link between activity and improved performance, through the development and application of metrics.

In several areas, the findings from this study did not match with findings in existing literature and thus identified key differences between academic perspectives and UK practice:

- Over four decades, the UK form of OD has diverged significantly from the traditional US model of OD. The content analysis profiles demonstrate that in the 1970s, OD in the UK was akin to the traditional US form of OD. The focus on *Change Management* grew in the next three decades. In the 1980s HR became the most prominent feature of UK OD, and in the 1990s this leading position was taken by HRD. In the period 2000–2010 OD became a broader discipline, and a *Strategic* broad *Organization-wide* approach was evident.
- The extent of the link with HR and HRD in the UK was not generally acknowledged by academics. Mention of OD by prominent HR academics was all but absent.
- OD is considered as being of higher status and perceived to be of higher importance than other specialist areas of HR/HRD in the UK.
- US-based scholars presented the OD profession as though there was no national difference in its form.
- Issues of ethics, values and organizational power differences are of importance in existing literature and the view was given by scholars that they will become more so in the future of OD. However, these issues were not expressed as being of concern to OD practitioners.
- Although not addressed in the literature, it was clear from the interview data that the relevance of the form of OD practice should be informed by the organizational context, particularly that of its size.

Other findings from this research were that:

- With the bank of written material produced, and embedded institutions such as the NTL (with a presence in the UK), US-based scholars continue to be the primary source for shaping what OD is considered to be.
- Traditional OD has developed with the increased use of techniques such as AI, large group and dialogical approaches. It has moved away from a positivist ontological base to embrace socially constructed reality.
- Whilst UK OD changed between 1970 and 2010, there were also many other changes of relevance in its environment. The nature of organizations and types of organizational change altered significantly. There were new categories of employees, such as *knowledge workers*, and the nature of employment (e.g. *flexible employee contract* categories) had developed. Other professions on the boundary of OD, such as Change Management, Consultancy and HR also changed in form.
- After 1980, interest in OD in academic publications waned in the US, UK and Germany. However, the post 2000 resurgence of interest in OD was much stronger in the UK and Germany than it was in the US, as

shown by the increased number of journal publications found in the bibliometric search. This raises questions on whether in the dissemination of ideas, scholars and UK publication in OD have been influenced by the rise in the practice community.

- A call for increased institutionalism for UK OD was identified, in terms of a need to complete recognized training and qualification in OD. Within this was an appeal for clarity in relation to separation of core and periphery OD, with a view to the field of OD becoming more distinct with clear boundaries and legitimate professionals.

- The most likely of Abrahams's (1991) perspectives in the adoption of OD were *fashions*, *fads* and *forced selection* rather than the take-up of OD being mainly as the rational *efficient choice*.

- In an increasingly unpredictable global business world, the lowest risk strategy for managers is to make decisions which mimic other higher status organizations in their field, with deference shown to the advice of acknowledged, institutionalized, professional groups in order to justify decisions. As such, advantage may be gained by the OD profession by becoming more institutionalized though professionalization.

- There is a need for more rigorous research in OD, particularly focusing on how it can contribute to successful change processes. This would legitimize OD as a profession and strengthen its institutional status.

- There is evidence of the application of agency to progress vested interests from a number of parties with respect to OD, including the CIPD and OD, HR, HRD professionals and academics, primarily within the context of isomorphic institutionalism.

- In a global business environment where there have been numerous financial crises and organizational scandals, the OD profession's acknowledged and long-standing association with professional values should be valued as a contributor to ethical sustainable long-term organizational change.

Return to the Research Questions and a Revised Definition

The research questions posed have been addressed as follows:

1 To what extent is there a difference between the academic literature and practitioners' perspective of the development of the OD profession in the UK?

The findings from this study suggest a significant difference between the academic literature and practitioners' perspectives of OD in the UK. In particular, there are few UK-based academics who publish in the subject area of OD. Furthermore, there is a lack of recognition of OD by UK-based HR academics. This completely at odds with OD's place in the practice world and the extent to which it is linked with HR and HRD in the UK.

2   What does the empirical data of this study evidence on the development of the OD profession in the UK in respect of its form, magnitude and perceived importance?

The UK form of OD was found to be much broader than traditional OD and the boundaries with HR and HRD particularly blurred. The OD profession was found to have grown in number over the four decades and appeared to be perceived as being of high status.

3   What are the forces at work which influence the development of the OD profession in the UK?

A range of forces were identified as being at work in influencing the development of the OD profession in the UK, with the most important factors accounted for in the key findings above. These include US-based scholars dominating the thought world of OD; traditional OD having developed in terms of increasing its focus on organizational-level issues; and the underlying philosophy of OD is declared to have moved from a positivist ontological to a socially constructed realist stance. In addition, the environment OD operates in has also developed. For example: organizational forms, the nature of employment arrangements, types of employees and other linked professions have changed. There are early signs of a resurgence of academic interest in the UK and Germany. In the UK this is arguably in reaction to growth in the practice of OD. The perceived need for OD practitioners to achieve legitimacy through formal qualification in OD is apparent and there is an appeal for clarity of its boundaries. The forces driving adoption of OD are not always rational and the application of agency by a range of stakeholders is evident. There is need for the application of more rigorous research to underpin OD practice. This would advantage the profession as would be an increase in its institutionalized professional status.

At the end of Chapter 2 the following definition of OD was developed by the author as informed by the literature: 'OD involves **planned change (at whole- or sub-) system level, with the goal of organizational effectiveness achieved through the application of OD—processes, tools and techniques and delivered by adhering to humanistic values'.**

In the light of the data collected in this study and some of the more unique views expressed in the literature the author has now revised this definition. Reference to *planned* change has been removed since there is no reason that this cannot be accompanied by e.g. emergent change, which was considered to be 'the first substantial alternative to OD' (Burnes and Cooke, 2012, 1408).

A further influence on the revised definition is that organization boundaries are increasingly porous and systems in themselves can be revolutionized, even the application of the description *transformation* is on occasion now not radical enough to describe changes in organizational forms. In the current era, there are now samples of organizations fundamentally changing their core purposes, such as in local government and health provision in the UK where organizations which once had the core purpose of providing service, are split into separate (and different core purpose) commissioning and provider organizations. Therefore, it is no longer simply *system* change, but could equally be *supra-* and/or *sub-*system change. In the light of the above, organization design must now be core to OD. Success cannot be achieved in the majority of OD endeavors, without active consideration of organization design as a priority.

The final influence in the author's revised definition is consideration that *humanistic values* for application within practice within the *system* is no longer sufficient. Whilst still important, *humanistic values* should now be superseded now by wider societal concerns.

Furthermore, the revised definition is now two-fold, including *Core OD* and *Non-Core OD*:

> Core OD involves change in the system (at supra- and/or sub-system level), with the goal of achieving organisational effectiveness, through responsive and transformational/radical design of structures, OD—processes, tools and techniques reflecting consideration of needs of all stakeholders including wider society and employees.'
>
> 'Non-Core OD is where recognized applications of core OD—design, processes, tools, and techniques are used by professionals in boundary professions (such as HR, HRD, Change Management and Consultancy) in support of enhancing the delivery in their own professional practice.

Both of these definitions should include the following addition: 'pertinent OD—design, processes, tools and techniques are those which result from rigorous academic research'. However not all of these, even if recognized as tried and tested design, processes, tools and techniques clearly meet this standard.

Adding to Previous Knowledge on OD

In an earlier stage of this research, the content analysis data was published in the *International Journal of Human Resource Management* (Gillon et al., 2014). The contribution to knowledge at that point was identified as being an extension of current thinking on OD by contrasting the research of academic scholars on the evolution of the HRM profession in the UK and the US.

Much has been written about the profession of OD, often in a prescriptive manner but with little empirical evidence to corroborate claims. Prior to this study, there was almost no substantiated information on the nature of the profession in the UK. This work makes a contribution to existing knowledge by presenting triangulated evidence on the nature of the form of the OD profession in the UK collected using transparent research methods. The review of job advertisements over a forty-year period provides robust data on the developing magnitude and form of OD and the nature of the elite interview sample supplies a richness of perspective.

This study has demonstrated that OD in the UK is not as described by the US-based scholars. This is also the first work which has investigated the development of OD through the lenses of Institutional Theory, Fads, Fashions and the Dissemination of Management Ideas. In doing so it has challenged the *given* understanding of the form of OD, the context of how it has developed and why it has changed. From this work there are caveats for OD practitioners, OD professional associations and for scholars: these are presented below.

Implications for Practitioners, Professional Associations and for Academics

Practitioners

The implications of this research for UK OD practitioners are somewhat contradictory in nature. On the one hand, findings indicated a more diverse form of OD that is linked to HR and HRD and this had contributed to its growth in magnitude in the UK: whilst in the US, stricter adherence to traditional OD, albeit with some new techniques and focus, resulted in challenge for the relevance of the profession.

On the other hand, there were potential benefits to be had by increasing the institutional status of OD through development of a more regulated qualification and professional association membership route. If this path was followed, then the profession was more likely to be able to manage a distinct boundary and be less open to being dismissed as a fad or fashion.

Professional Associations

Ultimately, it may be that in the UK OD has now reached sufficient critical mass through organic growth and that the time is ripe for OD to strengthen its institutional status through the European OD Network, or similar. The CIPD is considered by some to have been predatory in its approach to subsuming OD. However, the CIPD action of including OD in its professional map could be either a comparatively half-hearted reaction to a clearly growing trend, or a failed attempt: since many OD practitioners actively engaged in distancing themselves from HR and HRD.

A significant finding from this research is the idea that there should be two forms of OD professional. One would be the highly specialized *pure* OD professional and the other would be a hybrid type—HR/HRD with OD skills alongside their other generalist and specialist skills. Whether increased institutionalism is achieved through an OD professional association or the CIPD is less important, as long as the *pure* form of OD is not tied to, and subsumed by, all of the norms of the CIPD but instead treated as an equal, albeit small, partner in the isomorphic process.

Academics

One key implication of this research for business and management academics is the need for recognition of the growth in the OD professional group, and the need for action to follow from that. In order to remain relevant, academics should be outward focused and in a position to identify changes in business trends at an early stage. This would involve being less reactive and playing more of a leading and influential role in the development and shape of, for example, the profession of OD. There is something of a gap in leadership of the development of the profession in the UK, so that role is there for the taking.

For some time, there has been a focus on the need for relevance alongside rigor in academia (e.g. Starkey and Madan, 2001) and a focus on the necessity for the demonstration of research impact. This research study was by no means the first to identify that the embedded norms of career reward in academic publishing caused unhelpful behavior with regards to relevance and impact. However, in this study, the local academic subject domain effect identified was found to drive behavior which resulted in a divergence of the academic subjects of OD, HR and HRD, as these disciplines apply different theory bases and traditionally publish in different journal communities. Conversely, findings indicate that a more converged approach to people management was required in practice, and is therefore in place.

Finally, the call for increasing rigorous research in OD and Change Management, if heeded, would be of great benefit to both academic and practitioner communities. The production of valid, impactful and rigorous research would promote the relevance of the academic community and provide a source of legitimization for the practice community.

Future Potential for Research

A primary opportunity for further research would be to more rigorously examine the corresponding development of the OD profession in the US and other countries. The relationship of OD and its contribution to Change Management is also a possible area for further work, and a more in-depth study of the use of OD in specific sectors might also prove to be of interest and value.

Although methodologically difficult for comparison a follow up study on the development of OD during the period 2010–2020, would be of interest. However, the area which might be of most use to the practitioner community would be to utilize the data from this study as a starting point to clarify what is core and peripheral in OD.

Finally . . . the Puzzle Is Solved (But Not Resolved)

In the introductory chapter, I explained how I had uncovered a puzzle which had not made sense to me. In particular, my experience of OD as a thriving and growing profession in the UK was not reflected in the academic literature. At the end of this work, the puzzle has been solved. My experience of the nature of OD was indeed reflected in the volume of OD job roles found in the content analysis exercise, and further confirmed in the interview findings.

I now better understand the actions of the OD (and HR and HRD) professional community in the UK, and their underpinning motivation. For business leaders a more converged model to managing people issues makes sense. Often HR and HRD practitioners are keen to subsume OD within their fold. For OD professionals, it is a double-edged sword: convergence with HR and HRD could make them more relevant, but divergence could achieve a perceived status advantage. The researcher also now has a clearer grasp that the OD, HR and HRD academics in the UK have diverged in these subject areas and why that is the case.

However, whilst the puzzle has been solved, it has not been resolved, especially for community of scholars. The divergence of the subject areas, and the reasons for that, are now understood. Scholars have been dominated by the US thought on what constitutes OD. In the UK they appear to often have little meaningful interface with the world outside of universities, or at least they are not incentivized to make this a priority. Ultimately, in an era when there is rhetoric on an increasing focus on relevance and impact, the divergence in the communities of OD, HR and HRD, academics might yet prove to be their Achilles heel.

References

Abrahamson, A. (1991) 'Managerial Fads and Fashions: The Diffusion and Rejection of Innovations' *Academy of Management Review* 16 (3) 586–612.

Beer, M. (1976) 'On Gaining Influence and Power for OD' *Journal of Applied Behavioural Science* 12 (1) 44–51.

Beer, M., and Walton, A. E. (1987) 'Organization Change and Development' *Annual Review Psychology* (38) 339–367.

Bradford, D., and Burke, W. (2004) 'Introduction: Is OD in Crisis?' *Journal of Applied Behavioural Science* 40 (4) 369–373.

Bradford, D., and Burke, W. (2006) 'The Future of OD?' in Gallos, J. (ed.) *Organization Development—A Jossey-Bass Reader*. John Wiley & Sons: San Francisco, CA. Pp. 842–857.

Bunker, B, Alban, B., and Lewicki, R. (2004) 'Ideas in Currency and OD Practice: Has the Well Gone Dry?' *Journal of Applied Behavioral Science* 40 (4) 403–422.

Burke, W. (2011) 'A Perspective on the Field of Organization Development and Change: The Zeigarnik Effect' *Journal of Applied Behavioural Science* 47 (2) 143–167.

Burnes, B., and Cooke, B. (2012) 'Review Article: The Past, Present and Future of Organization Development: Taking the Long View' *Human Relations* 65 (11) 1395–1429.

Cummings, T., and Feyerherm, A. (2003) 'Reflections on Organization Development' *Journal of Applied Behavioral Science* 39 (1) 97–115.

French, W., and Bell, C. (1999) *Organization Development Behavioural Science Interventions for Organization Improvement* (6th edn.). Prentice Hall: Saddle River.

Gallos, J. (2006) in Gallos, J. (ed.) *Organization Development—A Jossey-Bass Reader*. John Wiley & Sons: San Francisco, CA.

Starkey, K., and Madan, P. (2001) 'Bridging the Relevance Gap: Aligning Stakeholders in the Future of Management Research' *British Journal of Management* 12 (S1) S3–S26.

Index

Boldface page references indicate tables. *Italic* references indicate figures.

Made in United States
North Haven, CT
12 April 2023